INTERNATIONAL HUMAN RIGHTS PROTECTION

INTERNATIONAL HUMAN RIGHTS PROTECTION

Balanced, Critical, Realistic

Marc Bossuyt

Prefaces
Theo van Boven
Paul Mahoney

intersentia

Cambridge – Antwerp – Portland

Intersentia Ltd
Sheraton House | Castle Park
Cambridge | CB3 0AX | United Kingdom
Tel.: +44 1223 370 170 | Fax: +44 1223 370 169
Email: mail@intersentia.co.uk
www.intersentia.com | www.intersentia.co.uk

Distribution for the UK and Ireland:
NBN International
Airport Business Centre, 10 Thornbury Road
Plymouth, PL6 7 PP
United Kingdom
Tel.: +44 1752 202 301 | Fax: +44 1752 202 331
Email: orders@nbninternational.com

Distribution for Europe and all other countries:
Intersentia Publishing nv
Groenstraat 31
2640 Mortsel
Belgium
Tel.: +32 3 680 15 50 | Fax: +32 3 658 71 21
Email: mail@intersentia.be

Distribution for the USA and Canada:
International Specialized Book Services
920 NE 58th Ave. Suite 300
Portland, OR 97213
USA
Tel.: +1 800 944 6190 (toll free) | Fax: +1 503 280 8832
Email: info@isbs.com

International Human Rights Protection. Balanced, Critical, Realistic
© Marc Bossuyt 2016

ISBN 978-1-78068-400-0
D/2016/7849/64
NUR 828

British Library Cataloguing in Publication Data. A catalogue record for this book is available from the British Library.

To Juliette, Celeste and Felix,
Louie and Viktor

PREFACE

A LIFETIME OF FIDELITY
AND PARTICIPATION

Theo VAN BOVEN*

This book brings together a remarkable selection of Marc Bossuyt's opinions and insights on specific areas of his interest and expertise. Marc's writings carry the imprint and consistency of legal precision. As also transpires from the farewell lecture delivered at the University of Antwerp under the telling title *At the Crossroads of Law and Politics*, other qualities and dimensions also come to the fore. A comprehensive and effective human rights policy requires, in addition to international and domestic judicial control, a variety of extra-judicial means of prevention, promotion and protection, particularly in situations where gross violations are imminent or rampant.

Some forty years cover Marc Bossuyt's intricate professional involvement in support of the cause of human rights and fundamental freedoms. As it happened, being myself Marc's country neighbour from the North and brought up in the same mother tongue, I shared with him, albeit not precisely concurrently, similar experiences in a series of United Nations human rights mechanisms in Geneva. Many of our footsteps were set around the Lac Léman, not physically walking together but in a common spirit of having the same objective in mind: helping to make the global human rights agenda more effective and credible.

Against this background I wish to single out two areas of an institutional and thematic nature which may serve as illustrations of contributions made by Marc Bossuyt to the United Nations human rights legacy. First, his membership and leadership as an independent expert of the United Nations Sub-Commission on the Prevention of Discrimination and the Protection of Minorities (in later years re-named Sub-Commission on the Promotion and the Protection of Human Rights). It was with the active input of Marc Bossuyt that the Sub-Commission, often withstanding the odds of political tensions, initiated major developments in the UN human rights arena, frequently in close concert with

---

*   Honorary Professor of International Law, University of Maastricht; honorary member of the International Commission of Jurists; former director of the UN Division of Human Rights; doctor *honoris causa* of Université Catholique de Louvain, Erasmus University Rotterdam, University of New York at Buffalo and Universidad de Buenos Aires.

civil society organisations and academia. A thorough examination of the various components of the UN human rights agenda is bound to reveal the pioneering role the Sub-Commission has played in the framing of normative standards, in giving new impetus to thematic issues of wide public concern and in taking on gross and consistent patterns of human rights violations. The name of Marc Bossuyt will always be associated with his role as the Sub-Commission's Special Rapporteur to whom the task was entrusted to draw up the text of the Second Protocol to the International Covenant on Civil and Political Rights, aiming at the world wide abolition of the death penalty.

A second area to demonstrate the impact of Marc Bossuyt on the priority agenda of the United Nations is his involvement in the elimination of racial discrimination. Marc is not only a former and current member of the Committee on the Elimination of Racial Discrimination (CERD – the first treaty body functioning within the UN human rights system), he also assumed the chair of one of the two plenary working groups of the World Conference against Racism held in Durban, South Africa, in 2001. In that capacity which he described as the most hectic days of his professional life, he was one of those negotiators who were instrumental against all political odds in steering a consensus text to its adoption. The Durban text deserves special mention as a tribute because, among other significant affirmations and overtures, it provided an unprecedented global framework and moral imperative for remedying and repairing historical racist and colonial wrongs. Alas, as Marc Bossuyt correctly recalls, the outcome of the Durban Conference was overshadowed in its immediate aftermath when three days after the closing of the conference the 9/11 dramatic terrorist attacks occurred against the New York Twin Towers which turned out to have a major adverse effect on the human rights situation at large.

While in the course of a lifetime of some forty years the promotion and protection of human rights moved from peripheral margins to more central areas of international law and international relations, what really counts at the end of the day is implementation at national and local levels. Marc Bossuyt is right in drawing particular attention to the role and the contribution of national judicial mechanisms, notably the courts, to uphold the rule of law. Access to an independent judiciary is undoubtedly a core component in addressing claims of human rights violations. In addition, as part of a public process of awareness building at national and international levels, the emergence, growth and recognition of other components that foster human rights accountability need to be kept in mind, among them independent national human rights institutions, ombudspersons, civil society organisations and educational institutions. All such organs of society operating *At the Crossroads of Law and Politics* are forming part of the contemporary human rights arsenal. Because of his many ventures in shedding light on a wide spectrum of challenging human rights issues Marc Bossuyt deserves much credit.

PREFACE

A PENETRATING AND SALUTARY ANALYSIS OF THE EUROPEAN SYSTEM OF HUMAN RIGHTS PROTECTION

Paul MAHONEY*

Marc Bossuyt's short book on international human rights protection is wide-ranging, covering both the United Nations system and the various existing regional systems, as well as the contribution made at national level by the domestic courts. Thus, a significant part of the book is devoted to examining the enforcement machinery set up under the European Convention on Human Rights, concentrating notably on the judicial activity of the European Court of Human Rights in Strasbourg, which is the driving force at the heart of that machinery.

There is an all too common intolerance in European human rights circles of anyone who dares to break ranks by questioning or, even worse, criticising the rulings or approach of the Strasbourg Court. Such persons are regarded almost as renegades or traitors; they are not true human rights "patriots". Sad to say, self-questioning and openness to criticism are generally lacking as qualities in many leading lights of the European human rights movement.

In his book, as in his writings throughout his distinguished career, Marc Bossuyt provides a refreshing breath of fresh air. In looking not only at the remarkable, ground-breaking achievements of the Strasbourg Court but also at its possible errors, he has not been afraid to break the taboo of human rights "patriotism".

The protection of human rights, Marc Bossuyt writes, brings us to the crossroads of law and politics. To the crossroads of law and morals, one might also add. It is no easy matter to draw the line between letting democracy work at local level in the many and diverse societies of a Convention community of 800 million people and imposing, in the cause of human rights, an ever-growing and ever-detailed corpus of Europe-wide rules elaborated by the judicial interpretation of a small group of judges in Strasbourg. Marc Bossuyt

---

*   Judge in respect of the United Kingdom on the European Court of Human Rights (2012–2016). Any views expressed sitting are personal.

fears that on occasions, in its enthusiasm to be "the Conscience of Europe" and to continually spread wider and yet wider the net of human rights protection, the Strasbourg Court has strayed outside its treaty-given international, judicial role under the Convention. The result being over-intervention into the normal workings of democratic processes at national level and over-expansion of the Convention rights and freedoms into domains not covered by the text of the treaty. As one of the most controversial areas of the Strasbourg Court's case-law he cites the development of positive obligations under the Convention, with the first casualty of this development being democracy. To the rallying cry that all is justified by the doctrine of the Convention being a living instrument, he replies that there must be some limits to evolutive interpretation of the Convention's text. And his book endeavours to identify those limits.

Whether or not one shares Marc Bossuyt's reservations, or fully shares all his reservations, his analysis is the fruit of an evidently deep commitment to the notion of the international protection of human rights. His voice speaks with the combined experience of a senior national judge, a university scholar and someone engaged in national and international human rights institutions from the beginning of his professional life; it is a voice that deserves to be heard. His penetrating analysis cannot but help all concerned to arrive at a clearer-sighted vision of both the role and the limits of the international judicial protection of human rights in Europe. He describes the debate in the UN Commission on Human Rights during his tenure as a member from 1986 to 1991 as being "essentially a confrontation of ideas". That is what this highly readable little book successfully sets out to stimulate in the section on the European system of human rights protection.

INTRODUCTION

The present book aims at assisting judges and lawyers, diplomats and other civil servants, professors and students alike, to become more familiar with the rapid developing field of the international protection of human rights. First, in order to better understand the normative framework, some fundamental questions are raised about the concept of (the different categories of) human rights and about the fundamental principle of equality and non-discrimination, including an analysis of the concept of affirmative action. Second, a short survey is given of the institutional framework (a true labyrinth) both at the universal level (UN Charter-based organs and UN treaty bodies) and at the regional level (Council of Europe, Organisation of American States and African Union).

To show the interrelatedness between the international and the national protection of human rights, attention has also been given to the contribution of national courts to human rights protection. This is in particular the case of the South African Constitutional Court with respect to social rights and the US Supreme Court with respect to the concept of affirmative action and (in the second part of this book) with respect to "self-executing" provisions of international human rights treaties. Brief references are also given to the case law of the Court of Justice of the European Union in Luxembourg, with respect to affirmative action, and (in the second part of this book) to EU Regulations and Directives in the framework of the Common European Asylum System.

In the second part of the present book some specific issues are dealt with. Some of them are procedural, such as the detailed analysis of the final day of the World Conference on Racism and the question of the internal applicability of international human rights provisions, while others are more substantive such as the issue of the death penalty and irreducible life sentences and the question of the interpretation of the European Convention on Human Rights by the European Court of Human Rights in Strasbourg with respect to both the scope of its jurisdiction and the normative provisions of the Convention to which it attributes positive obligations. Finally, attention is given to some specific legal regimes set up for refugees, minorities and victims of armed conflicts which are somewhat at the periphery of the international protection of human rights.

Besides an annex, the book contains 15 chapters, generally based on previous publications by the author. Some of them were previously presented at colloquia in Antwerp, Brussels and Leuven (Belgium), Budapest (Hungary), Geneva (Switzerland), Mexico City (Mexico), Paramaribo (Suriname), Poitiers and Strasbourg (France) or Thessaloniki (Greece). Several of those publications were not easily accessible or were not in English. For the purposes of this book, however, they have been translated and they have all been revised and updated. The basic treaty provisions are reproduced systematically and some fundamental questions going back to their origin are raised.

Variety is a key word that characterises this book, not only in the selection of the chapters but also in the way they are dealt with. Some chapters contain a lot of academic references, others only a few, particularly the ones dealing with the institutional framework. The choice of the chapters is generally based on personal research or personal involvement with the matters dealt with. The annex (the farewell speech of the author at the University of Antwerp) will help the reader to understand why some chapters are included and how the totality of the issues dealt with presents a coherent view on the development of the international protection of human rights.

While trying to adopt a universal approach, the European system nevertheless takes a prominent role, mainly because it is the oldest and most developed system of international protection. As is also the case with other issues, that system is examined in a critical way. It is not because human rights protection pursues laudable goals that it should be immune to criticism. In dealing on a daily basis with complaints of persons claiming to be victims of human rights violations, the European Court of Strasbourg is inclined to neglect quite often the limits put on the scope of its jurisdiction and of the normative provisions it has to apply. Its desire to make constant "progress" in the protection of human rights risks replacing the concept of universal human rights with a purely regional standard. It also loses track of the proper role judges should fulfil in a society governed by the rule of law and the separation of powers.

This is but one aspect of the critical approach taken by the author. It is his feeling that judges, in particular those belonging to courts specialised in human rights, have a tendency to systematically favour interpretations benefitting to the applicants, while overlooking too easily the far-reaching implications their judgments may have for the society as a whole. Continuously tilting the balance in favour of individual applicants, without taking fully into account the difficulties democratic governments experience in coping with the challenges of our present times, divorces human rights protection too much from the pressing needs of the realities of today's world.

Finally, the author wishes to express special thanks to the Stellenbosch Institute for Advanced Study (STIAS) in South Africa where he stayed as Research Fellow (in 2014 and 2016), to the College of Law of the National Taiwan University in Taipei where he stayed as Visiting Professor (in 2015/2016) and to his home university, the University of Antwerp (Belgium), where he is Emeritus Professor of International Law (since 2007).

Stellenbosch, 1 March 2016

The present book was finalised at the
Stellenbosch Institute for Advanced Study (STIAS)
Wallenberg Research Centre at Stellenbosch University
Stellenbosch 7600
South Africa

CONTENTS

"We hold these truths to be self-evident, that all men are created equal, that they are endowed by their Creator with certain unalienable Rights that among these are Life, Liberty and the Pursuit of Happiness"
(United States Declaration of Independence, 4 July 1776)

PART ONE

INTERNATIONAL PROTECTION
OF HUMAN RIGHTS IN GENERAL

The first part of this book deals with the international protection of human rights in general. It contains elements of the normative framework of present day international human rights protection as well as those necessary to understand the institutional framework, on the universal level and on the regional level.

A. THE NORMATIVE FRAMEWORK

On the basis of an analysis of the main international human rights instruments, the concept of human rights will be clarified by identifying different categories of human rights (Chapter I).

A more theoretical approach contributes to specify the characteristics of the socio-economic rights which are different from those of civil rights and fundamental freedoms, as also shown in the case law of the South African Constitutional Court (Chapter II).

The principle of equality is most fundamental. That is why all human rights instruments contain at least a non-discrimination clause and often also a general prohibition of discrimination (Chapter III).

A related question concerns the concept of affirmative action which has been strongly influenced by the case law of the US Supreme Court (Chapter IV).

CHAPTER I

THE CONCEPT OF HUMAN RIGHTS[1]

Quite often little attention is given to the exact meaning of the concept of "human rights".[2] Nowadays, considerable efforts are undertaken to expand the list of human rights with one or another novelty. A preliminary question should be raised as to the conditions that should be fulfilled by a given interest to transform it into a human right. What quality requirements should be satisfied to qualify as human right? As its denomination itself indicates, one may assume that human rights are rights everyone is entitled to, purely and only because he or she is a human being.

Inflation, a negative phenomenon in economics, is unfortunately also not unknown in relation to legal concepts. A few examples illustrate how difficult it may be to stick to a pure terminology. Not all ill-treatment is inhuman treatment and certainly not torture. Not every alien staying illegally in a country is an asylum seeker and certainly not every asylum seeker is a refugee. Not every massacre is genocide. And not every right is a human right. Sometimes it is assumed that every legitimate aspiration is a human right. If the concept of human rights has any meaning, it should only apply to "rights". What is not a right is *a fortiori* not a human right. According to the classical definition of Rudolf von Jhering, a right is a "legally protected interest". Consequently, it must be an interest recognised, protected or guaranteed by the national legislation, by the Constitution or by international treaties. This is a formal requirement. But there are also substantive requirements.

A legitimate aspiration, however important or desirable, is not necessarily a right. Here too, some examples may clarify this. Nothing is more looked after than the "pursuit of happiness". Every human being attaches high importance to loving and being loved. But, however much we may regret it, there is, at least in the legal meaning of the concept of "right", no "right to happiness" and no "right to be loved", no more so than a "right to fair weather". Of course, anybody may claim the contrary but this is without legal consequences whatsoever. Non-lawyers sometimes pretend that they favour a non-legal definition of the concept

---

[1] Based on Bossuyt, Marc, *L'interdiction de la discrimination dans le droit international des droits de l'homme,* Brussels, Bruylant, 1976, 262 p.

[2] See Bossuyt, Marc, "Social rights: a specific category of human rights?", in Mexican Supreme Court of Justice, *Dialogue between judges. Writings of the Summit of Presidents of Constitutional, Regional and Supreme Courts,* Mexico, 2014, pp. 359–373, at pp. 359–361.

of "right". They simply overlook that, in doing so, the very concept of a right loses its significance and becomes entirely worthless.

In its classical meaning, a "human right" is not only a right everybody – whoever, wherever and whenever – is entitled to, but also a right the public authorities are supposed to be capable to respect, whatever the available resources may be, and foremost, it is a right a judge can legally enforce. A State where those classical human rights are not respected is – by definition – not a State abiding by the rule of law. Those human rights are the "civil rights" as enshrined in the oldest human rights declarations: the French Declaration of the Rights of Man and of the Citizen of 1789 and the American Bill of Rights of 1791.

Civil rights are "fundamental freedoms" which impose *in essence* (but – and it should be underlined – not exclusively) negative obligations every State *can* respect. Even States with scarce resources are capable of respecting civil rights and fundamental freedoms. Those rights are universal because they ought not only to be respected but they also *can* be respected anywhere in the world. Those are characteristics typical of the concept of "human rights" in its classical meaning.

The identification of the human rights, as recognised in positive law, can be based on an analysis of the international instruments on human rights adopted at the universal level (the Universal Declaration of Human Rights of 10 December 1948, the International Covenant on Civil and Political Rights, and the International Covenant on Economic Social and Cultural Rights of 16 December 1966) and at the regional level (the European Convention on Human Rights of 4 November 1950, the European Social Charter of 18 October 1961, revised on 3 May 1996, the American Convention on Human Rights of 22 November 1969, and the African Charter on Human and Peoples' Rights of 26 June 1981). The main division is between civil and political rights, on the one hand, and socio-economic rights, on the other hand.

A. CIVIL AND POLITICAL RIGHTS

The category of civil and political rights, as indicated by its name, is composed of two sub-categories: civil rights and political rights. The latter sub-category is the smallest.

1. POLITICAL RIGHTS[3]

While belonging – in opposition to social rights – to the general category of civil rights, political rights differ from civil rights *stricto sensu* in that they may be

---

[3]   BOSSUYT, *supra* note 1, pp. 194–195.

reserved to the nationals of the State concerned. Those political rights are the right to vote,[4] the right to be elected[5] and the right to have access to public services in one's country.[6] The right to enter one's own country also is reserved to the nationals of the country concerned.[7] Not "everyone", but "every citizen" is entitled to those rights. A State may, of course, confer those rights on non-nationals but, contrary to what is the case for civil rights *stricto sensu*, to exclude non-nationals from the enjoyment of political rights is not discriminatory. Moreover, the right to be elected and the right to have access to public services are clear examples which show that the notion of "right" does not necessary imply that every citizen who so wishes will be elected or will become a civil servant. It is a mere possibility: an equal chance should be given to every citizen, not the effective acquisition of the desired status.

2. CIVIL RIGHTS[8]

The sub-category of civil rights consists of fundamental rights, fundamental freedoms and fundamental guarantees and the fundamental principle of non-discrimination which applies to all those rights, freedoms and guarantees.

a. Fundamental Rights

The (most) fundamental rights are the right to *life*[9] and the right to *liberty* and security.[10] However, to avoid any misunderstanding, the right to life is not the right to obtain life but the right to be free to live. It is also obvious that "the right to liberty" is both a right and a freedom. The right to life and the right to liberty are to be analysed as the right of everybody not to be arbitrarily deprived of his or her life or liberty. Those rights are accompanied by the absolute prohibition of torture and inhuman or degrading punishment or treatment[11] and the absolute prohibition of slavery and servitude[12] and

---

4   Art. 25(b) of the International Covenant on Civil and Political Rights (hereafter: Civ. Cov.), Art. 3 of the (First) Protocol to the European Convention on Human Rights (hereafter: Eur. Prot. No. 1), Art. 23.1(b) of the American Convention on Human Rights (hereafter: Am. Conv.), Art. 13.1 of the African Charter on Human and Peoples' Rights (hereafter: Afr. Ch.), Art. 21.1 of the Universal Declaration of Human Rights (hereafter: Univ. Decl.).

5   Art. 25(b) Civ. Cov., Art. 3 Eur. Prot. No. 1, Art. 23.1(b) Am. Conv.

6   Art. 25(c) Civ. Cov., Art. 13.2 Afr. Ch., Art. 23.1(c) Am. Conv. (Art. 21.2 Univ. Decl.).

7   Art. 12.4 Civ. Cov., Art. 2.2 Eur. Prot. No. 4, Art. 22.5 Am. Conv., Art. 12.2 Afr. Ch.

8   BOSSUYT, *supra* note 1, pp. 195–207.

9   Art. 6 Civ. Cov., Art. 2 of the European Convention on Human Rights (hereafter: Eur. Conv.), Art. 4 Am. Conv., Art. 4 Afr. Ch. (Art. 3 Univ. Decl.).

10   Art. 9 Civ. Cov., Art. 5 Eur. Conv., Art. 7.1 Am. Conv., Art. 6 Afr. Ch. (Art. 3 Univ. Decl.).

11   Art. 7 Civ. Cov., Art. 3 Eur. Conv., Art. 5.2 Am. Conv., Art. 5 Afr. Ch. (Art. 5 Univ. Decl.).

12   Art. 8.1–2 Civ. Cov., Art. 4.1 Eur. Conv., Art. 6.1 Am. Conv., Art. 5 Afr. Ch. (Art. 4 Univ. Decl.).

Table 1. Analysis of Civil Rights

			European Convention	Civil Covenant	American Convention	African Charter	Universal Declaration
Fundamental RIGHTS		LIFE – torture & inhuman treatment	2 (d) 3 (d)	6 (d) 7 (d)	4 (d) 5.2 (d)	4 5	3 5
		LIBERTY & security + contractual obligation – slavery & servitude – forced labour	5 1 Protocol No. 4 4.1 (d) 4.2	9 11 (d) 8.1 & 2 (d) 8.3	7,1 7,7 6.1 (d) 6.2	6 5	3 4
		Juridical Personality + name + nationality		16 (d)	3 (d) 18 (d) 20 (d)		6 15
Fundamental FREEDOMS	Private	To marry	12	23.2	17.2 (d)		16
		Private and family life, home, correspondence	8	17 (d)	11.2		12
		Thought, conscience and religion (manifest)	9 (r)	18 (r)	12 (d) (r)	8	18
	Public	Expression	10 (r)	19 (r)	13 (r)		19
		Assembly	11 (r)	21 (r)	15 (r)	11	20
		Association	11 (r)	22 (r)	16 (r)	10	20
		Movement, residence, to leave	2 Prot. No. 4 (r)	12 (r)	22 (r)	12	13
Fundamental GUARANTEES		Fair trial + presumed innocent + non-retroactivity Effective remedy	6.1 6.2 7 (d) 13	14.1 14.2 15 (d) 2, 3	8.1 8.2 9 (d) 25	7.1 7.1(b) 7.2	10 11.1 11.2 8
Fundamental PRINCIPLE		NON-DISCRIMINATION	14	2.1	1.1	2–3	2

(d): Article allowing no derogation even in time of war or other public emergency threatening the life of the nation.

(r): Article allowing for limitations or restrictions under certain conditions.

forced labour.[13] Those prohibitions are absolute in the sense that they are the only human rights which do not allow for any limitation, any exception or any derogation.

Indeed, some of those rights belong to the category which does not allow for any derogation, not even "in time of war or other public emergency threatening the life of the nation".[14] Only a few of the rights to which that prohibition applies are mentioned both in the Civil Covenant and in the European and the American Convention: the right to life, the prohibition of torture, the prohibition of slavery and the non-retroactivity of criminal laws.[15] One right (the right to recognition as a person before the law)[16] is mentioned in the Civil Covenant and in the American Convention. Other rights are only mentioned in either the Civil Covenant (the prohibition of interference with privacy, family, home or correspondence[17] and the prohibition of imprisonment merely on the ground of inability to fulfil a contractual obligation)[18] or the American Convention (the freedom of conscience and religion,[19] the right of the family,[20] the right to a name,[21] the rights of the child,[22] the right to nationality[23] and the right to participate in government).[24] It appears from that list that, with the exception of the right to life and the prohibition of torture and slavery, no derogation is allowed for, not because those rights are considered more fundamental than others, but because a public emergency has no relevance for the respect of those rights or principles.

b. Fundamental Freedoms

Among the fundamental freedoms, one may distinguish, on the one hand, the fundamental freedoms concerning the private life (or privacy) of a person and, on the other hand, the fundamental freedoms which are exteriorised in public. The *"private freedoms"* are the freedom of thought, conscience and religion,[25] the right to privacy, family, home or correspondence[26] and the right (of men and women of marriageable age) to marry and to found a family.[27] No limitations of

---

13   Art. 8.3 Civ. Cov., Art. 4.2 Eur. Conv., Art. 6.2 Am. Conv.
14   Art. 4 Civ. Cov., Art. 15 Eur. Conv., Art. 27 Am. Conv.
15   Art. 15 Civ. Cov., Art. 7 Eur. Conv., Art. 9 Am. Conv. (and Art. 7.1(b) Afr. Ch.).
16   Art. 16 Civ. Cov. (and Art. 3 Am. Conv. and Art. 6 Univ. Decl.).
17   Art. 17 Civ. Cov., Art. 8 Eur. Conv., Art. 11.2 Am. Conv.
18   Art. 11 Civ. Cov. (and Art. 1 Eur. Prot. No. 4 and Art. 7.7 Am. Conv.).
19   Art. 12 Am. Conv. (and Art. 18 Civ. Cov. and Art. 9 Eur. Conv. and Art. 8 Afr. Ch.).
20   Art. 17.2 Am. Conv. (and Art. 23.2 Civ. Cov. and Art. 12 Eur. Conv.).
21   Art. 17 Am. Conv. (and Art. 23 Civ. Cov. and Art. 12 Eur. Conv.).
22   Art. 19 Am. Conv. (and Art. 24 Civ. Cov.).
23   Art. 20 Am. Conv. (Art. 15 Univ. Decl.).
24   Art. 23 Am. Conv. (and Art. 25 Civ. Cov. and Art. 3 Eur. Prot. No. 1).
25   Art. 18 Civ. Cov., Art. 9 Eur. Conv., Art. 12 Am. Conv., Art. 8 Afr. Ch. (Art. 18 Univ. Decl.).
26   Art. 17 Civ. Cov., Art. 8 Eur. Conv., Art. 11.2 Am. Conv. (Art. 12 Univ. Decl.).
27   Art. 23.2 Civ. Cov., Art. 12 Eur. Conv., Art. 17.2 Am. Conv. (Art. 16 Univ. Decl.).

those private freedoms are allowed for. The *"public* freedoms" are the freedom of expression,[28] the freedom of peaceful assembly,[29] the freedom of association[30] and the freedom of movement.[31] The freedom to *manifest* one's religion or beliefs also is a public freedom subject to limitations.[32]

The exercise of those public freedoms may be subjected to limitations or restrictions but only under strict conditions:

(1) they must be "provided by law";[33]
(2) they must be "necessary in a democratic society";[34] and
(3) they must pursue a legitimate interest, such as "the protection of the rights and freedoms of others", the "protection of public health or morals", "national security or public safety",[35] and the "prevention of disorder or crime".[36]

A typical example of such a clause is contained in Article 11.2, 1st sentence, of the European Convention concerning the right to freedom of peaceful assembly and to the freedom of association with others:

> "No restrictions shall be placed on the exercise of these rights other than such as are prescribed by law and are necessary in a democratic society in the interests of national security or public safety, for the prevention of disorder or crime, for the protection of health or morals or for the protection of rights and freedoms of others".

All those fundamental freedoms are rights and those (civil) rights are freedoms. For example, the expression "freedom of thought" is only the abbreviation of the "right to freedom of thought". They are "rights" because they are "legally protected interests". The protected interest is a freedom and the protection of those freedoms by the law (international and/or domestic) transforms them into rights. That protection does not provide the beneficiaries with something they did not yet possess (*cf.* Jean-Jacques Rousseau: "Man is born free"), but it provides them with a legal protection of those interests they possess by requiring from the State not to interfere arbitrarily in the exercise of those freedoms. It is

---

28   Art. 19 Civ. Cov., Art. 10 Eur. Conv., Art. 13 Am. Conv., Art. 9.2 Afr. Ch. (Art. 19 Univ. Decl.).
29   Art. 21 Civ. Cov., Art. 11 Eur. Conv., Art. 15 Am. Conv., Art. 11 Afr. Ch. (Art. 20 Univ. Decl.).
30   Art. 22 Civ. Cov., Art. 11 Eur. Conv., Art. 16 Am. Conv., Art. 10 Afr. Ch. (Art. 20 Univ. Decl.).
31   Art. 12 Civ. Cov., Art. 2 Eur. Prot. No. 4, Art. 22 Am. Conv., Art. 12 Afr. Ch. (Art. 13 Univ. Decl.).
32   Art. 18.3 Civ. Cov., Art. 9.2 Eur. Conv., Art. 12.3 Am. Conv. (Art. 18 Univ. Decl.).
33   In the articles mentioned in notes 17 and 20–23 *supra,* except Artt. 8, 9.2 and 10 Afr. Ch.
34   In the articles mentioned in the notes 17 and 20–23 *supra,* except Artt. 12, 18 and 19 Civ. Cov., Artt. 12–13 Am. Conv. and Artt. 8, 9.2 and 10–12 Afr. Ch.
35   In the articles mentioned in notes 17 and 20–23 *supra.* As far as the Afr. Ch. is concerned, only its Art. 11 (right to assembly) mentions legitimate interests ("national security, the safety, health, ethics and freedom of others").
36   Only in Artt. 8, 10 and 11 Eur. Conv. and Art. 2 Eur. Prot. No. 4.

in that sense that the recognition of civil rights and fundamental freedoms is declaratory.

Table 2. Synthesis of Civil Rights

	RIGHTS		FREEDOMS	
NON-DISCRIMINATION	LIFE (d) – no torture (d)	LIBERTY – no slavery (d)	Private	public
	Juridical Personality (d) + name (d) + nationality (d)	Fair trial + presumed innocent + non-retroactivity (d)	(1) conscience & religion (2) private and family life, home, correspondence (3) to marry	(1) 'manifest' (r) conscience & religion = expression (r) (2) assembly & association (r) (3) movement (r)
	Effective remedy			

(d): Article allowing no derogation even in time of war or other public emergency threatening the life of the nation.

(r): Article allowing for limitations or restrictions under certain conditions.

c.   *Fundamental Guarantees*

Nobody may be arbitrarily deprived of his life or liberty. That is why their deprivation requires the strict observance of a regular procedure. As far as the deprivation of life is concerned, Article 2.1 of the European Convention states that:

> "No one shall be deprived of his life intentionally save in the execution of a sentence of a court following his conviction of a crime for which this penalty[37] is provided by law".

Moreover, the same article provides for exceptions:

> "Deprivation of life is not inflicted in contravention of [the Convention] when it results from the use of force which is no more than absolutely necessary a) in defence of any person from unlawful violence [self-defence]; b) in order to effect a lawful arrest or to prevent the escape of a person lawfully detained; c) in action lawfully taken for the purpose of quelling a riot or insurrection".

As far as the deprivation of liberty is concerned, it is provided that:

> "In the determination of any criminal charge against him or of his [civil][38] rights and obligations in a suit a law, everyone shall be entitled to a fair and public hearing

---

[37]   The death penalty was only outlawed by the Protocol No. 6 to the European Convention on Human Rights (28 April 1983) in time of peace, by the Second Optional Protocol to the International Covenant on Civil and Political Rights (15 December 1989), by the Protocol to the American Convention on Human Rights to Abolish the Death Penalty (8 June 1990) and by Protocol No. 13 to the European Convention (3 May 2002) in all circumstances (see *infra*, Chapter X, A).

[38]   Art. 6.1 Eur. Conv.

[within a reasonable time][39] by a [competent],[40] independent and impartial tribunal established by law".[41]

This guarantee applies both in determining civil rights and obligations and in determining any criminal charge. As only the criminal procedure may lead to deprivation of liberty (or even life), the guarantees in this matter are more explicit and comprise "the right to be presumed innocent until proved guilty according the law"[42] and the principle of non-retroactivity of criminal laws:[43]

> "No one shall be held guilty of any criminal offence on account of any act or omission which did not constitute a criminal offence, under national or international law, at the time when it was committed".[44]

A more general guarantee is the one providing an "effective remedy" or an "effective recourse" if a right is violated:

> "any person whose rights or freedoms as here-in recognized are violated shall have an effective remedy".[45]

When limited to the rights and freedoms recognised in the convention concerned, as in the Civil Covenant or in the European Convention, that guarantee reinforces the efficacy of the protection of those rights and freedoms. When it applies to all fundamental rights recognised "by the constitution or laws of the State concerned or by this Convention", as is the case in the American Convention, it is itself a right applicable to rights recognised in domestic law, even when they are absent in that Convention itself. This guarantee differs from the one of a fair trial[46] in that it does not require a judicial procedure before a tribunal.

d. A Fundamental Principle

The principle of non-discrimination[47] applies to all the provisions (rights, freedoms and guarantees) of the international instruments on human rights. It is

---

[39]   *Ibid.*
[40]   Art. 14.1 Civ. Cov.
[41]   Art. 14.1 Civ. Cov., Art. 6.1 Eur. Conv., Art. 8.1 Am. Conv., Art. 7.1 Afr. Ch. (Art. 10 Univ. Decl.).
[42]   Art. 14.2 Civ. Cov., Art. 6.2 Eur. Conv., Art. 8.2 Am. Conv., Art. 7.1(b), Afr. Ch. (Art. 11.1 Univ. Decl.).
[43]   Art. 15 Civ. Cov., Art. 7 Eur. Conv., Art. 9 Am. Conv., Art. 7.2 Afr. Ch. (Art. 11.2 Univ. Decl.).
[44]   Art. 14.1 Civ. Cov., Art. 6.1 Eur. Conv., Art. 8.1 Am. Conv., Art. 7.2 Afr. Ch.
[45]   Art. 2.3 Civ. Cov., Art. 13 Eur. Conv., Art. 25 Am. Conv. (Art. 8 Univ. Decl.).
[46]   Art. 14.1 Civ. Cov., Art. 6.1 Eur. Conv., Art. 8.1 Am. Conv., Art. 7.1 Afr. Ch. (Art. 10 Univ. Decl.).
[47]   Art. 2.1 Civ. Cov., Art. 14 Eur. Conv., Art. 1.1 Am. Conv., Artt. 2–3 Afr. Ch. (Art. 2 Univ. Decl.).

not in itself a right that belongs to the one or the other category of rights, but it is a principle applicable to both social rights and civil rights.[48] It is *the* fundamental principle of human rights. Its effects, however, are more far reaching when applied to social rights rather than to civil rights.

B. SOCIO-ECONOMIC AND CULTURAL RIGHTS

There seems to be no legal criterion to distinguish between economic and social rights. Moreover, there is less homogeneity among the different international conventions on socio-economic rights. The International Covenant on Economic, Social and Cultural Rights protects the right to work (Art. 6), the right to just and favourable conditions of work (Art. 7), the right to form trade unions and join the trade union of his choice (Art. 8), the right to social security (Art. 9), the right to protection of the family (Art. 10), the right to an adequate standing of living (Art. 11), the right to the highest attainable standard of physical and mental health (Art. 12), the right to education (Art. 13) and the right to take part in cultural life (Art. 15).

The main rights protected by the (Revised) European Social Charter are the right to work (Art. 1), the right to organise (Art. 5), the right to bargain collectively (Art. 6), the right of children and young persons to protection (Art. 7), the right to social security (Art. 12), the right to social and medical assistance (Art. 13), the right of the family to social, legal and economic protection (Art. 16), the right of migrant workers and their families to protection and assistance (Art. 19) and the right to equal opportunities and equal treatment in matters of employment and occupation without discrimination on the grounds of sex (Art. 20).

In the African Charter, besides civil rights and fundamental freedoms, the following socio-economic rights are included: the right to work (Art. 15), the right to enjoy the best attainable state of physical and mental health (Art. 16) and the right to education (Art. 17). Also in the Universal Declaration of Human Rights, socio-economic rights are included along with civil rights and fundamental freedoms: the right to social security (Art. 22), the right to work (Art. 23), the right to leisure (Art. 24), the right to a standard of living adequate to health and well-being (Art. 25) and the right to education and the right to freely participate in the cultural life of the community (Art. 27). This coexistence in the Universal Declaration can be explained by the non-binding character of that instrument. One may wonder whether that coexistence in the African Charter really reinforces the protection of social rights therein or is

---

48   See *infra*, Chapter III, B, 2.

rather made possible by the weak system of control for the rights enshrined in that Charter.

A special place is taken by "the right to form and to join trade unions". It is mentioned both in Article 11.1 of the European Convention and in Article 22 of the Civil Covenant. Both articles state that this right is included in "the right of peaceful assembly and to freedom of association with others for the protection of his interests". Article 8.1(a) of the Social Covenant also ensures "[t]he right of everyone to form trade unions and join the trade union of his choice". This right is often quoted as an example of the difficulty of distinguishing between civil and social rights. A right, however, is not a social right because it is of special interest to workers, trade unions or labour law professors. It is the content of the right that is decisive and that content depends on the interpretation given to it. If that right is interpreted as being limited to the right of anybody to form with others a trade union and the freedom to join (or not to join) the trade union of one's choice, it is clearly a civil right. If it is interpreted as including "such things as consultation with unions, negotiation with them, the conclusion of agreements, etc.",[49] it becomes a social right.

The same is true for the right to education. If its content is limited to the freedom anybody has to establish with others a school, at his or her own expense, and to have his or her children sent to the school of his or her choice, it is a civil right. If its content is extended to the obligation of the State to establish schools and to subsidise schools set up by private initiative, it is a social right. The distinction is important to determine the obligations of the State and the extent to which the State may interfere in the exercise of that right by fixing school curriculum, the diplomas the school awards, the qualifications of teachers, etc.

A paramount example of a social right is the right to work. In itself, it is not sufficient for judicial determination. Many questions have to be answered first, such as what kind of work, where, when, how long, at what price and who will pay for it? Without a legal framework determining the modalities of the exercise of that right, a judge is powerless. The same is true for the social security of persons that do not work because of their age (too low or too high) or their health or because they are unemployed. To become effective, the right to social security requires huge resources and an often complex set of regulations determining the modalities and the conditions for its exercise. Social rights are not less important than civil rights and fundamental freedoms but they require different legal techniques to ensure their realisation.[50]

On the basis of an analysis of the international instruments on human rights, one may conclude that life and liberty are considered to be the most

---

49   *Cf.* the separate opinion (§15) of Judge Sir Gerald Fitzmaurice (the United Kingdom) in ECtHR, Case of *National Union of Belgian Police v. Belgium*, Pl. Ct., 27 October 1975.
50   See *infra*, Chapter II, A.

precious interests of every human being. The protection of human rights aims at guaranteeing that everybody enjoys "the right to *live in freedom*". The fundamental freedoms guaranteed by international conventions can be considered as modalities of the right to liberty and the socio-economic rights as conditions making it possible to exercise the right to life according to adequate standards.

CHAPTER II

SOCIAL RIGHTS: A SPECIFIC CATEGORY OF HUMAN RIGHTS?[51]

Social rights are generally included in other conventions than civil rights because they have different characteristics and because the role of judicial supervision, if any, is different with respect to social rights than with respect to civil rights. First, we will turn to the role of international supervisory organs with respect to social rights before examining the judgments of a prominent national constitutional court (the South African one) in the field of social rights.

A. SOCIAL RIGHTS IN INTERNATIONAL CONVENTIONS[52]

If we speak about human rights in their classical meaning, it is because modern developments have given a different meaning to those rights. Since the Universal Declaration of Human Rights of 10 December 1948, the catalogue of human rights has been expanded with the inclusion of social rights, such as the right to social security, the right to work, the right to health care, the right to education, etc. This expansion has changed the very concept of human rights. Those social rights are not less legitimate or less important than classical civil rights but their legal characteristics are different.

---

51   Based on a contribution to the Summit of Presidents of Constitutional, Regional and Supreme Court Justices in Mexico City on 8–9 November 2012 mentioned *supra* note 2; see also: BOSSUYT, Marc, "La distinction juridique entre les droits civils et politiques et les droits économiques, sociaux et culturels", *Revue des droits de l'homme/Human Rights Journal*, 1975, pp. 783–820; *id.*, "Les droits sociaux: une catégorie spécifique de droits de l'homme?", in Leif BERG ET AL. (Eds.), *Cohérence et impact de la jurisprudence de la Cour européenne des droits de l'homme (Liber amicorum Vincent Berger)*, Oisterwijk, Wolf Legal Publ., 2013, pp. 43–58.

52   *Cf. supra* note 2, pp. 361–365.

1. THE DIFFERENT CHARACTERISTICS OF SOCIAL RIGHTS[53]

The existence of different conventions for civil rights and social rights is not the result of a conscious and deliberate choice of lawyers, diplomats and politicians. It is even less the result of an old-fashioned liberalism blind to social needs. Nor does it result from the ignorance of real life or from a regretful negligence. It is the intrinsic difference between those two categories of rights that made a different treatment necessary and unavoidable. Those categories have nothing to do with notions familiar to civil codes or to social legislation. They have an autonomous meaning in the field of human rights. The distinction is based on the importance of the means necessary to ensure their implementation requiring an active role of the State. It is not because a right has a civil or a social connotation that is has different characteristics. It is the other way round: it is appropriate to qualify a right as civil or a social right in function of the characteristics it is considered to have. Once a right is interpreted as requiring means unavailable in many States or requiring the setting up of priorities between different rights or different categories of persons, they qualify as social rights.

A more theoretical approach can contribute to a better understanding of the scope of the different categories of rights and of the extent of the obligations resting upon States in the implementation of those rights. Civil rights require, in essence, an *abstention* of the State by imposing *negative* obligations, while social rights require an active *intervention* by imposing *positive* obligations. Consequently, the content of civil rights is *invariable,* regardless of the available resources, while social rights have a *variable* content. The recognition of civil rights tends to legally protect interests (generally called "freedoms") which every human being inherently possesses. That legal protection consists in prohibiting the State from arbitrarily depriving anybody of those rights and freedoms or to interfere in their exercise, except under strictly limited conditions. The granting of social rights provides someone with goods and services he otherwise would not enjoy. An individual, however, can only claim a social right to the extent the State has determined the modalities and the conditions of their enjoyment.

The recognition in international or domestic law of civil rights implies the respect of *all* those rights, *immediately* and for *everybody*. On the contrary, not all social rights of all persons can be implemented at once. The realisation of social rights, to the maximum of the available resources, can only be ensured progressively. That is also why the mechanisms of protection are more developed with respect to civil rights, sometimes even entrusted to judicial bodies, than with respect to social rights since the realisation of the latter rights requires choices to be made by political responsible bodies. The function of a system

---

[53]   Bossuyt, *supra* note 1, pp. 184–191.

of protection of civil rights is mainly *institutional* (setting up a mechanism of control), while for social rights its function is *normative* (providing new rights to the beneficiaries). In that sense, recognition of civil rights is *declaratory* in nature while the attribution of (new) social rights is *constitutive*.

It is true that, in its Chamber judgment of 9 October 1979 in the case of *Airey v. Ireland*, the European Court of Human Rights, "aware that the further realisation of social and economic rights is largely dependent on the situation – notably financial – reigning in the State in question", stated that:

> "Whilst the Convention sets forth what are essentially civil and political rights, many of them have implications of a social or economic nature" (§26).

The Court also considered that:

> "the mere fact that an interpretation of the Convention may extend into the sphere of social and economic rights should not be a decisive factor against such an interpretation; there is no water-tight division separating that sphere from the field covered by the Convention" (*ibid.*).

In its Declaration and Programme of Action, adopted in Vienna on 25 June 1993, the World Conference on Human Rights also stated, in point 5, that:

> "All human rights are universal, indivisible and interdependent and interrelated. The international community must treat human rights globally in a fair and equal manner, on the same footing, and with the same emphasis".

Nevertheless, social rights can only be enforced by a judge when sufficiently precise regulations indicate which rights, under what conditions and in which ways ought to be granted to which categories of persons. Even though a State may want to realise them all, and however much the legislative, the executive and the judicial power of the State may be willing to support their realisation, it will not always be possible to ensure at once the enjoyment of all those rights for everybody when the State does not have the necessary resources to do so.

Social rights are not less legitimate and not less important than civil rights and fundamental freedoms – and it is not superfluous to stress this. But in particular the role that can be fulfilled by courts in the realisation of social rights is – without being non-existent – nevertheless different when they deal with those rights rather than with civil rights and fundamental freedoms. It is erroneous to believe that by labelling socials rights as human rights they acquire the same legal characteristics as civil rights and fundamental freedoms.[54]

---

[54]   Bossuyt, Marc, "Should the Strasbourg Court exercise more self-restraint? On the extension of the jurisdiction of the European Court of Human Rights to social security regulations", *Human Rights Law Journal*, 2007, pp. 321–332, at p. 329.

2.   THE DEFINITION OF SOCIAL RIGHTS

As mentioned already,[55] a right is not, as far as its legal characteristics are concerned, a social right because it concerns a social matter or because it is included in a treaty concerning social rights. Reference has already been made[56] to "the right of everyone to form trade unions and join the trade union of his choice" which has, when strictly interpreted, all the characteristics of a fundamental freedom. However, when a right or a prohibition is interpreted in a way that imposes positive obligations upon States that require considerable resources, it becomes a social right. One of the consequences this entails is that its realisation may come into competition with the realisation of other rights. As far as civil rights and fundamental freedoms are concerned, which everybody is entitled to enjoy, the discretionary margin of the State is very limited. That margin is confined to the extent that some of those civil rights and fundamental freedoms may be subjected to restrictions under strict conditions (prescribed by law, necessary in a democratic society and in the interest of a limited number of objectives). Moreover, as a result of the prohibition of discrimination, certain categories of persons may even be granted rights not prescribed by the national legislator, nor by a treaty (the rights creating effect).[57] This can result in a considerable increase of expenditures, possibly at the expense of the realisation of other social rights with respect to the same or other categories of persons.

It is not because the difference between the two categories of human rights is not minimised[58] – contrary to the contemporary trend in the field[59] – that it is presented as a black-and-white distinction. There is a grey zone, both pale grey and dark grey. Indeed, civil rights and fundamental rights may also entail positive obligations and expenditures. Only when those positive obligations result in expenditures that many States cannot afford, and when they require making choices and setting priorities at the expense of other rights or other categories of persons, can those rights no longer be considered to be civil

---

[55]   See *supra*, Chapter I, B.

[56]   *Ibid.*

[57]   Bossuyt, *supra* note 1, pp. 218–219.

[58]   See *ibid.*, pp. 169–191, and *supra* note 51, pp. 783–820, and *id.*, "International Human Rights Systems: Strengths and Weaknesses", in Kathleen Mahoney & Paul Mahoney, *Human Rights in the Twenty-first Century*, Dordrecht, Kluwer Acad. Publ., 1993, pp. 52–55; Vierdag, Egbert W., "The Legal Nature of the Rights granted by International Covenant on Economic, Social and Cultural Rights", *Netherlands Yearbook of International Law*, 1978, pp. 69–105.

[59]   See van Hoof, G.J.H., "The Legal Nature of Economic, Social and Cultural Rights: a Rebuttal of Some Traditional Views", in Philip Alston & Katharina Tomasevski, *The Right to Food*, The Hague, M. Nijhoff, 1990, pp. 97–110; Meyer-Bisch, Patrice, *Le corps des droits de l'homme. L'indivisibilité comme principe d'interprétation et de mise en œuvre des droits de l'homme*, Freiburg, 1992, 401 p., at pp. 135–155; Arambulo, Kitty, *Strengthening the Supervision of the International Covenant on Economic, Social and Cultural Rights. Theoretical and Procedural Aspects*, Antwerp, Intersentia, 1999, 449 p., at pp. 71–81.

rights but rather to have become social rights. It is the degree to which positive obligations and expenditures are required that is important. When interpreting civil rights and fundamental freedoms, international courts in particular must be aware that the scope of those rights and freedoms is not unlimited.

3. THE ROLE OF INTERNATIONAL COURTS WITH RESPECT TO SOCIAL RIGHTS

When recognising the competence of international courts to verify the respect of treaty obligations in the field of human rights, the transfer of competences from the national legislator to the international judge is much greater with respect to social rights than with respect to civil rights and fundamental freedoms. That is the reason why States are very reluctant to confer jurisdiction to international courts in controlling the realisation of social rights. It suffices to refer to the control mechanism of the European Social Charter and to that of the International Covenant on Economic, Social and Cultural Rights which are much more modest than those set up by the European Convention on Human Rights and the International Covenant on Civil and Political Rights.

It is sometimes claimed that it was due to the opposition between western and socialist States during the Cold War that the two categories of rights are contained in two different treaties. The *travaux préparatoires* of the two International Covenants on Human Rights do not confirm this. They show precisely that the differences in the nature of the rights and in the obligations of States led the drafters of the International Bill of Human Rights to opt for two covenants.[60] The Member States of the Council of Europe were exclusively western and did not wage a Cold War among themselves, and nevertheless they also opted for two conventions: the European Convention on Human Rights for civil rights and fundamental freedoms and the European Social Charter for social rights.

Questions may be raised when an international court does interpret a civil right or a fundamental freedom in a manner which amounts to the transformation of such a right or freedom into a social right. At the international level it also falls to the States to set out the applicable regulations and to international courts to interpret and apply those regulations, bound however by the limits the States parties have set on their jurisdiction. To affirm that those courts are competent, in particular as far as their jurisdiction is concerned, to

---

60   BOSSUYT, Marc, "Les travaux préparatoires", in Emmanuel DECAUX (Dir.), *Le Pacte international relatif aux droits civils et politiques, Commentaire article par article*, Paris, Economica, 2011, pp. 1–9, at pp. 5–6.

disregard the intentions of the States parties and that they are only bound by the limits they impose themselves, undermines the rule of law.

This does not imply that civil rights and fundamental rights should not be interpreted "in the light of present-day conditions",[61] quite the contrary. But, for example, an interpretation extending the jurisdiction of the European Court of Human Rights to social rights is difficult to reconcile with the respect of the intention of the States parties as required by the rules of interpretation applicable to treaties. The so-called "teleological" or "dynamic" interpretation favoured by European courts is sometimes inclined to lose sight of the boundaries of their jurisdiction. The more the norms of reference are open and abstract, as is the case with those contained in the European Convention on Human Rights and in the more recent Charter on Fundamental Rights of the European Union, the more caution and restraint is required.

B. THE SOUTH AFRICAN CONSTITUTIONAL COURT AND SOCIAL RIGHTS[62]

The South African experience in dealing with social rights presents an interest far beyond the country or even the continent concerned. Those rights were included in the Bill of Rights of the South African Constitution and gave rise to several important cases dealt with by the South African Constitutional Court. Even admitting that the difference between civil and political rights, on the one hand, and social rights, on the other hand, is one of degree rather than one of nature (a largely academic dispute),[63] the question remains what the extent of that difference is and what are its implications. The cases relating to social rights dealt with by the South African Constitutional Court provide interesting elements to answer those questions.

At the time of drafting of the South African Bill of Rights (1991–1993), the so-called "anti-constitutionalisers" opposed the inclusion of social rights, because they believed that those rights were not justiciable and that entrusting judges to enforce those rights would violate the principle of separation of powers.[64] On 6 September 1996, the South African Constitutional Court, called upon to "certify" the final Constitution which was adopted on 8 May 1996,

---

61   ECtHR, *Tyrer v. the United Kingdom*, 25 April 1978, §31.
62   Bossuyt, Marc, "The South African Constitutional Court and socio-economic rights", in *Liège, Strasbourg, Bruxelles: parcours des droits de l'homme (Liber amicorum Michel Melchior)*, Limal, Anthemis, 2010, pp. 281–309.
63   Bossuyt, *supra* note 54, pp. 328–329.
64   *Cf.* Christiansen, Eric, "Adjudicating non-justiciable rights: socio-economic rights and the South African Constitution", *Columbia Human Rights Law Review*, 2007, pp. 324–325; Mureinik, Etienne, "Beyond a Charter of Luxuries: Economic Rights in the Constitution", *South African Journal on Human Rights,* 1992, pp. 464–474.

rejected both objections:[65] it considered the task of enforcing social rights not "so different from that ordinarily conferred upon them by a bill of rights that it results in a breach of the separation of powers" and, in its opinion, the fact that those rights "will almost inevitably give rise to [budgetary] implications does not seem to be a bar to their justiciability".[66]

In cases concerning social rights, the South African Constitutional Court admitted a variability of the obligations of the State uncommon to civil rights. In the *Grootboom* judgment of 4 October 2000, Justice Zak Yacoob stated that "[t]he state's obligation [...] may differ from province to province, from city to city, from rural to urban areas and from person to person".[67] It is difficult to imagine that this could be the same with respect to civil rights or fundamental freedoms as the enjoyment by everyone of all those rights and freedoms should be respected at once. In the *Mazibuko* judgment of 8 October 2009, Justice Kate O'Regan also stressed that what is required by a social right "will vary over time and context" (§60) and, more particularly, that the obligation "in relation to the right of access to sufficient water will vary depending upon circumstance" (§62).[68]

1. THE MINIMUM CORE APPROACH v. PRIORITISATION AND ACCOUNTABILITY

In legal doctrine much effort has been put into trying to convince the South African Court to adopt the minimum core approach favoured by the UN Committee on Economic, Social and Cultural Rights.[69] That Committee had in 1990 expressed the view that:

> "a minimum core obligation to ensure the satisfaction of, at the very least, minimum essential levels of each of the rights is incumbent upon every State party".[70]

---

65   *Certification of the Republic of South Africa*, CCT 32/96, [1996] ZACC 26; 1196 (4) SA 744 (CC); 1196 (10) *BCLR* 1253 (CC) (6 September 1996).

66   *Ibid.*, §§77–78.

67   *Government of the Republic of South Africa and Others v. Grootboom and Others*, §76, CCT 11/00, [2000] ZACC 19; 2001 (1) SA 46 (CC); 2000 (11) *BCLR* 1169 (4 October 2000).

68   *Lindiwe Mazibuko and Others v. City of Johannesburg and Others*, §§60 and 62, CCT 39/09, [2009] ZACC 28; 2010 (3) *BCLR* 239 (CC); 2010 (4) SA 1 (CC) (8 October 2009).

69   SCOTT, Craig & ALSTON, Philip, "Adjudicating Constitutional Priorities in a Transnational Context: a Comment on *Soobramoney*'s Legacy and *Grootboom*'s Promise", *South African Journal on Human Rights*, 2000, pp. 206–268. See also BOLLYKY, Thomas, "R IF C > P + B: A Paradigm for Judicial Remedies of Socio-Economic Rights Violations", *South African Journal on Human Rights*, 2002, pp. 161–200; PIETERSE, Marius, "Coming to Terms with Judicial Enforcement of Socio-Economic Rights", *South African Journal on Human Rights*, 2004, pp. 383–417 and "Resuscitating Socio-Economic Rights: Constitutional Entitlements to Health Care services", *South African Journal on Human Rights*, 2006, pp. 473–502.

70   General Comment No. 3, UN Doc E/1991/23, Annex III, §§9–10, December 1990.

In an article published in 2003,[71] David Bilchitz stated:

> "It is by no means clear that the problems in South Africa arise from an absolute scarcity of resources; in this context, the problems seem to be rather about the highly unequal distribution of resources".

Should social rights be used by judges as a tool to engage in a major programme of redistribution of resources? It is one question whether this is the ultimate purpose of provisions on social rights in international conventions and in national constitutions. It is another question whether such a revolutionary task should be entrusted, if ever, to the judiciary rather than to the legislative or to the executive. In other countries with enormous differences in distribution of wealth, there seems to be not even a beginning of an awareness that the social rights enshrined in the International Covenant on Economic, Social and Cultural Rights or in their own national Constitution would have that purpose. It would nevertheless be the logical outcome of the minimum core approach.

As stated in Section 26(2) of the South African Constitution, the State has to achieve the progressive realisation of social rights "within its resources". In his concurring opinion in the *Soobramoney* of 27 November 1997, Justice Albie Sachs had stated that "[u]nfortunately, the resources are limited".[72] In the book[73] he wrote at the end of his 15 years at the South African Constitutional Court, he refers in his chapter[74] on social rights to that opinion when he states:

> "Socio-economic rights in this respect were different in their mode of enjoyment, if not in their essence, from civil and political rights";[75]

> "the exercise of a right that by its nature is shared, often competitively, with other holders of the right, must have different legal characteristics from the exercise of a classical individual civil right that is autonomous and complete in itself".[76]

The main question is:

> "Should the Constitution be read as handing over to each judge in each court the right and duty to decide who should have priority access to social goods in short supply?"[77]

---

71 BILCHITZ, David, "Towards a Reasonable Approach to the Minimum Core: Laying the Foundations for Future Socio-Economic Rights Jurisprudence", *South African Journal on Human Rights*, 2003, pp. 1–26, at p. 17, note 52.

72 *Soobramoney v. Minister of Health KwaZulu-Natal*, §59, CCT 32/97, [1997] ZACC 17; 1998 (1) SA 765 (CC); 1997 (12) BCLR 1696 (27 November 1997).

73 SACHS, Albie, *The Strange Alchemy of Life and Law*, Oxford, Oxford Univ. Pr., 2009, 306 p.

74 *Ibid.*, Chapter 7 ("The Judge Who Cried: The Judicial Enforcement of Socio-Economic Rights"), pp. 161–201.

75 *Ibid.*, p. 176.

76 *Ibid.*

77 *Ibid.*, p. 182.

The realisation of social rights is an exercise in prioritisation. The inability to realise all social rights for all persons at once, due to the insufficient availability of resources, makes it essential to determine which social rights of which persons will be realised first. By adopting the minimum core approach the Court should establish which classes of needs enjoy priority over others.[78] National courts, conscious of the immensity and the eminently political sensitivity of that task,[79] will not engage easily[80] in such an endeavour. That does not mean that they cannot fulfil a meaningful role in providing guidelines to the responsible political authorities.[81] They may certainly judge the reasonableness of the programmes and the policies set out by the legislature and by the executive,[82] but that is different from determining precisely which persons are entitled at a given moment to which social right.

Justice O'Regan eloquently stated the purpose of that approach in the *Mazibuko* judgment:

> "[T]o determine precisely what the achievement of any particular social and economic right entails [...] is a matter, in the first place, for the legislature and executive [...] for it is their programme and promises that are subjected to democratic popular choice" (§61).

In her view, it is mainly a matter of accountability:

> "[T]he social and economic rights enable citizens to hold government to account for the manner in which it seeks to pursue the achievement of social and economic rights" (§59); "[T]he social and economic rights entrenched in our Constitution [...] enable citizens to hold government accountable not only through the ballot box but also, in a different way, through litigation" (§71).

---

[78] Cf. WESSON, Murray, *"Grootboom* and beyond: Reassessing the Socio-Economic Jurisprudence of the South African Constitutional Court", *South African Journal on Human Rights*, 2004, pp. 284–308, at p. 298.

[79] As stressed by Justice Sachs in *Soobramoney*, such choices may be "agonising" (§59).

[80] Cf. in *Soobramoney* (§29), President Arthur Chaskalson: "A court will be slow to interfere with rational decisions taken in good faith by the political organs and medical authorities whose responsibility it is to deal with such matters" (§29), and Justice Sachs: "Courts are not the proper place to resolve the agonising personal and medical problems that underlie [the tragic medical choices to be made]" (§58); and in *Treatment Action Campaign*, the Court: "Courts are ill-suited to adjudicate upon issues where court orders could have multiple social and economic consequences for the community" (§38).

[81] Cf. WESSON, *supra* note 78, p. 295: "[The Court] therefore does not dictate exactly what the state should do to assist people in the position of the respondents but instead gives it broad guidelines".

[82] Cf. Justice Yacoob in *Grootboom*: "These policies and programmes [implemented by the executive] must be *reasonable* both in their conception and their implementation" (§42), and Justice O'Regan in *Lindiwe Mazibuko*: "The purpose of the constitutional entrenchment of social and economic rights [is] to ensure that the state continue to take *reasonable* legislative and other measures progressively to achieve the realisation of the rights to the basic necessities of life" (§59) and "the government agency must explain why the policy is *reasonable*" (§161) (emphasis added).

In adopting an approach of accountability, the Court is not encroaching upon the greater democratic legitimacy of the legislature and the executive but, on the contrary, it enhances the democratic quality of the separation of powers. Moreover, as stated by Murray Wesson in an article published in 2004:

> "In this way, the Court is able to fulfil functions for which it is well suited (protecting the interests of vulnerable groups and holding the state to standards of justification) while the state is accorded primary responsibility for organising and implementing socio-economic programs".[83]

2. STOCK-TAKING OF THE JUDGMENTS RENDERED

In no case dealt with up to now has the Court determined the minimum core of a social right everyone should be entitled to.[84] In *Soobramoney*[85] (1997) and in *Mazibuko* (2009), the Court rejected the contentions of the applicants. In *Grootboom* (2000), the Court required only the progressive implementation of "a comprehensive and coordinated programme [providing also] relief for people in intolerable conditions or crisis situation". In two cases, the Court ordered the authorities to take action: in the case of the *Hoërskool Ermelo*[86] (2009), the Court ordered the high school to report within a specified period of time on the reasonable steps it has taken in reviewing its language policy, having regard not only to its own interests and those of its learners but also to the interests of the community in which the school is located and the needs of other learners; in the *Blue Moonlight Properties* case[87] (2011), the Court, considering that the eviction of unlawful occupiers was lawful, nevertheless ordered the City of Johannesburg to provide the occupiers with temporary accommodation.

---

[83] WESSON, *supra* note 78, p. 305.

[84] See also LEHMANN, Karin, "In Defense of the Constitutional Court: Litigating Socio-Economic Rights and the Myth of the Minimum Core", *American University International Law Review*, 2006, pp. 163–197.

[85] In a more recent judgment (*Oppelt v. Head: Health, Department of Health Provincial Administration: Western Cape*, CCT 185/14, [2015] ZACC 33; 2016 (1) SA 325 (CC) (14 October 2015) concerning the right of access to health care, Acting Justice Mahube Molema (with seven concurring and two dissenting Justices) found that the negligence of the Health Department – in not transferring the applicant within four hours of the injury to a hospital specialised in spinal cord injuries – had violated his right to emergence medical treatment.

[86] Deputy Chief Justice Dikgang Moseneke, writing for a unanimous Court, in *Head of Department: Mpumalanga Department of Education and Another v. Hoërskool Ermelo & Others*, CCT 40/09, [2009] ZACC 32; 2010 (2) SA 415 (CC); 2010 (3) BCLR 177 (CC) (14 October 2009).

[87] Justice Johann van der Westhuizen, writing for a unanimous Court, in *City of Johannesburg Metropolitan Municipality v. Blue Moonlight Properties 39 (Pty) Ltd and Another*, (CC) [2011] ZACC 33; 2012 (2) BCLR 150 (CC); 2012 (2) SA 104 (CC) (1 December 2011).

In a few cases, the Court imposed procedural requirements. It did so (a) in its judgment in *Occupiers of Olivia Road*[88] of 19 February 2008, by prohibiting the eviction of any person from his home in the absence of an appropriate court order, (b) in its judgment in *Leon Joseph*[89] of 9 October 2009, by prohibiting the termination of electricity supply in the absence of a pre-termination notice, and (c) in its judgment in *Abahlali Besamjondolo Movement SA*[90] of 14 October 2009, by requiring evictions in KwaZulu-Natal to comply with the national Housing Act and the National Housing Code.

In other cases, the Court decided that a particular social right as defined by the legislator should be extended to additional categories of persons: in its judgment in *Treatment Action Campaign*[91] of 5 July 2002, the Court ordered the removal of the exclusion, at public hospitals and clinics that are not research and training sites, of the use of a particular medicine for pregnant mothers infected by HIV; in its judgment in *Khosa* of 4 March 2004, the Court ordered the extension of social assistance to permanent residents regardless of their nationality.

The European Court had also rejected, in its judgment in *Gaygusuz v. Austria* of 16 September 1996, the argument of the Austrian Government based on "the idea that the State has special responsibility for its own nationals". Similarly, the South African Constitutional Court rejected in *Khosa* the argument that "the state has an obligation toward its own citizens first" (§57). The modern tendency is to favour the responsibility of a State for persons present on its territory rather than based on their nationality.[92]

The argument that "this would impose an impermissibly high financial burden on the state" (§60) was rejected in *Khosa*[93] by Justice Yvonne Mokgoro because:

> "the state can protect itself against persons becoming financial burdens by thorough, careful consideration in the admission of immigrants [(§64)...; i]f a mistake is made in this regard, [...] that may be a cost we have to pay for the constitutional commitment to developing a caring society" (§65).

---

88   *Occupiers of Olivia Road, Berea Township, and 197 Main Street, Johannesburg. v. City of Johannesburg and Others*, CCT 24/07, [2008] *ZACC* 1; 2008 (3) SA 208 (CC); 2008 (5) *BCLR* 475 (CC) (19 February 2008).

89   *Leon Joseph and Others v. City of Johannesburg and Others*, CCT 43/09, [2009] *ZACC* 30; 2010 (3) *BCLR* 212 (CC); 2010 (4) SA 55 (CC) (9 October 2009).

90   *Abahlali Basemjondolo Movement SA and Sibusiso Zikode v. Premier of the Province of KwaZulu-Natal*, CCT 12/09, [2009] *ZACC* 31; 2010 (2) *BCLR* 475 (CC) (14 October 2009).

91   *Minister of Health and Others v. Treatment Action Campaign and Others (No. 1)*, CCT 9/02, [2002] *ZACC* 16; 2002 (5) SA 703; 2002 (10) *BCLR* 1075 (5 July 2002).

92   On the ground "nationality", see Bossuyt, *supra* note 54, pp. 324–325.

93   *Khosa and Others v. Minister of Social Development and Others; Mahlaule and Another v. Minister of Development and Others*, CCT 13/03, CCT 12/03, [2004] *ZACC* 11; 2004 (6) SA 505 (CC); 2004 (3) *BCLR* 569 (CC) (4 March 2004).

On the other hand, Justice Sandile Ngcobo, with Justice Tholie Madala concurring, believes that "[n]o careful immigration policy can foresee that an immigrant once admitted will fall upon hard times and thus become unable to provide for him or herself" (§132). Knowing that immigration, in South Africa as well as in Europe, is rarely the result of "careful consideration in the admission of immigrants" but rather of the State being confronted with situations of *fait accompli* on a large scale, the opinion of the minority seems to come closer to reality than that of the majority.

Contrary to Louis Khosa and others, who contended that the exclusion of all non-citizens was inconsistent with the State's obligations to provide access to social security to "everyone" (§38), the majority of the Court admitted that:

> "social benefits should not be made available to all who are in South Africa *irrespective of their immigration status* [(§58) …] It may be reasonable to exclude from the legislative scheme workers who are citizens of other countries, *visitors and illegal residents, who have only a tenuous link with this country*" (§59) (emphasis added).[94]

Even if nationality is considered irrelevant in matters of social benefits, the immigration status of the applicant and the quality and extent of the links he has with the country concerned certainly are relevant. The Court did not decide that everybody, but only foreigners who are "permanent residents", should also qualify for social assistance.

3. INTERNATIONAL SUPERVISORY ORGANS v. NATIONAL COURTS

It may be useful to stress some of the differences between an international supervisory committee making recommendations to governments on social rights and national courts rendering binding judgments on the same matter. An international committee addresses itself to all powers of a State without being concerned with the respective roles of the legislative, the executive and the judiciary in the implementation of the measures required. Even if the distinction between categories of rights is minimised,[95] it cannot be denied that the judiciary undoubtedly has a greater role to play in ensuring the respect for civil and political rights than in the implementation of social, economic and cultural rights. With respect to the latter, the national court is fully aware

---

94 In a comment on the judgment in ECtHR, *Koua Poirrez v. France*, 30 September 2003, the present author did express a similar view by stating that nothing indicated that the European Court "might have come to the same conclusion if the case had concerned a foreigner who had refused to comply with an order to leave the country or who had been staying in the country as a tourist. […] it seems justified to link entitlements to social allowances to the nature and the length of his entitlement to stay in the country" (Bossuyt, *supra* note 54, p. 327).

95 *Ibid.*, pp. 328–329.

that, as a matter of principle, it is not its role to substitute itself for the legislator and the government, particularly since social rights can only be sanctioned as subjective rights by a court of law when there are national regulations defining the content, the modalities and the beneficiaries of the rights concerned.[96] It is only on the basis of sufficiently precise national legislation and regulation that a court can enforce individual social rights. Finally, familiar as it is with the legal, political and economic framework of its own national State, the national court is undoubtedly better qualified than any international body to render binding decisions on the implementation of social rights.

---

[96]   *Ibid.*, p. 328.

CHAPTER III
THE PROHIBITION
OF DISCRIMINATION[97]

In the international human rights instruments, a distinction has to be made between the discrimination clauses and the provisions containing a (more) general prohibition of discrimination.

A. THE DISCRIMINATION CLAUSES IN INTERNATIONAL HUMAN RIGHTS INSTRUMENTS

In Article 2, 1st sentence, of the Universal Declaration of Human Rights it is stated that:

> "Everyone is entitled to all the rights and freedoms set forth in this Declaration, without *distinction* of any kind, such as race, colour, sex, language, religion, political or other opinion, national or social origin, property, birth or other status" (emphasis added).

Article 2.2 of the International Covenant on Economic, Social and Cultural Rights reads as follows:

> "The States Parties to the present Covenant undertake to guarantee that the rights enunciated in the present Covenant will be exercised without *discrimination* of any kind as to race, colour, sex, language, religion, political or other opinion, national or social origin, property, birth or other status" (emphasis added),

while Article 2.1 of the International Covenant on Civil and Political Rights states that:

---

[97] Based on a contribution to the Summer Session of the Institute of International Public Law and International Relations of Thessaloniki entitled "L'interdiction de la discrimination et l'action positive" in Kalliopi KOUFA (Ed.), *Might and Right in International Relations, Thesaurus Acroasiun,* vol. XXVIII, Athens, Sakkoulas Publ., 1999, pp. 325–344, at pp. 331–337; see also: BOSSUYT, Marc, "The Principle of Equality in Article 26 of the International Covenant on Civil and Political Rights", in Armand DE MESTRAL ET AL. (Eds.), *The Limitation of Human Rights in Comparative Constitutional Law,* Québec, Y. Blais, 1986, pp. 269–288; *id.,* "Prohibition of Discrimination and the Concept of Affirmative Action", in *Bringing International Human Rights Law Home,* New York, United Nations, 2000, pp. 93–106.

"Each State Party to the present Covenant undertakes to respect and to ensure to all individuals within its territory and subject to its jurisdiction the rights recognized in the present Covenant, without *distinction* of any kind, such as race, colour, sex, language, religion, political or other opinion, national or social origin, property, birth or other status" (emphasis added).

In Article 14 of the European Convention on Human Rights,[98] discrimination is prohibited solely with respect to the rights and freedoms set forth in the Convention. Article 14 of the European Convention, like Article 2 of both Covenants, forbids discrimination only with respect to the rights "enunciated", "recognized" or "set forth" in the treaties concerned. In other words, the prohibition is limited to the rights guaranteed by the Convention.

This is also the case with the American Convention and the African Charter. Article 1.1 of the American Convention on Human Rights, reads as follows:

"The States Parties to this Convention undertake to respect the rights and freedoms recognized herein and to ensure to all persons subject to their jurisdiction the free and full exercise of those rights and freedoms, without any *discrimination* for reasons of race, color, sex, language, religion, political or other opinion, national or social origin, economic status, birth, or any other social condition" (emphasis added),

while Article 2 of the African Charter on Human and Peoples' Rights states that:

"Every individual shall be entitled to the enjoyment of the rights and freedoms recognized and guaranteed in the present Charter without *distinction* of any kind such as race, ethnic group, colour, sex, language, religion, political or any other opinion, national and social origin, fortune, birth or any status" (emphasis added).

1. QUESTIONS OF TERMINOLOGY

As far as the terminology is concerned, there seems to be some confusion in that Article 2 of the Universal Declaration and Article 2.1 of the Civil Covenant use the term "distinction", while in the other human rights instruments the term "discrimination" is used. The confusion is even greater when looking to the French version of those instruments where the term "*distinction*" is, in addition, used in Article 7, 1st sentence, of the Universal

---

[98]   "The enjoyment of the rights and freedoms set forth in this Convention shall be secured without *discrimination* on any ground such as sex, race, colour, language, religion, political or other opinion, national or social origin, association with a national minority, property, birth or other status" (emphasis added).

Declaration,[99] in Article 2.2 of the Social Covenant and in Article 14 of the European Convention. On the latter, the European Court of Human Rights stated in its judgment of 23 July 1968 in the case *"relating to certain aspects of the laws on the use of languages in education in Belgium (merits)"* (Series A, p. 34) that:

> "In spite of the very general wording of the French version (*'sans distinction aucune'*), [... t]his version must be read in the light of the more restrictive text of the English version ('without discrimination')."

It is quite obvious that not every "distinction" is prohibited but only "discrimination", which is the term most frequently used when referring to unjust, unreasonable, illegitimate or arbitrary distinctions. The use of the term "distinction" in the first human rights instruments can be explained by its use (in English and in French) in the UN Charter of 26 June 1945 which states, in its Article 55, as one of the goals of the United Nations the promotion of "universal respect for, and observance of, human rights and fundamental freedoms for all without *distinction* as to race, sex language, or religion" (emphasis added). Progressively, with the exception of the African Charter, the term "distinction" has been replaced by the more appropriate term "discrimination", first in English, as shown by the European Convention of 4 November 1950, and later also in French.

It appears from the *travaux préparatoires* of the Covenants that the Third Committee of the General Assembly replaced in 1963, at the initiative of the Italian representative Professor Francesco Capotorti,[100] the term "distinction" in the draft Social Covenant by the term "discrimination". It was expected that the terminology in the draft Civil Covenant would be made uniform with the Social Covenant but, undoubtedly due to the great number of Articles that had to be adopted in 1966 before the final adoption of the Covenants on 16 December 1966, the term "distinction" was not replaced in the Civil Covenant. It emerges, however, from the consideration of the preparatory work that by using the term "distinction", the scope of the prohibition in the Civil Covenant is not larger than in the Social Covenant, which uses the term "discrimination".

Nowadays it is generally accepted that the term "distinction" is neutral and used to indicate a difference of treatment which has not (yet) been qualified as justified or not, while the term "discrimination" is reserved, at least in the international law of human rights, for a distinction considered unjustified. More and more, the term "differentiation" is used to indicate a difference of treatment which is considered to be justified.

---

[99]   See *infra*, Chapter III, B.
[100]   A/C.3/SR.1257, p. 260.

2. THE DETERMINATION OF A DISCRIMINATION

An important element in determining a discrimination is the ground on which the difference of treatment is based. The enumeration of those grounds in the international instruments protecting human rights in general is not exhaustive but exemplary. The contrary impression given by the four grounds mentioned in the UN Charter ("race, sex, language, or religion") is contradicted by their enlargement to 12 in the Universal Declaration (additional grounds are "[...], colour, [...] political or other opinion, national or social origin, property, birth or other status") and even to 13 in the European Convention (the additional ground is: "association with a national minority") as well as by having the enumeration of those ground preceded by the words "such as" (in French: "*notamment*"). The enumeration of the grounds mentioned in those international instruments is very homogenous, with the exception of the ground "property" which is replaced by "economic status" in the American Convention and by "fortune" in the African Charter. Only the latter Charter mentions the ground "ethnic group". The last mentioned ground ("or other status") in those enumerations becomes in the American Convention "or any social condition" and in the African Charter "or any status". Grounds are included in those enumerations not so much because they are the most heinous[101] but because they are the most likely to be the basis of a discrimination.[102]

Since their enumeration is non-exhaustive, the grounds, though important, are not in themselves the decisive element in determining the arbitrary character of a discrimination. A difference of treatment based on a ground not mentioned in the convention concerned can nevertheless be discriminatory and, vice versa, a difference of treatment based on a ground mentioned in a convention is not necessarily discriminatory.[103] To find out whether a difference of treatment is discriminatory, the relationship has to be examined between that ground and the right (or freedom) in which the difference of treatment is operated. It is necessary that the matter concerned by the difference of

---

[101] Discrimination on the basis of the colour of eyes or hair would not be less arbitrary but is less likely to happen in legal regulations.

[102] When e.g. the Constitutions of India (1949: Art. 15), Pakistan (1973: Art. 26.1) and Nepal (1990: Art. 11.4) mention "caste", it does not mean that this ground is only prohibited in those countries but only that in those countries the need was felt more than elsewhere to mention this ground because discrimination on that basis was not unlikely to happen.

[103] As far as "race" is concerned, it is difficult to imagine this ground to be relevant for any legally protected interest (with the possible exception of the recruitment of actors having to play the role of a person of African descent). The International Convention on the Elimination of All Forms of Racial Discrimination is a convention aimed at outlawing discriminations based on a limited number of "racial" grounds: "race, colour, descent, or national or ethnic origin". In that case, the finding of a difference of treatment in a right or freedom based on such a ground will, in general, be sufficient to qualify it as discriminatory.

treatment is a right or a freedom; in other words, it has to be a legally protected interest. When a difference of treatment does not concern a matter not protected by the law, because it has not (yet) been subjected to legal regulation, it is not a discrimination prohibited by law.

Private life, for example, is reserved for private acts of an individual in which the State may not interfere. In the private domain (e.g. love relations) an individual may act according to his preferences, even when based on grounds which would not be justifiable if they would concern rights or freedoms. It is, however, the law that fixes the borders of private life and, if the need is felt, the legislator may regulate new fields of human activity as long as the right to privacy does not become void of its substance. An example can be the admission to and the functioning of clubs which can be regulated to some extent. Once a matter is subject to legal regulations, discrimination in that matter is prohibited. There is an absolute incompatibility between law and arbitrariness.

A difference of treatment is arbitrary when the ground on which it is based is not relevant for the right concerned. A sufficient connexion is needed between the one and the other. It is perfectly possible that a ground is relevant for a given right and not for another, like it may be that a difference of treatment is justified when based on a given ground but not on another. In its judgment of 23 July 1968 in the *Belgian linguistic* case (Series A, p. 34), the European Court of Human Rights held that:

> "the principle of equality of treatment is violated if the distinction has no *objective and reasonable justification*. The existence of such a justification must be assessed in relation to the aim and effects of the measure under consideration, regard being had to the principles which normally prevail in democratic societies. A difference of treatment in the exercise of a right laid down in the Convention must not only pursue a *legitimate aim*: article 14 is likewise violated when it is clearly established that there is no *reasonable relationship of proportionality between the means employed and the aim sought to be realized*" (emphasis added).

When judging a difference of treatment in a legal provision, there is generally little disagreement on the legitimacy of the goal pursued or on the objectivity – and even on the relevance – of the ground on which the difference is based. On the contrary, opinions may easily diverge as far as the "proportionality" is concerned.[104]

---

[104] On the concept of proportionality, see MARTENS, Paul, "L'irrésistible ascension du principe de proportionnalité", in *Présence du droit public et des droits de l'homme (Mélanges offerts à Jacques Velu)*, Brussels, Bruylant, 1992, vol 1, pp. 49–68.

B.   THE GENERAL PROHIBITION OF DISCRIMINATION

Article 7 of the Universal Declaration of Human Rights reads as follows:

"All are equal before the law and are entitled without any *discrimination* to equal protection of the law. All are entitled to equal protection against any *discrimination* in violation of this Declaration and against any incitement to such *discrimination*" (emphasis added).[105]

Article 26 of the International Covenant on Civil and Political Rights also contains a general prohibition of discrimination, which reads as follows:

"All persons are equal before the law and are entitled without any *discrimination* to the equal protection of the law. In this respect, the law shall prohibit any *discrimination* and guarantee to all persons equal and effective protection against *discrimination* on any ground such as race, colour, sex, language, religion, political or other opinion, national or social origin, property, birth or other status" (emphasis added).

Article 1.1 of Protocol No. 12 to the European Convention on Human Rights, adopted on 4 November 2000, contains also a more general prohibition than guaranteed in Article 14 of that Convention:

"The enjoyment of any right set forth by law shall be secured without *discrimination* on any ground such as sex, race, colour, language, religion, political or other opinion, national or social origin, association with a national minority, property, birth or other status" (emphasis added).

It is mainly with respect to Article 26 of the Civil Covenant that we will examine the scope of the general prohibition of discrimination. First, we will see whether that prohibition covers both "equality in the law" and "equality before the law" and what is meant by the non-independent existence of the prohibition of discrimination and by its autonomous violation. Second, we will examine whether Article 26 of the Civil Covenant is applicable to social rights.

1.   EQUALITY BEFORE AND IN THE LAW

There is no doubt that, in its first sentence, Article 26 of the Civil Covenant guarantees and "equality before the law" and "equality in the law" in the sense given to those expressions by Hans Kelsen.[106] Strictly speaking, "equality

---

[105]   In French, the term "*distinction*" is used once and the term "*discrimination*" is used twice in that Article.

[106]   *The Pure Theory of Law* (translated into English by Max Knight), Berkeley, University of California Press, 1962, p. 141: "The guarantee of this equality [before the law] means only

before the law" concerns the application of the law, while "equality *in* the law" concerns the creation of the law. Equality before the law requires (only) that the law be applied without discrimination. As far as fundamental freedoms to which "everyone" is entitled are concerned, a judge that would not equally apply the law to all would not only violate the principle of equality before the law but would also violate the right of the person not to be deprived of that freedom.

The drafters of national constitutions or international conventions are not always aware of Kelsen's distinction between equality *before* and equality *in* the law. By adding, in Article 26, 1ˢᵗ sentence, 2ⁿᵈ part, of the Civil Covenant, to the expression "equal before the law" the expression "[all persons ...] are entitled without any discrimination to the equal protection of the law", the drafters of that Covenant made it clear that it also prescribes "equality in the law". "Equality in the law", which means that the law itself may not itself contain any discriminatory element, is a principle not addressed to judges but to legislators. There is no doubt that the prohibition of discrimination – which meaning is not different from the principle of equality, but formulated negatively instead of positively – covers equality both *in* and *before* the law. The international judge will not only verify whether the law has been applied without discrimination but also whether the law itself is not discriminatory.

In an article published in 1981, Christian Tomuschat[107] nevertheless expressed the view that: "Article 26 is confined to equality before the law". An examination of the relevant proceedings in the Commission on Human Rights[108] reveals that the main point at issue was whether or not the provision (which would later become Article 26) should protect rights not guaranteed by the Civil Covenant. At no time it was contended that the wider scope of application would entail that the level of protection provided by the clause for the rights not guaranteed by the Covenant (Article 26) would be different from that for the rights guaranteed by the Covenant (Article 2.1).

It was during the proceedings in the Third Committee of the General Assembly[109] that Article 26 was completed. The logical conclusion to be drawn from the explanations given by the proponents of the Indian amendment[110] to add the words "and are entitled to equal protection of the law" is that the first sentence contains two distinct concepts – (a) "equality before the law" and (b)

---

[107]   that the law-applying organs are permitted to consider only those differences which the statutes to be applied by them expressly recognize. Thereby nothing else is stipulated but the general principle of the lawfulness of the application of the law, immanent in all law; and the principle of the legality of the application of statutes, immanent in all statutes: the tautological principle that a norm ought to be applied in conformity with this norm".

[107]   Tomuschat, Christian, "Equality and Non-Discrimination under the International Covenant on Civil and Political Rights", in I. von Muench (Ed.), *Festschrift für Hans-Jürgen Schlochauer*, Berlin, de Gruyter, 1981, p. 698, note 27.

[108]   Bossuyt, *supra* note 97, pp. 269–287, at pp. 273–275.

[109]   *Ibid.*, pp. 275–277.

[110]   A/C.3/L.945.

"equal protection of the law" – which cannot be understood otherwise than covering the notion of "equality in the law". The main purpose of another amendment proposed by Greece and the United Kingdom,[111] to introduce the second sentence of Article 26 with the words "in this respect", was to avoid a prohibition of discrimination, which would extend to discrimination in private and social relations. If any meaning should be given to the second sentence, it should require the States parties to adopt legislative measures providing effective protection against discrimination of any kind.

However, it is the essence of any legal protection that it provides safeguards against discrimination in the enjoyment of *all* rights, but also in the enjoyment of *rights* only. The principle of equality does not prescribe material equality among all persons, but equality before *the law* and in *the law*. All persons – how different they all may be – are equal *in rights*. Consequently, the second sentence of Article 26 can only be understood as requiring the extension of the protection of the law to matters which hitherto did not enjoy its protection.

By requiring the intervention of the legislature, it is obvious that the second sentence of Article 26 is not "self-sufficient" as it is not formulated in a manner sufficiently complete and precise to enable a judge to apply it in the absence of the intervention of the legislature. Contrary to the first sentence of Article 26, its second sentence does not provide any individual with a judicial enforceable new right, nor can it have third party effects ("*Drittwirkung*"). Moreover, that requirement is limited by the fundamental right of respect for the privacy of everyone, albeit that it is the law that fixes the borders of that privacy.[112] In doing so, the law also fixes the limits of the scope of application of a general prohibition of discrimination. The general prohibition of discrimination contained in Article 26 of the Civil Covenant does not confer a new right to individuals but it extends the prohibition of discrimination (and the competence of the supervising organs) to rights not guaranteed by the Civil Covenant.

It is in that sense that neither the general prohibition of discrimination (as in Article 26 of the Civil Covenant or in Protocol No. 12 to the European Convention), nor the limited prohibition clause (as in Article 2 of both Covenants and in Article 14 of the European Convention) have an "independent existence". They are always to be examined in relation to a substantive right or freedom. The absence of an independent existence does not imply that it cannot be autonomously violated. It is not because the prohibition of discrimination

---

[111] A/C.3/L.946.
[112] In the Explanatory Report to Protocol No. 12 to the European Convention, it is emphasised that Article 1 of that Protocol "is not intended to impose a general positive obligation on the Parties to prevent or remedy all instances of discrimination in relations between private persons" (§25) and "[i]t is understood that purely private matters would not be affected. Regulations of such matters would also be likely to interfere with the individual's right to respect for his private and family life, his home and his correspondence, as guaranteed by Article 8 of the Convention" (§28).

has no "independent existence" that there can be no "autonomous violation" of the prohibition of discrimination without a simultaneous violation of the right concerned.

As long as the right concerned is a fundamental freedom requiring essentially from the State a negative obligation of no (arbitrary) interference in the enjoyment of that freedom, it is hard to imagine a violation of the prohibition of discrimination with respect to that freedom without a simultaneous violation of that freedom itself. The simple fact that someone is deprived of a fundamental freedom, to which everyone is entitled, is a violation of the right to the enjoyment of that freedom as well as a violation of the prohibition of discrimination.

If the right concerned is a social right requiring from the State a positive intervention "to the maximum of its available resources", the fact that someone is deprived of such a right is not necessarily a violation of that right, but there will be a violation if someone is deprived of that right on a discriminatory basis. In that case, someone who, on the basis of the applicable regulations regarding that social right, is not entitled to it, will be entitled to invoke that right on the basis of the prohibition of discrimination, which in that case has a creative effect.

2.   THE APPLICABILITY OF ARTICLE 26 OF THE CIVIL COVENANT TO SOCIAL RIGHTS

The question of the applicability of Article 26 of the Civil Covenant did arise with respect to social rights "enunciated" in the Social Covenant. Two cases were brought before the Human Rights Committee by two Dutch women, Ms S.W.M. Broeks[113] and Ms F.H. Zwaan de Vries,[114] who complained that they were receiving a lesser benefit because they were married. In its views adopted on 9 April 1987, the Human Rights Committee found a violation of Article 26 of the Civil Covenant as applied to the field of social security. In those cases, the Netherlands Government had taken the view that Article 26 could only be invoked, under the Optional Protocol to the Civil Covenant, in the sphere of civil and political rights, albeit not necessarily limited to those civil and political rights embodied in that Covenant. The complaints, however, concerned the enjoyment of economic, social and cultural rights dealt with by the Social Covenant, which deliberately does not provide for an individual complaints procedure.

In the Committee's view, however, the Civil Covenant applies even if any of the matters referred to therein is mentioned or incorporated in the provisions of other international instruments. Notwithstanding the interrelatedness of the two Covenants, it is necessary to apply fully the terms of the Civil Covenant.

---

[113]   A/42/40, pp. 139–150.
[114]   *Ibid.*, pp. 160–169.

The provisions of Article 2 of the Social Covenant do not detract from the full application of Article 26 of the other Covenant. Article 26 is thus concerned with the obligations imposed on States in regard to their legislation and its application. The fact that a married woman had to prove that she was a "breadwinner", a condition that did not apply to married men, constituted, according to the Committee, a difference of treatment which was in fact based on sex, placing married women at a disadvantage compared with married man. In its views, the Committee stated that such difference of treatment was not reasonable.

It is questionable whether the drafters of Article 26 of the Civil Covenant really intended to entrust the Human Rights Committee with monitoring its application in the sphere of economic, social and cultural rights. However, the text adopted clearly encompasses all the various rights and freedoms, without making any exception in the case of economic, social and cultural rights. Therefore, the Committee had to recognise the general character of the prohibition of discrimination. One of the consequences of the broad scope of Article 26 is that it expands the supervisory power of the judges.

CHAPTER IV

THE CONCEPT OF
AFFIRMATIVE ACTION[115]

Before mentioning the justifications given for affirmative action and analysing the different forms of it, it is useful to make a survey of the international provisions dealing with affirmative action and of case law concerning that concept. The crucial question is to know whether affirmative action is an exception to the prohibition of discrimination or is limited by that prohibition. As far as terminology is concerned, it is important to ban the expression "positive discrimination". Once it is admitted that in the international law of human rights the term "discrimination" is reserved for a difference of treatment that cannot be justified,[116] the expression "positive discrimination" is a *contradictio in terminis*: if the difference is discrimination, it cannot be positive and, if it is justified, it cannot be discrimination. That is why expressions such as "affirmative action" (in US law) or "positive action" should be used. In UN human rights treaties the expression "special measures" is frequently used.

A. INTERNATIONAL PROVISIONS AND CASE LAW CONCERNING AFFIRMATIVE ACTION

A brief survey of international provisions concerning affirmative action, will be followed by one of the jurisprudence concerning that concept, mainly in the United States and in the European Union.

---

[115] Based on the UN Working Paper (E/CN.4/Sub.2/1998/5, Geneva, 1998, 10 p.) and the Final Report (E/CN.4/Sub.2/2002/21, Geneva, 2002, 40 p.) on the Concept of Affirmative Action; see also: Bossuyt, Marc, "The concept and practice of affirmative action", in Ineke Boerefijn et al. (Eds.), *Temporary Special Measures. Accelerating* de facto *equality of women under article 4(1) UN Convention on the Elimination of all forms of Discrimination against Women*, Antwerp, Intersentia, 2003, pp. 65–74; *id.*, "La notion d'action positive", in *La pauvreté: un défi pour les droits de l'homme*, Paris, Pedone, 2009, pp. 97–102.

[116] See *supra*, Chapter III, A, 1.

1. INTERNATIONAL PROVISIONS DEALING WITH AFFIRMATIVE ACTION

Among the most important international provisions dealing with "affirmative action", the following may be mentioned:

- Article 5 of the Convention (No. 111) concerning Discrimination in Respect of Employment and Occupation, adopted on 25 June 1958 by the International Labour Organization, which reads:

  "1. *Special measures of protection or assistance* provided for in other conventions or recommendations adopted by the International Labour Conference shall not be deemed to be discrimination.
  2. Any member may, after consultation with representative employers' and workers' organizations, where such exist, determine that *other special measures designed to meet the particular requirements of persons* who, for reasons such as sex, age, disablement, family responsibilities or social or cultural status, are generally recognized to require special protection or assistance, shall not be deemed to be discrimination" (emphasis added).

- Article 2.3 of the United Nations Declaration on the Elimination of All Forms of Racial Discrimination, adopted on 20 November 1963, which reads:

  "*Special concrete measures* shall be taken in appropriate circumstances *in order to secure adequate development or protection of individuals belonging to certain racial groups* with the object of ensuring the full enjoyment by such individuals of human rights and fundamental freedoms. These measures shall in no circumstances have as a consequence the maintenance of unequal or separate rights for different racial groups" (emphasis added).

- Article 1.4 of the International Convention on the Elimination of All Forms of Racial Discrimination, adopted on 21 December 1965, which reads:

  "*Special measures taken for the sole purpose of securing adequate advancement of certain racial or ethnic groups or individuals requiring such protection as may be necessary* in order to ensure such groups or individuals equal enjoyment or exercise of human rights and fundamental freedoms shall not be deemed racial discrimination, provided, however, that such measures do not, as a consequence, lead to the maintenance of separate rights for different racial groups and that they shall not be continued after the objectives for which they were taken have been achieved" (emphasis added).

- Article 9.2 of the UNESCO Declaration on Race and Racial Prejudice, adopted on 27 November 1978, which reads:

  "Special measures must be taken to ensure equality in dignity and rights for individuals and groups wherever necessary, while ensuring that they are not such as to appear racially discriminatory. In this respect, particular attention should be paid to *racial or ethnic groups which are socially or economically disadvantaged*, so as to afford them, on a completely equal footing and without discrimination or restriction, the protection of the laws and regulations and the advantages of the social measures in force, in particular in regard to housing, employment and health; to respect the authenticity of their culture and values; and to facilitate their social and occupational advancement, especially through education" (emphasis added).

– Article 4 of the Convention on the Elimination of All Forms of Discrimination against Women, adopted on 18 December 1979, which reads:

"1. Adoption by States parties of *temporary special measures aimed at accelerating* de facto *equality between men and women* shall not be considered discrimination as defined in the present Convention, but shall in no way entail as a consequence the maintenance of unequal or separate standards; these measures shall be discontinued when the objectives of equality of opportunity and treatment have been achieved.
2. Adoption by States parties of special measures, including those measures contained in the present Convention, aimed at protecting maternity shall not be considered discriminatory" (emphasis added).

2. THE CONCEPT OF AFFIRMATIVE ACTION IN US AND EU CASE LAW

There have been situations in the past where specific groups of individuals, who may be identified by reference to grounds mentioned in the texts prohibiting discrimination, have been subjected to systematic discrimination. It may be justified – or even necessary – in such situations to take affirmative measures in order to help such groups to overcome the unfavourable situation in which they are placed.

a. Affirmative Action in the Case Law of the US Supreme Court[117]

There is no way of considering the question of "affirmative action" without referring to the jurisprudence of the United States Supreme Court in the matter of discrimination and more particularly racial discrimination. The first example of such jurisprudence is the judgment passed in 1896 in the famous *Plessy v. Ferguson* case (163 U.S. 537), in which the US Supreme Court legitimated the "separate but equal" doctrine. Almost 60 years were to pass before that doctrine was reversed by the judgment delivered in 1954 in the equally famous case of *Brown v. Board of Education* (374 U.S. 483), in which the Supreme Court held that separate schools inevitably created a feeling of inferiority. Even before that case arose, the Supreme Court had held in its judgment in 1944 in *Korematsu v. United States* (323 U.S. 214) that any legal restrictions limiting the civil rights of a single racial group were

---

[117] See also McWhirther, Darien, *The End of Affirmative Action: Where do we go from there?*, New York, Birch Lane Press Books, 1996, 188 p.

immediately suspect and had to be submitted to very "strict scrutiny". On the other hand, with respect to distinctions on the ground of sex, the Supreme Court subsequently considered only "intermediate scrutiny" to be necessary.

In American law, the expression "affirmative action" appears for the first time in Executive Order 10925, signed by President John F. Kennedy in 1961, requiring federal employers to hire more employees belonging to minorities. Two major Civil Rights Acts were signed, one in 1964 by President Lyndon B. Johnson and one in 1972 by President Richard M. Nixon.

In 1974, the Supreme Court considered that it did not have to rule on affirmative action measures in the matter of admission to university in the *DeFunis v. Odegaard* case (416 U.S. 312), on the grounds that the White Jewish student, who had been denied access to the Law School of the University of Washington, had meanwhile been admitted. In the *Regents of the University of California v. Bakke* case (438 U.S. 265), the Supreme Court was very divided. Justice Lewis F. Powell, who agreed partly with the four judges in favour and partly with the four judges against the affirmative action programme of the School of Medicine of the University of California in Davis, issued a judgment in 1978 in which he held that such a programme had to be subject to very strict scrutiny, but that one of the arguments mentioned in favour of the programme, namely the wish to obtain the benefits derived from an ethnically diversified body of students, was sufficiently compelling for the university to apply it as one of the factors to be taken into consideration in the selection of students.

In the years that followed, the Supreme Court issued many judgments, some accepting and some rejecting the affirmative action programmes that came before it. The judgments in favour of affirmative action programmes which had been challenged included the following:

- *Steelworkers v. Weber*, 443 U.S. 193 (1979);
- *Fullilove v. Klutznick*, 448 U.S. 149 (1980);
- *Sheet Metal Workers v. EEOC (Equal Employment Opportunity Commission)*, 478 U.S. 421 (1986);
- *United States v. Paradise*, 480 U.S. 149 (1987);
- *Johnson v. Santa Clara County*, 480 U.S. 1442 (1987);
- *Metro Broadcasting Inc. v. FCC (Federal Communications Commission)*, 497 U.S. 547 (1990).

In the *Steelworkers* case (1979), the Supreme Court accepted the affirmative action programme reserving training places for Black workers, on the grounds that the programme had been set up by a private employer and was intended to apply to job categories traditionally affected by segregation. In the *Sheet Metal Workers* (1986), *Paradise* (1987) and *Johnson* (1987) cases, affirmative action programmes were accepted because they were intended to remedy cases of intentional discrimination practised in the past to the detriment of Black workers in the metal workers' union of the City of New York and in the Alabama police corps and to the detriment of women belonging to the skilled craft category in Santa Clara County (California).

In other judgments, the Supreme Court turned down action programmes which were brought before it. The cases concerned were:

- *Firefighters v. Stotts*, 476 U.S. 561 (1984);
- *Wygant v. Jackson Board of Education*, 476 U.S. 267 (1986);
- *City of Richmond v. Croson*, 488 U.S. 469 (1989).

In the *Firefighters* (1984) and *Wygant* (1986) cases, the affirmative action programmes called respectively for the dismissal of fire fighters of the township of Memphis and of teachers in a school in Michigan, all Whites and senior to their Black colleagues. In the *Croson* (1989) case, the programme reserved 30 per cent of the contracts issued by the township of Richmond (Virginia) to companies belonging to minorities, namely "Blacks, Hispanics, Orientals, Indians, Eskimos and Aleuts". The Court held that such a measure was not "narrowly tailored" to the objective pursued and that it was unconnected with any past discrimination against Eskimos in Virginia.

In 1995, the Supreme Court passed judgment in the important case *Adarand Constructors, Inc. v. Peña* (515 U.S. 200). The Adarand Company was complaining that it had lost a public works contract to a company belonging to a Hispanic on account of a federal law whereby 10 per cent of all public works contracts had to be attributed to minorities. Writing on behalf of a majority of six, Judge Sandra O'Connor held three propositions derived from former Court judgments concerning race-based programmes:

(1) scepticism: preferences based on racial or ethnic criteria needed to be subjected to the closest scrutiny;
(2) consistency: the control standard should not depend on the race of those who benefit or suffer from the plan concerned; and
(3) coherence: equal protection should be the same regardless of the level of government (federal or otherwise) involved.

On 18 March 1996, the Fifth Circuit held in its judgment in *Hopwood v. Texas* (78 F.3d 932) that "the University of Texas School of Law may not use race as a factor in deciding which applicants to admit in order to achieve a diverse a diverse student body, to combat the perceived effects of a hostile environment at the law school, to alleviate the law school's poor reputation in the minority community, or to eliminate any present effects of past discrimination by actors other than the law school". On 1 July 1996, the Supreme Court declined to review that case. On 23 June 2003, the Supreme Court abrogated *Hopwood* in *Grutter v. Bollinger* (539 U.S. 306) by stating that the US Constitution "does not prohibit the law school's narrowly tailored use of race in admissions decisions to further a compelling interest in obtaining the educational benefits that flow from a diverse student body".

The Supreme Court is expected to decide in 2016 in the case of *Fisher v. University of Texas* (570 U.S. ___) concerning the affirmative action admission policy of the University of Texas at Austin. In that case, the Supreme Court had on 24 June 2013 vacated the decision of the Fifth Circuit court and remanded the case for further consideration. The case was reargued on 9 December 2015.

b.   Affirmative Action in the Case Law of the EU Court of Justice

As far as the jurisprudence of the Court of Justice of the (then) European Communities is concerned, the Luxembourg Court, passing judgment in the *Kalanke v. Freie Hansestadt Bremen* case (C-450/93) on 17 October 1995, held that:

> "National rules which guarantee women *absolute and unconditional priority* for appointment or promotion go beyond promoting equal opportunities and overstep the limits of the exception in Article 2 (4) of the Directive" (ECLI:EU:C:1995:322) (emphasis added).

According to EU Council Directive 76/207/EEC of 9 February 1976, the latter shall be "without prejudice to measures to promote equal opportunity for men and women, in particular by removing existing inequalities which affect women's opportunities" in the areas of access to employment, including promotion, and to vocational training. At the same time, the Directive was held to preclude national rules concerning equal treatment for men and women in public services:

> "which, where candidates of different sexes shortlisted for promotion are equally qualified, *automatically* give priority to women in sectors where they are underrepresented, underrepresentation being deemed to exist when women do not make up at least half of the staff in the individual pay brackets in the relevant personnel group or in the function levels provided for in the organization chart" (emphasis added).

However, in the *Marschall v. Land NordrheinWestfalen* case (C-409/95), the Court of Justice issued a judgment on 11 November 1997, in which it ruled that the above-mentioned Directive did not preclude:

> "A national rule which, in a case where there are fewer women than men at the level of the relevant post in a sector of the public service and both female and male candidates for the post are equally qualified in terms of their suitability, competence and professional performance, requires that priority be given to the promotion

of female candidates *unless reasons specific to an individual male candidate tilt the balance in his favour* [...] provided that:

> In each individual case the rule provides for male candidates who are equally as qualified as the female candidates a guarantee that the candidatures will be the subject of an objective assessment which will take account of all criteria specific to the candidates and will override the priority accorded to female candidates where one or more of those criteria tilts the balance in favour of the male candidate, and such criteria are not such as to discriminate against the female candidates" (ECLI:EU:C:1997:533) (emphasis added).

The controversial provision of the *Beamtengesetz* (Law on Civil Servants of the *Land*) of 1 May 1981 provides:

> "Where, in the sector of the authority responsible for promotion, there are fewer women than men in the particular higher grade post in the career bracket, women are to be given priority for promotion in the event of equal suitability, competence and professional performance, *unless reasons specific to an individual [male] candidate tilt the balance in his favour*" (emphasis added).

In the Court's view, unlike in the *Kalanke* case, owing to the "saving clause" ("*Öffnungsklausel*"), the automatic preference allowed to women may be waived "if reasons specific to an individual male candidate tilt the balance in his favour".

In its judgment in the *Briheche* case (C-319/03) of 30 September 2004, the Court stated that the above-mentioned Directive precludes

> "a national provision [...] which reserves the exemption from the age limit for obtaining access to public-sector employment to widows who have not remarried who are obliged to work, excluding widowers who have not remarried who are in the same situation" (ECLI:EU:C:2004:574).

The Court sanctioned the French provision which "automatically and unconditionally" gave priority to widows over widowers.

B. JUSTIFICATIONS AND FORMS OF AFFIRMATIVE ACTION

Before identifying the different forms of affirmative action, it may be useful to make a brief inventory of the justifications given for it.

1. JUSTIFICATIONS GIVEN FOR AFFIRMATIVE ACTION

When introducing an affirmative action policy, States try to justify it vis-à-vis public opinion. The grounds given as justification will mainly depend on the specific social context of the State in question. The following justifications have been given:

(a) to remedy or redress historical injustices: to compensate for intentional or specific discrimination in the past that still has repercussions today;

(b) to remedy social/structural discrimination: equality for all before the law establishes formal equality but is insufficient to address adequately practices in society that lead to structural discrimination;

(c) to create diversity or proportional group representation: the presence of racial and ethnic diversity within the academy and workplace is a necessary component of a just society;

(d) social utility: professionals from a disadvantaged group have a better understanding and knowledge of problems affecting disadvantaged groups and their interests will be better perceived and protected;

(e) to pre-empt social unrest: to promote the interests of underprivileged members of society and to balance internal inequalities of economic and political power, with the hope of pre-empting social unrest;

(f) better efficiency of the socio-economic system: the working of the labour market can be optimised if the present imperfections caused by irrational prejudices are corrected;

(g) a means of nation building: efforts are made to create a more egalitarian society and a common nationality to strengthen its sovereignty;

(h) – equality of *opportunity* is consistent with the view that the aim of anti-discrimination law is to secure the reduction of discrimination by eliminating or cleansing from the decision-making processes illegitimate considerations based on race, gender or ethnicity which have harmful consequences for individuals. This approach is markedly individualistic and comes from a liberal vision of society, reflecting respect for efficiency, merit and achievement;

– equality of *results* is more controversial because of its methods, which are open-ended and unmanageable, such as the adoption of quotas. This approach takes insufficient account of the extent to which the burden of helping disadvantaged groups falls on third parties who may be "innocent" of past wrongdoing, who may have gained no benefit from discrimination against these groups in the past and who comprise some of the least advantaged sections of the community.

2. FORMS OF AFFIRMATIVE ACTION

Affirmative action is often treated under a generic heading, as though affirmative action measures are uniform. Some forms of affirmative action will be more effective or appropriate to promote equality than others, depending on the particular context and the political choice that has been made. As long as "affirmative action" takes the form of "affirmative mobilisation" or of "affirmative fairness", such special measures give no rise to controversy, contrary to measures which take the form of "affirmative preference".

a.   "Affirmative Mobilisation" and "Affirmative Fairness"

The special measures may be called measures of "affirmative mobilisation" when, through affirmative recruitment, the targeted groups are aggressively encouraged and sensitised to apply for a social good, such as a job or a place in an educational institution. This can occur through announcements or other recruitment efforts, where it has been made sure that they actually reach the targeted groups. An example would be the setting up of job-training programmes to enable members of minorities to acquire the skills that would allow them to compete for jobs and promotion.

Special measures may be called measures of "affirmative fairness", when a meticulous examination takes place in order to make sure that members of target groups have been treated fairly in the attribution of social goods, such as entering an educational institution, receiving a job or promotion. When it comes to how people are hired or promoted, decision-making has to be colour-blind and people must be treated on the basis of their individual merits rather than on their status as a member of a particular group. It boils down to the idea that the "best qualified" ought always to be hired.

Affirmative mobilisation and affirmative fairness both entail measures dedicated to overcome the social problems of a target group, but the measures do not themselves entail discrimination against people who are not members of that group. Rather, they place the costs of affirmative action on the whole society. In that way, these measures are colour-blind, but when it comes to the motivation of the measures or their strategic planning or monitoring, the approach is definitely race-conscious. It is probably for that reason, among others, that affirmative recruitment and affirmative fairness are well received and accepted.

b.   "Affirmative Preference"

"Affirmative preference" means that someone's gender or race will be taken into account in the granting or withholding of social goods. Affirmative preference measures can mean two things: first, they can mean that, when two equally qualified persons apply for a job, promotion, grant, etc., preference will be given to the person belonging to a designated group that is the beneficiary of affirmative action measures; second, they can also include other more radical measures, such as prohibiting members of non-designated groups from applying for opportunities. Alternatively, they can be allowed to compete, but even if they are better qualified, preference will still be given to designated groups. Members of designated groups can be automatically given additional points in competitive examinations, which is called "race-norming". Lower standards can be applied to them when evaluating their applications for university or employment. Informal percentages, guidelines, goals, quotas or reservations can be imposed that fix the proportions of social goods the designated groups must receive. Affirmative preference is the most controversial form of affirmative action. It treats people as members of groups or categories without regard to individual merit. Although persons have validly satisfied the criteria, they will be nonetheless denied what would otherwise be their just due.

***

There is no doubt that a persistent policy in the past of systematic discrimination of certain groups of the population may justify – and in some cases may even require – special measures intended to overcome the sequels of a condition of inferiority which still affects members belonging to such groups. "Affirmative action" or "positive action" is the proper term which covers such special measures. A wide variety of measures are labelled measures of affirmative action. Indeed, measures presented as such may take very different forms. Those measures do not give rise to controversy as long as they take the form of "affirmative mobilisation", when, through affirmative recruitment, the targeted groups are aggressively encouraged and sensitised to apply for a job, or "affirmative fairness", when a meticulous examination takes place in order to make sure that the members of a targeted group have been treated fairly in the attribution of a job. The matter is more delicate when the measures take the form of "affirmative preference". But even those measures are not objectionable as long as preference is given to members of the targeted group only if they are equally qualified as others not belonging to that group.

In matters of human rights, a preference may only be justified if it is based on a ground which is relevant to the right at stake. For instance, in matters of employment and education, the principal criterion is competence. A classic example is the hiring of a violinist for an orchestra. The decisive criterion has to be the competence of the candidate in playing the violin. It is not relevant to take into account the colour, sex, religious faith, language or political persuasion of the candidate. Only the competence of the candidate in playing the violin should be the determining factor. In order to avoid members of the jury being influenced by irrelevant factors, the violin test may even be taken behind a closed curtain. If someone needs life-saving surgery, it is in the interest of the patient to care about the capacity of the surgeon to perform the operation, while all other factors have at the most only a peripheral importance.

Nevertheless, for certain matters, other criteria than competence may also be relevant and be taken into account. Some criteria are relevant for some matters and not for other matters. Particularly in the public sector, other criteria than competence, such as the proportional representation of the different groups composing a given society, may be considered relevant. In the field of politics, members of the Government are appointed on the basis of the confidence they enjoy from the political groups that constitute the majority in Parliament. The determining factor is "representativity". In a diverse society, proportional representation of specific groups may be considered desirable. In some cases, the electorate may even be divided on the basis of criteria which are considered particularly relevant in the exercise of political power. Sometimes such criteria may even be taken into account in large sectors of public life, including the civil service, the military, the police, the judiciary, etc.

It is not appropriate to make sweeping general statements as to the extent to which such criteria may be taken into account. It depends on the specific circumstances of the society in which the measures are taken. Different historical, cultural, sociological, economic and other elements which are specific to the society in question have to be taken into account. It is the proper role of judges – administrative, judicial or even constitutional or international judges – to verify in each particular case whether the rule or its application respects the principle of equality and non-discrimination to which everybody is entitled.

It is quite obvious that no measure intended to favour members of groups which were previously in a disadvantaged position may be justified simply by referring to the intent of the measure taken, however legitimate that intention may be. Everyone is entitled to the enjoyment of fundamental rights and freedoms and nobody may be discriminated against in the enjoyment of his or her fundamental rights and freedoms, regardless of the objective pursued by the discriminatory measure. The discriminatory effect depends on the characteristics of a specific measure used to pursue a given objective and not solely on the objective itself.

The principle of equality and non-discrimination would be without any normative value if any distinction could be justified by qualifying it as a measure of affirmative action. This most basic principle of human rights, which applies to all rights, freedoms and guarantees, would become meaningless if measures which clearly and manifestly deprive persons of a right, a freedom or a guarantee on the basis of a criterion which is not relevant to the right or freedom in question, were justified by labelling such measures as affirmative action. Good intentions or legitimate objectives are not sufficient to justify a distinction based on whatever ground in whatever matter. It is not sufficient that the persons favoured by the measure taken belong to a group whose members were previously the victims of exactly the same kind of measures. An injustice cannot be repaired by another injustice. It is not because the descendants of the victims of the past are substituted for the descendants of the oppressors of the past that a discriminatory measure becomes legitimate and consistent with the requirements of the protection of human rights and fundamental freedoms.

The prohibition of discrimination also applies to all measures regardless of whether they are qualified by national authorities as measures of affirmative action or not. It is up to the national authorities to find ways and means to adopt measures of affirmative action which are designed to help members of groups previously discriminated against to overcome the lasting consequences of past policies of discrimination. In general, national authorities should take measures which help those persons to acquire the same qualifications as members of groups which were favoured in the past. Through measures of affirmative action, the former should be helped to acquire the qualifications asked for, rather than by lowering the level of those qualifications. Efforts should be undertaken to improve the qualifications of target groups rather than creating different sets of requirements on the basis of criteria which are not relevant to the particular matter.

In a society where persons belonging to certain groups still suffer from past discriminatory practices, States should pursue a policy of affirmative action. This does not mean, however, that whatever measure those States may take under the heading of affirmative action is compatible with its human rights obligations. The State may help persons belonging to such groups to overcome those handicaps, but this has to be done in a manner which does not violate the fundamental rights and freedoms of persons not belonging to such groups. The simple fact that a particular category of the population has suffered from disadvantageous economic or social conditions does not mean that, in order to upgrade its material position, any distinction based on the characteristic defining the group should be considered legitimate, even when this ground is irrelevant as a basis of distinction with regard to that particular right. It would not be justifiable to provide special social benefits to persons who do not need them but who belong to a category which formerly was in a disadvantaged position, and to deny the same benefits to persons who do need them but belong to a category which previously enjoyed better conditions in society.

Affirmative action should be centred on taking measures expected to meet the needs of the category it is intended to favour, rather than on restricting the benefits of the measures on the basis of the element which distinguishes that category from the other members of the population, but which is not relevant to the right concerned. It is through the choice, timing and location of the measures that the policy can favour the target category without violating the rights – including the right to equal protection of the law – of persons not belonging to that category. In no case may someone be deprived of a basic right on the pretext that doing so would help particularly disadvantaged groups to better overcome the consequences of previous discrimination.[118]

---

[118]   As illustrated by the example given by Lord Denning: "So here if this education authority were to allocate boys to particular schools according to the colour of their hair or, for that matter, the colour of their skin, it would be so unreasonable, so capricious, so irrelevant to any proper system of education that it would be *ultra vires* altogether and this Court would strike it down at once. But, if there were valid educational reasons for a policy, as, for instance in an area

Affirmative action policies are only admissible insofar as they do not contravene the principle of non-discrimination. This means that, if a distinction is made, due attention should be given to the ground on which the distinction is based in deciding whether it amounts to discrimination or not. However, it is not the ground itself that is decisive, but the connection between the ground and the right with regard to which the distinction is practised. There has to be a sufficient connection between the right and the ground. The ground has to be deemed relevant to the specific right on which the distinction is based. The aim or goal pursued is not decisive. The judicial assessment of whether distinctions are arbitrary goes a step further than the assessment undertaken at a purely political level. Thus, affirmative action to ensure full equality is not always legitimate. Affirmative action should not be interpreted as justifying any distinction based on any ground with respect to any right merely because the object of the distinction is to improve the situation of disadvantaged individuals or groups. Affirmative action is no exception to the principle of non-discrimination. Rather, it is the principle of non-discrimination that establishes the limits to each affirmative action.

---

where immigrant children were backward in the English tongue and needed special teaching, then it would be perfectly right to allocate those in need to special schools where they would be given extra facilities for learning English" (Quoted by McKean, William, *Equality and Discrimination under International Law*, Oxford, Clarendon, 1983, 333 p., at p. 246).

B. THE INSTITUTIONAL FRAMEWORK

Understanding international protection of human rights requires knowledge of the institutional framework in which those norms have been adopted and of the mechanisms set in place to favour respect of those norms. A brief survey will be given of the most important instruments, organs and procedures developed both in the framework of the United Nations and in the framework of regional organisations

In the framework of the United Nations, attention is given, first, to the UN Charter-based organs, in particular the UN Commission on Human Rights and its successor the Human Rights Council, including the confidential procedure for the examination of communications and the special procedures (country-oriented and thematic) (Chapter V), and, second, to the treaty-based UN organs established by the International Covenants on Human Rights, by the conventions prohibiting discrimination, in particular discrimination based on race and against women, and by other conventions such as those against torture and enforced disappearance and on the rights of the child, of migrant workers and of persons with disabilities (Chapter VI).

At the regional level (Chapter VII) attention is given to the protection of human rights in the framework of the Council of Europe, more particularly by the European Convention on Human Rights (1950) and the European Social Charter (1961), revised in 1996; of the Organisation of American States, by the American Convention on Human Rights (1978); and of the Organisation of the African Union, by the African Charter on Human and Peoples' Rights (1981).

Until the 20th century, the protection of human rights was, with the exception of slavery, considered to belong to the domestic jurisdiction of each State. Before the end of the Second World War, the only precedents for international protection of human rights were the minimum standard for foreigners, the humanitarian intervention and the protection of minorities in the framework of the League of Nations. The breakthrough was the adoption at San Francisco on 26 June 1945 of the Charter of the Organisation of the United Nations, which contains a number of provisions referring to human rights.

CHAPTER V

THE UN CHARTER-BASED HUMAN RIGHTS BODIES[119]

The principal organ to deal with human rights within the Organisation of the United Nations, the UN Commission on Human Rights,[120] was set up in 1946. It was one of the eight functional commissions of the UN Economic and Social Council (ECOSOC), itself consisting of 54 States. The UN Commission on Human Rights was often criticised, mainly for its so-called "politicisation". That organ has nevertheless succeeded in adopting an impressive number of international human rights instruments and a great variety of procedures enabling the international community to exercise pressure on States to improve their human rights record. It is precisely because those instruments have been adopted by that political body that the norms contained therein are universally recognised as the standards of reference of human rights everywhere in the world.

A first reform in 1990 led to the enlargement of the Commission (since 1992) from 43 to 53 members (ten additional members from Africa, Asia and Latin America) and to the possibility of convening special sessions. After the Vienna Conference on Human Rights in June 1993, the mandate of a UN High Commissioner for Human Rights[121] was established by the General Assembly in its resolution 48/141 of 20 December 1993.

A second reform took place in 1999–2000 modifying the confidential procedure to examine communications on human rights violations by requesting the Working Group on communications of the Sub-Commission on the Promotion and the Protection of Human Rights to report directly to the Commission. Moreover, the Sub-Commission could not adopt anymore country

---

[119] Based on lectures given in French at the Summer Session of the International Institute of Human Rights at Strasbourg, 8–10 July 2014.

[120] See also MARIE, Jean-Bernard, *La Commission des droits de l'homme de l'O.N.U.*, Paris, Pedone, 1975, 352 p.; BOSSUYT, Marc, "The U.N. Human Rights Commission", in Karel WELLENS (Ed.), *Peace and Security: Justice and Development*, The Hague, Instituut Asser, 1986, pp. 77–80; *id.*, "La Belgique et la Commission des Droits de l'Homme de l'ONU (1986–1991)", in *La Belgique et 50 Ans de Nations Unies*, Brussels, Vif éd., 1995, pp. 47–56.

[121] The successive High Commissioners were Mr José Ayala-Lasso (Ecuador, 1994–1997), Mrs Mary Robinson (Ireland, 1997–2002), Mr Sergio Vieira de Mello (Brazil, 2002–2003), Ms Louise Arbour (Canada, 2004–2008), Ms Navanethem Pillay (South Africa, 2008–2014) and, at present, Mr Zeid Ra'ad Al Hussein (Jordan, 2014–present).

specific resolutions and the meeting time of its annual session was reduced from four to three weeks.

A third reform replaced the Commission with a Human Rights Council,[122] established by the General Assembly in its resolution 60/251 of 15 March 2006. That resolution was adopted by 170 votes to four (Israel, Marshall Islands, Palau and USA) with three abstentions (Belarus, Iran and Venezuela). The Human Rights Council consists of 47 States, elected by secret ballot by the majority of the members of the General Assembly. They serve for a period of three years and shall not be eligible for immediate re-election after two consecutive terms.

The seats in the Human Rights Council are distributed as follows: 13 African States, 13 Asian States, eight Latin American and Caribbean States, six Eastern European States and seven States belonging to the Group of Western European and other States. The latter Group, which occupied in 1991 ten seats out of 43 (23%) and since 1992 ten out of 53 (18%), now occupies only seven seats out of 47 (14%) and the African and Asian States which occupied in 1991 twenty seats out of 43 (46%) and since 1992 27 out of 53 (50%), occupies henceforth 26 seats out of 47 (55%). Consequently, the ratio Western Group / African and Asian Groups evolved from 10/20 to 7/26.

The General Assembly, by a two-thirds majority of the members present and voting, may suspend the rights of membership in the Council of a member of the Council that commits gross and systematic violations of human rights. However, it is important to be aware that the Council is not a tribunal of independent judges, nor an academy of human rights experts or a club of human rights activists. It is a political organ composed of States represented by their governments and reflecting the political forces of the world as it is (and not as we would like it to be).

The Human Rights Council meets regularly throughout the year and schedules three *sessions* per year (four weeks in March, three in June and three in September) instead of one session of six weeks in February/March as it used to be at the time of the Commission on Human Rights. Moreover, special sessions may be hold at the request of a member of the Council with the support of one third of the membership (instead of half of the membership before). The Commission hold five special sessions on the former Yugoslavia (1st and 2nd sessions in 1992), Rwanda (3rd in 1994), East Timor (4th in 1999) and the occupied Palestinian territories (5th in 2000).

The Council hold already 24 special sessions on the occupied Palestinian territories (1st and 3rd in 2006, 6th in 2008, 9th and 12th in 2009 and 21st in 2014),

---

122   See also BOSSUYT, Marc, "The New Human Rights Council: A first appraisal", *Netherlands Human Rights Quarterly*, 2006, pp. 551–555; *id.*, "Le Conseil des droits de l'homme: une réforme douteuse?", in *Droit du pouvoir, pouvoir du droit (Mélanges offerts à Jean Salmon)*, Brussels, Bruylant, 2007, pp. 1183–1192; CALLEJON, Claire, *La réforme de la Commission des droits de l'homme des Nations Unies: de la Commission au Conseil des droits de l'homme*, Paris, Pedone, 2008, 427 p.; FREEDMAN, Rosa, *The United Nations Human Rights Council: A Critique and Early Assessment*, Abingdon, Routledge, 2013, 332 p.

on Lebanon (2nd in 2006), on Darfur (4th in 2006), on Myanmar (5th in 2007), on the world food crisis (7th in 2008), on the Democratic Republic of Congo (8th in 2008), on the economic and financial crisis (10th in 2009), on Sri Lanka (11th in 2009), on Haiti (13th in 2010), on the Côte d'Ivoire (14th in 2010), on the Libyan Arab Jamahiriya (15th in 2011), on the Syrian Arab Republic (16th, 17th and 18th in 2011 and 19th in 2012), on the Central African Republic (20th in 2014), on the "Islamic State" in Iraq (22nd in 2014), on Boko Haram (23rd in 2015) and on Burundi (24th in 2015).

A new procedure of Universal Periodic Review (UPR) has been established. The review of the human rights situation of each State is based on three documents: (a) a report (20 p.) presented by the State concerned; (b) a report (10 p.) of the High Commissioner for Human Rights summarising the information gathered by the United Nations on that State; and (c) a report (10 p.) of the High Commissioner on the views of the non-governmental organisations and the national human rights institutions. During the first cycle (2008–2012), all Member States of the United Nations were reviewed. The second cycle started in May 2012. 42 States are being reviewed every year *a rato* of 14 each session. Each State will be the object of a debate of three hours and a half. For each State, a group of three different States (troika) is drawn by lot and will be responsible for conducting the drafting of the report of the working group.

The Commission had one Sub-Commission, the name of which was changed in 1999 from "Sub-Commission on the Prevention of Discrimination and the Protection of Minorities" into "Sub-Commission on the Promotion and the Protection of Human Rights". This Sub-Commission, consisting of 26 independent experts elected for four years by the Commission, met every year during four or three weeks in Geneva in August. The Sub-Commission undertook mainly studies on a great variety of problems relating to human rights and established three working groups on contemporary forms of slavery, on indigenous populations and on minorities. The Sub-Commission hold its last session in 2006 and was replaced in 2008 by an Advisory Committee of the Human Rights Council, consisting of 18 independent experts meeting twice a year during a week in February and August. The Advisory Committee functions as a think-tank for the Council and works at its direction. It provides expertise to the Council in the manner and form requested by it and focuses on studies and research-based advice. It may also propose suggestions for research proposals. Unable, however, to adopt resolutions or decisions, it is no more than a shadow of what the Sub-Commission was.

The Commission on Human Rights drafted the most important human rights instruments, starting with the Universal Declaration of Human Rights. That Declaration was followed by a number of conventions which set up treaty based organs to supervise the respect by the States parties of the normative provisions of those conventions.[123] The Commission on Human Rights – followed in that by

---

123   See *infra*, Chapter VI.

the Human Rights Council – also examines, in the framework of a confidential procedure, human rights complaints, euphemistically called "communications", and establishes special procedures (country mandates and thematic mandates).

A. THE EXAMINATION OF "COMMUNICATIONS"

From its beginnings, the Organisation of the United Nations received communications from individuals and from non-governmental organisations complaining about human rights violations. In 1947, the Commission on Human Rights, followed in that by the Economic and Social (ECOSOC), has expressed the opinion that it was not competent to undertake any action concerning human rights complaints. However, later developments led to the adoption on 27 May 1970 by ECOSOC of its resolution 1503 (XLVIII). This resolution established a confidential procedure for dealing with communications relating to violations of human rights and fundamental freedoms. The United Nations Secretariat makes a summary of all the communications received and send a copy of each communication to the government concerned requesting a reply.

A Working Group of five members of (now) the Advisory Committee, designated by their geopolitical group, meets annually for two weeks to examine those communications and decides whether they appear to reveal "a consistent pattern of gross and reliably attested violations of human rights and fundamental freedoms". Since the adoption by ECOSOC of its resolution 2000/3 of 19 June 2000, it is no longer the Sub-Commission but the Working Group itself which takes the decision – by a majority of at least three of its five members – to bring to the attention of the Working Group on Situations of (now) the Human Rights Council the communications that correspond to the criteria of resolution 1503 (XLVIII). The present procedure is governed by Human Rights Council resolution 5/1 of 18 June 2007.

According to Sub-Commission resolution 1 (XXIV) of 13 August 1971, the communications must originate from a person or group of persons, who, it can be reasonably presumed, are victims of such violations and are clearly identified. Their language may not be essentially abusive and, in particular, may not contain insulting reference to the State against which the complaint is directed. They may not have manifestly political motivations, nor be based exclusively on report disseminated by mass media. Domestic remedies have to be exhausted.

The Working Group on Situations, consisting of five members of the Human Rights Council, also meets twice annually. It has the following options: to discontinue consideration of the matter, to keep the situation under review and to appoint or not appoint an independent expert or to take up the matter under public procedure. Only in the last situation does the procedure cease to be confidential. At the time of the Commission on Human Rights, this happened only once with complaints concerning Equatorial Guinea. The Human Rights Council did the same in 2012 concerning Eritrea. Since 2006, the Council has examined, moreover, the human rights situation in the framework of that confidential procedure in Kyrgyzstan (2006), in the Islamic Republic of Iran (2007), in Uzbekistan (2007), in Turkmenistan (2008–2009 and 2012), in the Maldives (2008), in the Democratic Republic of Congo (2009 and 2011–2012), in Guinea (2009–2010), in Tajikistan (2011), in Iraq (2012) and in Cameroon (2014).

B. THE SPECIAL PROCEDURES[124]

In the framework of the human rights violations procedure, based on resolution 1235 (XLII) of 6 June 1967 of the Economic and Social Council, the members of the Commission or the Sub-Commission could in a public debate mention violations of human rights of which they had cognisance. This could lead to the adoption of resolutions and sometimes to the establishment of a special procedure. Those special procedures concerned either the human rights situation in particular countries (country-oriented procedures) or specific thematic issues (thematic procedures). More recently, the Human Rights Council also established Commissions of Inquiry or mandated the High Commissioner to set up Investigations.

1. THE COUNTRY-ORIENTED PROCEDURES

Some procedures have been established at the time of the Commission on Human Rights; some of those have been maintained by the Human Rights Council while others have been initiated by that Council:

(a) Country mandates established by the Commission on Human Rights:
   1967: a Special Group of Experts on violations of human rights in *southern Africa*;
   1968: a Special Committee of Enquiry on *Israeli* practices in the *occupied territories*;
   1975: a Special Working Group on *Chile*; this Group travelled to Chile in July 1978, and was replaced in
   1979: by a Special Rapporteur on *Chile* (and by a Special Rapporteur on involuntary disappearances);

---

[124] See also Bossuyt, Marc, "The Development of Special Procedures of the United Nations Commission on Human Rights", *Human Rights Law Journal*, 1985, pp. 179–210; Lempinen, Miko, *Challenges facing the system of special procedures of the United Nations Commission on Human Rights*, Turku, Abo Akademi, 2001, 307 p.; Ramcharan, Bertrand, *The Protection Roles of UN Human Rights Special Procedures*, Leiden, Brill, 2009, 224 p.

1981: a Special Envoy on *Bolivia* and a Special Representative on *El Salvador*;

1982: a Special Rapporteur on *Guatemala*; moreover, the Secretary General has been requested to make a report on the human rights situation in *Poland* and to establish direct contacts with *Iran*;

1984: a Special Rapporteur on *Afghanistan* and a Special Representative on *Iran*;

1989: a Special Rapporteur on *Romania*;

1991: Special Rapporteurs on occupied *Kuwait* and on *Iraq* and a Special Representative on *Cuba*;

1992: Special Rapporteurs on *Cuba*, *Haiti* (an Independent Expert since 1995), *Myanmar* and the former *Yugoslavia* (since 2001: a Special Representative for Bosnia-Herzegovina and the Federal Republic of Yugoslavia) and a Representative of the Secretary General for the *Western Sahara*;

1993: Special Rapporteurs on Equatorial *Guinea* (Special Representative since 2001), *Cambodia*, *Somalia*, *Sudan* and the occupied *Palestinian territories*;

1994: Special Rapporteurs on *Rwanda* and on the Democratic Republic of *Congo* and a Special Representative on *Bougainville*;

1995: a Special Rapporteur on *Burundi*;

1997: a Special Rapporteur on *Nigeria*;

2003: an Independent Expert on technical cooperation and advisory services on *Liberia*;

2004: a Special Rapporteur on *Belarus* and on the Democratic People's Republic of *Korea* and an Independent Expert on *Chad*;

(b) Country mandates maintained by the Human Rights Council:

1992: the Special Rapporteur on *Myanmar*;

1993: the Special Rapporteurs on *Cambodia* and on the *Palestinian territories* occupied since 1967 and Independent Experts on *Somalia* and on the *Sudan*;

1995: the Independent Expert on *Haiti*;

2004: the Special Rapporteur on the *Democratic People's Republic of Korea*;

(c) Country mandates established by the Human Rights Council:

(1) Independent Experts or Special Rapporteurs:

2011: an Independent Expert on the *Côte d'Ivoire* (since 2013: on capacity building and technical cooperation), Special Rapporteurs on the Islamic Republic of *Iran* and on the *Syrian* Arab Republic (which will start once the mandate of the Commission of Inquiry ends);

2012: Special Rapporteurs on *Belarus* and on *Eritrea*;

2013: Independent Experts on *Central African Republic* and on *Mali*;

(2) Commissions of Inquiry or Investigations:

2011: Independent International Commission of Inquiry on the *Syrian Arab Republic*;

2014: Commission of Inquiry on Human Rights in *Eritrea*;

2014: Independent Commission of Inquiry on the 2014 *Gaza* Conflict;

2014: OHCHR Investigation on *Sri Lanka*;

2015: OHCHR Investigation on *Libya*.

2. THE THEMATIC PROCEDURES[125]

There are Working Groups, composed of five members, Special Rapporteurs and Independent Experts:

(a) Working Groups on:

1980: Enforced or Involuntary Disappearances;

1991: Arbitrary Detention;

2002: People of African Descent;

2005: The Use of Mercenaries;

2010: Discrimination against women in law and in practice;

2011: Human rights and transnational corporations and other business enterprises;

(b) Special Rapporteurs on:

1982: Extrajudicial, summary or arbitrary executions;

1985: Torture and other cruel, inhuman or degrading treatment and punishment;

1986: Freedom of religion or belief;

1990: Sale of children, child prostitution and child pornography;

1993: Freedom of opinion and expression and on Contemporary forms of racism;

1994: Independence of judges and lawyers and on Violence against women, its causes and consequences;

1995: The environmentally sound management and disposal of hazardous substances and wastes;

1998: The right to education and on Extreme poverty and human rights;

1999: The human rights of migrants;

2000: Human rights defenders and on the Right to food and on Adequate housing;

2001: The rights of indigenous peoples;

2002: The right of everyone to the enjoyment of the highest attainable standard of physical and mental health;

---

125   See also FROUVILLE, Olivier DE, *Les procédures thématiques: une contribution efficace des Nations Unies à la protection des droits de l'homme*, Paris, Pedone, 1996, 139 p.

2004: The human rights of internally displaced persons and on Trafficking in persons;

2005: Minority issues and on the promotion and protection of human rights while countering Terrorism;

2007: Contemporary forms of slavery;

2008: Safe drinking water and sanitation;

2009: Cultural rights;

2010: Freedom of peaceful assembly and of association;

2011: The promotion of truth, justice, reparation and guarantees of non-recurrence;

2012: A safe, clean, healthy and sustainable environment;

2014: The rights of persons with disabilities and on the Negative impact of the unilateral coercive measures on the enjoyment of human rights;

2015: The right to privacy;

(c) Independent experts on

2000: The effects of foreign debt;

2005: Human rights and international solidarity;

2011: A democratic and equitable international order;

2012: A safe, clean, healthy and sustainable environment;

2013: The rights of older persons;

2015: The human rights of persons with albinism.

∗∗∗

It is difficult to evaluate the effects of UN procedures. These effects vary in function of the country concerned. The more the country is open to the outside world, the more UN procedures may influence its human rights behaviour. While evaluating these effects, one should not lose sight of the fact that the organs concerned are not judicial, but political. Action in the field of human rights can be undertaken only when there is a political majority in the United Nations to do so. The United Nations does not always succeed in acting wherever this would be necessary or useful. That is, however, no reason not to act when it is possible to act. Looking carefully, one will find out that the United Nations is less selective than people often think. The United Nations does not possess efficient means to put an end to human rights violations, but its procedures and organs make it possible to exercise pressure on governments. States are generally very sensitive to maintaining their good reputation in the field of human rights and they try to avoid becoming the object of a UN procedure that could tarnish their reputation. Progressively, those UN procedures have become more and more sophisticated.

CHAPTER VI

THE UN HUMAN RIGHTS
TREATY BODIES[126]

The Charter of the Organisation of the United Nations, adopted on 26 June 1945, contains a number of provisions referring to human rights. Most important are Articles 55 and 56, which constitute the basis of the international law obligation to respect human rights and fundamental freedoms. According to those articles, all Members pledge themselves to take joint and separate action in co-operation with the Organisation for the achievement of "universal respect for, and observance of, human rights and fundamental freedoms for all without distinction as to race, sex, language, or religion". Presently, 193 States, nearly all the sovereign States, are Members of the United Nations and did, by becoming Members, accept the obligations of the UN Charter. The obligation, enshrined in that Charter, to respect human rights and fundamental freedoms was, however, weakened by the absence of an enumeration and of a definition of those rights and freedoms. That obligation has been clarified by the adoption of various instruments for the protection of human rights.

The first task of the Commission on Human Rights was the elaboration of an Universal Declaration of Human Rights, adopted in Paris by the General Assembly in its resolution 217 A (III) of 10 December 1948.[127] While

---

[126]   Based on lectures given in French at the Summer Session of the International Institute of Human Rights at Strasbourg from 8 till 10 July 2014; see also: ALSTON, Philip & CRAWFORD, James, *The Future of UN Human Rights Treaty Monitoring*, Cambridge, Cambridge Univ. Pr., 2000, 563 p.; BAYEFSKY, Anne, *The UN Human Rights Treaty System in the 21st Century*, The Hague, Kluwer Law International, 2000, 1116 p.; O'FLAHERTY, Michael, *Human Rights and the UN: Practice Before the Treaty Bodies* (Nijhoff Law Specials), 1st Ed., The Hague, Springer, 2002, 256 p.; YOUNG, Kirsten, *The Law and Process of the U.N. Human Rights Committee,* Ardsley, Transnational Publ., 2002, 355 p.; BAYEFSKY, Anne, *How to Complain to the UN Human Rights Treaty System,* The Hague, Kluwer Law International, 2003, 384 p.; VANDENHOLE, Wouter, *The Procedures Before the UN Human Rights Treaty Bodies: Divergence or Convergence?,* Antwerp, Intersentia, 2004, 331 p.; EGAN, Suzanne, *The UN Human Rights Treaty System: Law and Procedure,* London, Bloomsbury Professional, 2011, 550 p.; KELLER, Helen & ULFSTEIN, Geir (Eds.), *UN Human Rights Treaty Bodies: Law and Legitimacy,* Cambridge, Cambridge Univ. Pr., 2015, 490 p.

[127]   See also VERDOODT, Albert, *Naissance et signification de la Déclaration universelle des droits de l'homme,* Louvain, Nauwelaerts, 1964, 356 p. The Universal Declaration was adopted by 48 to 0, with 8 abstentions (the Byelorussian SSR, Czechoslovakia, Poland, Saudi Arabia, South Africa, the Ukrainian SSR, the USSR and Yugoslavia).

providing an interpretation of the obligation to respect human rights taken up by the Members of the United Nations, the Universal Declaration, which is a recommendation of the General Assembly, does not have as such binding legal force and does not establish an international supervisory mechanism of that obligation.

That is why the Commission on Human Rights has pursued its endeavours by elaborating draft international human rights conventions, the legally binding character of which would be beyond dispute for all States becoming parties to it. Those drafts were adopted by the Commission on Human Rights on 16 April 1954 and forwarded to the Third Committee of the General Assembly. It took no less than twelve years before the General Assembly adopted on 16 December 1966, in its resolution 2200 A (XXI), the International Covenants on Human Rights and the (First) Optional Protocol to the International Covenant on Civil and Political Rights.

A. THE INTERNATIONAL COVENANTS ON HUMAN RIGHTS

It still took more than nine years from adoption before the entry into force of the International Covenant on Economic, Social and Cultural Rights (on 3 January 1976), to which 164 States are parties (status of ratification as of 1 January 2016), and of the International Covenant on Civil and Political Rights[128] and the (First) Optional Protocol to that Covenant (both on 23 March 1976), to which respectively 168 States and 115 States are parties.

Originally, the supervision of the implementation of the International Covenant on Economic, Social and Cultural Rights (hereafter: the Social Covenant) was exercised by the Economic and Social Council who had set up a Working Group of 15 governmental experts in charge of examining the implementation of that Covenant. The Economic and Social Council decided in 1985 to transform this Working Group into a "Committee of Economic, Social and Cultural Rights" (CESCR)[129] consisting of 18 experts, starting in 1987. On 10 December 2008, an Optional Protocol to that Covenant recognising the competence of that Committee to receive and examine communications submitted by individuals or groups of individuals or on their behalf has been adopted. It entered into force on 5 May 2013 and 21 States are parties to it.

---

128   See also BOSSUYT, Marc, *Guide to the 'travaux préparatoires' of the International Covenant on Civil and Political Rights,* Dordrecht, M. Nijhoff, 1987, 851 p.; NOWAK, Manfred, *U.N. Covenant on Civil and Political Rights: CCPR Commentary,* 2nd Ed., Kehl, Engel, 2005, 1277 p.; JOSEPH, Sarah & CASTAN, Melissa, *The International Covenant on Civil and Political Rights: Cases, Materials, and Commentary,* 3rd Ed., Oxford, Oxford Univ. Pr., 2013, 1042 p.

129   See also ODELLO, Marco & SEATZU, Francesco, *The UN Committee on Economic, Social and Cultural Rights: The Law, Process and Practice,* Abingdon, Routledge, 2012, 328 p.

The study of the reports submitted by the States parties under the International Covenant on Civil and Political Rights (hereafter: the Civil Covenant) is entrusted to the Human Rights Committee (HRC),[130] established by that Covenant and consisting of 18 members. The Committee has decided that the States parties should submit such a report every five years. The study of those reports is concluded by the adoption of "General Comments". By making a declaration under Article 41 of the Civil Covenant, the States parties to that Covenant may recognise, under the condition of reciprocity, the competence of the Human Rights Committee to receive inter-State communications. The latter procedure entered into force on 28 March 1979 and 50 States have made such a declaration. As yet, no inter-State case has been submitted to the Human Rights Committee. Moreover, the 115 States parties to the (First) Optional Protocol recognise the competence of the Human Rights Committee to receive "individual" communications. A Second Optional Protocol, adopted by the General Assembly on 15 December 1989, aiming at the abolition of the death penalty, entered into force on 11 July 1991 and 81 States are parties to it.[131] The so-called "International Bill of Human Rights" now consists of the Universal Declaration, the two International Covenants and two Optional Protocols to the Civil Covenant and the Optional Protocol to the Social Covenant.

B. INSTRUMENTS PROHIBITING DISCRIMINATION

Besides the International Covenants on Human Rights, mention should be made of some other instruments aiming at the explicit prohibition of discrimination based on certain grounds such as race, sex and religion or in certain fields such as education, employment and occupation.

Following the adoption of a United Nations Declaration on the Elimination of All Forms of Racial Discrimination in its resolution 1904 (XVIII) on 20 November 1963, the General Assembly adopted on 21 December 1965 in

---

[130] See also Bossuyt, Marc, "Chronique de jurisprudence du Comité des droits de l'homme (1993–1997)", *Revue trimestrielle des droits de l'homme*, 1998, pp. 507–570; Ando, Nisuke, *Toward Implementing Universal Human Rights. Festschrift for the Twenty-Fifth Anniversary of the Human Rights Committee*, Leiden, Brill, 2004, 279 p; Bair, Johann, *The International Covenant on Civil and Political Rights and its (first) Optional Protocol: A Short Commentary based on Views, General Comments, and Concluding Observations by the Human Rights Committee*, New York, P. Lang, 2005, 222 p.; Hennebel, Ludovic, *La jurisprudence du Comité des droits de l'homme des Nations Unies*, Brussels, Bruylant, 2007, 512 p.; Möller, Jacob & Zayas, Alfred de, *United Nations Human Rights Committee Case Law 1977–2008: A Handbook*, Kehl, Engel, 2009, 604 p.; Conte, Alex & Burchill, Richard, *Defining civil and political rights: the jurisprudence of the United Nations Human Rights Committee*, 2nd Ed., Burlington, Ashgate, 2010, 359 p.; Tyagi, Yogesh, *The UN Human Rights Committee: Practice and Procedure*, Cambridge, Cambridge Univ. Pr., 2011, 909 p.

[131] See *infra*, Chapter X, A.

its resolution 2106 A (XX) an International Convention on the Elimination of All Forms of Racial Discrimination (ICERD).[132] That Convention entered into force on 4 January 1969 and 177 States are parties to it. Under Article 9 of the above-mentioned Convention, all States parties have undertaken to submit every two years a report on the measures taken giving effect to the provisions of the Convention. Contrary to the optional procedure for inter-State communications in the Civil Covenant, the inter-State procedure in that Convention is compulsory under Article 11. Under Article 14, any State party may recognise the competence of the Committee on the Elimination of Racial Discrimination (CERD),[133] consisting of 18 members, to receive individual communications. That procedure entered into force on 3 December 1982 and 57 States have made such a declaration. The Committee established also "early warning measures and urgent action procedures" which allow it to intervene in order to prevent or limit serious violations of the Convention.

On 18 December 1979, the General Assembly has adopted in its resolution 34/180 a Convention on the Elimination of Discrimination against Women.[134] That Convention entered into force on 3 September 1981 and 189 States are parties to it. Under Article 18 of that Convention, the Committee on the Elimination of Discrimination against Women (CEDAW), consisting of 18 (and later 23) members, examines the reports submitted every four years by the States on the measures they have taken to give effect to the provisions of that Convention and on the progress made. Initially, the Convention did not provide for the examination of individual or inter-State communications, but any dispute between two or more States Parties concerning that Convention shall be submitted to arbitration or, if they are unable to agree on the organisation of the arbitration, to the International Court of Justice. An Optional Protocol to that Convention, adopted on 6 October 1999, recognises the competence of that Committee to examine "individual" communications. That Protocol also establishes an inquiry procedure that allows the Committee to initiate a confidential investigation by one or more of its members where it has received reliable information of grave or systematic violations by a State Party of rights established in the Convention. Where warranted and with the consent of the State Party, the Committee may visit the territory of the State party. That Protocol entered into force on 22 December 2000 and 106 States are parties to it.

---

132   See also LERNER, Natan, *The U.N. Convention on the Elimination of All Forms of Racial Discrimination*, 2nd Ed., Alphen a/d Rijn, Sijthof & Noordhoff, 1980, 259 p.

133   See also KRUCKENBERG, Lena, *The UNreal World of Human Rights: An Ethnography of the UN Committee on the Elimination of Racial Discrimination*, Baden-Baden, Nomos Publ., 2012, 186 p.

134   See also FREEMAN, Marsha, CHINKIN, Christine & RUDOLF, Beate, *The UN Convention on the Elimination of All Forms of Discrimination Against Women: A Commentary*, Oxford, Oxford Univ. Pr., 2012, 292 p.

On 25 November 1981, the General Assembly adopted in its resolution 36/55 a Declaration on the Elimination of All Forms of Intolerance and Discrimination based on Religion or Belief. There is not yet a convention on this matter.

As far as instruments are concerned aiming at prohibiting discrimination in certain fields, mention should be made of the Convention (No. 111) concerning Discrimination in Respect of Employment and Occupation adopted by the General Conference of the International Labor Organization on 25 June 1958, which entered into force on 15 June 1960 and to which 172 States are parties, and of the Convention against Discrimination in Education, adopted by the General Conference of UNESCO on 14 December 1960, which entered into force on 24 October 1968 and to which 101 States are parties.

C. OTHER HUMAN RIGHTS CONVENTIONS

On 10 December 1984, the General Assembly of the United Nations adopted in its resolution 39/46 the Convention against Torture and Other Cruel, Inhuman or Degrading Treatment.[135] This Convention contains the principle of universal jurisdiction by providing that each State party has jurisdiction, when the offences are committed on its territory, when the offender or the victim is its national or when the offender is present on its territory and not extradited (Article 5). In the latter event and in accordance with the principle "*aut dedere, aut judicare*", it shall submit the case to its competent authorities for the purpose of prosecution (Article 7). Moreover, any statement made as a result of torture may not be invoked as evidence in any proceedings (Article 15).

A Committee against Torture (CAT), consisting of ten experts, examines reports of States parties and may designate one or more of its members to make a confidential inquiry, if it receives reliable information which appears to contain well-founded indications that torture is systematically practised in the territory of a State party. The Convention also provides for an optional procedure for dealing with inter-State (Article 21) or individual communications (Article 22), recognised respectively by 63 and 66 States parties. This Convention, to which 158 States are parties, entered into force on 26 June 1987.

On 18 December 2002, an Optional Protocol to the Convention against Torture was adopted. That Protocol entered into force on 22 June 2006 and 80 States are parties to it. Under that Protocol, a Sub-Committee on Prevention (SPT) consisting of 25 members was established, authorised to undertake regular

---

[135] See also Burgers, Hermann, *The United Nations Convention Against Torture: A Handbook on the Convention Against Torture and Other Cruel, Inhuman, Or Degrading Treatment or Punishment*, The Hague, M. Nijhoff, 1988, 271 p.; Novak, Manfred & McArtur, Elizabeth, *The United Nations Convention against Torture: A Commentary*, Oxford, Oxford Univ. Pr., 2008, 600 p.; Dewulf, Steven, *The Signature of Evil: (Re)defining Torture in International Law*, Antwerp, Intersentia, 2011, 617 p.

visits to places where people are deprived of their liberty. Each State party shall also maintain, designate or establish one or several independent national preventive mechanisms for the prevention of torture at the domestic level.

On 20 November 1989, the General Assembly adopted the Convention on the Rights of the Child,[136] which entered into force on 2 September 1990 and to which 196 States are parties. This Convention has established a Committee on the Rights of the Child (CRC), consisting of ten experts and entrusted with the examination of reports submitted by the States parties every five years. On 25 May 2000, two Optional Protocols to that Convention have been adopted: the first, which entered into force on 18 January 2002 and to which 171 States are parties, concerns the sale of children, child prostitution and child pornography; the second, which entered into force on 12 February 2002 and to which 162 States are parties, concerns the involvement of children in armed conflicts. On 19 December 2011, a third Optional Protocol to that Convention on a communication procedure was adopted. It entered into force on 14 April 2014 and 24 States are parties to it.

On 18 December 1990, an International Convention on the Protection of the Rights of All Migrant Workers and Members of Their Families[137] was adopted. This Convention, which entered into force on 1 July 2003 and to which 48 States are parties, has established a Committee on Migrant Workers (CMW), consisting of ten (later 14) members, to examine reports submitted by the States parties every five years.

On 13 December 2006, a Convention on the Rights of Persons with Disabilities was adopted. This Convention, which entered into force on 3 May 2008 and to which 161 States are parties, has established a Committee on the Rights of Persons with Disabilities (CRPD), consisting of 12 (later 18) experts to receive reports submitted by the States parties at least every four years. On 13 December 2006, an Optional Protocol to that Convention, recognising the competence of the Committee to receive "individual" communications was adopted. It also entered into force on 3 May 2008 and 87 States are parties to it.

On 20 December 2006, an International Convention for the Protection of All Persons from Enforced Disappearance was adopted. It entered into force on 23 December 2010 and 51 States are parties to it. A Committee on Enforced Disappearances (CED), consisting of ten experts, examines an initial report submitted by the States parties and may request States parties to provide additional information on the implementation of this Convention. A request that a disappeared person should be sought may be submitted to the Committee, as

---

[136] See also DETRICK, Sharon, *A Commentary on the United Nations Convention on the Rights of the Child*, The Hague, M. Nijhoff, 1999, 790 p.

[137] See also CHOLEWINSKI, Ryszard, GUCHTENEIRE, Paul DE & PECOUD, Antoine, *Migration and Human Rights. The United Nations Convention on Migrant Workers' Rights*, Cambridge, Cambridge Univ. Pr., 2009, 474 p.

a matter of urgency, by any person having a legitimate interest. The Committee may consider communications from or on behalf of individuals subject to its jurisdiction and also communications in which a State party claims that another State party is not fulfilling its obligations under this Convention. It may request one or more of its members to undertake a visit and report back to it and, when enforced disappearance is being practised on a widespread or systematic basis, it may urgently bring the matter to the attention of the General Assembly of the United Nations.

***

The Committees also publish their interpretation of the content of human rights provisions, known as General Comments on thematic issues or methods of work. An annual meeting of Chairpersons of the (ten) Human Rights Treaty Bodies provides a forum for those chairpersons to discuss their work, share best practices, and consider ways to enhance the effectiveness of the treaty system as a whole.

On 9 April 2014, the General Assembly adopted its resolution 68/268 entitled "Strengthening and enhancing the effective functioning of the human rights treaty body system". This resolution encourages a simplified reporting procedure to facilitate the preparation of State reports, the adoption of short, focused and concrete concluding observations, an enhancement of the efficiency, transparency, effectiveness and harmonisation of the working methods and a balanced representation in the composition of the treaty bodies. Moreover, the General Assembly has decided to limit the number of words for each document, to allocate a maximum of three official languages for the work of the human right treaty bodies, to issue summary records in (only) one of the working languages and to make live webcasts of the public meetings of those organs. These measures will allow an increase of the meeting time of those organs taking into account their respective needs.

Table 3. United Nations Human Rights Instruments

A. THEMATIC ORDER	Adoption	In force	Committees	States parties[138]
Universal Declaration	*10.12.1948*			
Declaration Racial Discrimination.	*20.11.1963*			
Convention Racial Discrimination	**21.12.1965**	04.01.1969	CERD (18)	177
" Individual Communications	"	03.12.1982		57
Economic-Social Covenant	**16.12.1966**	03.01.1976	CESCR (18)	164
" Opt. Prot. Ind. Com.	10.12.2008	05.05.2013		21
Civil & Political Covenant	**16.12.1966**	23.03.1976	HRC (18)	168
" Art. 41 Interstate Com.	"	28.03.1979		50
" 1st Opt. Prot. Ind. Com.	16.12.1966	23.03.1976		115
" 2nd Opt. Prot. Death Penalty	15.12.1989	11.07.1991		81
Convention Discrimination Women	**18.12.1979**	03.09.1981	CEDAW (23)	189
" Opt. Prot. Ind. Com.	06.10.1999	22.12.2000		106
Declaration Religious Discrimination	*25.11.1981*			
Convention against Torture	**10.12.1984**	26.06.1987	CAT (10)	158
" Art. 20 Interstate Com.	"	"		63
" Art. 21 Individual Com.	"	"		66
" Opt. Prot. Prevention	18.12.2002	22.06.2006	SPT (25)	80
Convention Rights of the Child	**20.11.1989**	02.09.1990	CRC (10)	196
" Opt. Prot. Selling Children	25.05.2000	18.01.2002		171
" Opt. Prot. Armed Conflicts	25.05.2000	12.02.2002		162
" Opt. Prot. Ind. Com.	19.12.2011	14.04.2014		24
Convention Migrant Workers	**18.12.1990**	01.07.2003	CMW (14)	48
Convention Persons Disabilities	**13.12.2006**	03.05.2008	CRPD (18)	161
" Opt. Prot. Ind. Com.	13.12.2006	03.05.2008		87
Convention Enforced Disappearance	**20.12.2006**	23.12.2010	CED (10)	51

Conv. ILO Discr. Empl. & Occ.	*25.06.1958*	*15.06.1960*		172
Conv. UNESCO Discr. Education	*14.12.1960*	*24.10.1968*		101

---

138   Status of ratification as of 1 January 2016.

B. Chronological order			
Adoption	In force	States parties	Instruments
12.10.1948			*Universal Declaration*
25.06.1958	15.06.1960	172	*Conv. ILO Discr. Empl. & Occupation*
14.12.1960	24.10.1968	101	*Conv. UNESCO Discrim. Education*
20.11.1963			*Declaration Racial Discrimination*
21.12.1965	04.01.1969	177	**Convention Racial Discrimination**
21.12.1965	03.12.1982	57	Conv. Rac. Discrimination Ind. Com.
16.121966	03.01.1976	164	**Economic-Social Covenant**
16.12.1966	23.03.1976	168	**Civil & Political Covenant**
16.12.1966	28.03.1979	49	Civ. & Pol. Cov. Art. 41 Int.-State Com.
16.12.1966	23.03.1976	115	Civ. & Pol. Cov. 1st Opt. Prot. Ind. Com.
18.12.1979	03.09.1981	189	**Convention Discrimination Women**
25.11.1981			*Declaration Religious Discrimination*
10.12.1984	26.06.1987	158	**Convention against Torture**
10.12.1984	26.06.1987	63	Conv. Tort. Art. 21 Int.-St. Com.
10.12.1984	26.06.1987	66	Conv. Tort. Art. 22 Ind. Com.
20.11.1989	02.09.1990	196	**Convention Rights of the Child**
15.12.1989	11.07.1991	81	Civ. & Pol. Cov. 2nd Opt. Pr. Death Pen.
18.12.1990	01.07.2003	48	**Convention Migrant Workers**
06.10.1999	22.12.2000	106	Conv. Women Opt. Prot. Ind. Com.
25.05.2000	18.01.2002	171	Conv. Child. Opt. Prot. Selling Children
25.05.2000	12.02.2002	162	Conv. Child. Opt. Prot. Armed Conflicts
18.12.2002	22.06.2006	80	Conv. Torture Opt. Prot. Prevention
13.12.2006	03.05.2008	161	**Convention Persons Disabilities**
13.12.2006	03.05.2008	87	Conv. Disabilities Opt. Prot. Ind. Com.
20.12.2006	23.12.2010	51	**Convention Enforced Disappearance**
10.12.2008	05.05.2013	21	Econ.-Soc. Cov. Opt. Prot. Ind. Com.
19.12.2011	14.04.2014	24	Conv. Rights Child. Opt. Prot. Ind. Com.

C. Number of States parties			
States parties	Adoption	In force	Instruments
196	20.11.1989	02.09.1990	**Convention Rights of the Child**
189	18.12.1979	03.09.1981	**Convention Discrimination Women**
177	21.12.1965	04.01.1969	**Convention Racial Discrimination**
172	25.06.1958	15.06.1960	*Conv. ILO Discrim. Empl. & Occupation*
171	25.05.2000	18.01.2002	Conv. Child Opt. Prot. Selling Children
168	16.12.1966	23.03.1976	**Civil & Political Covenant**
164	16.12.1966	03.01.1976	**Economic-social Covenant**
162	25.05.2000	12.02.2002	Conv. Child Opt. Prot. Armed Conflicts
161	13.12.2006	03.05.2008	**Convention Persons Disabilities**
158	10.12.1984	26.06.1987	**Convention against Torture**
115	16.12.1966	23.03.1976	Civ. & Pol. Cov. 1st Opt. Pr. Ind. Com.
106	06.10.1999	22.12.2000	Conv. Women Opt. Prot. Ind. Com.
101	14.12.1960	24.10.1968	*Conv. UNESCO Discrim. Education*
87	13.12.2006	03.05.2008	Conv. Disabilities Opt. Prot. Ind. Com.
81	15.12.1989	11.07.1991	Civ. & Pol. Cov. 2nd Opt. Pr. Death Pen.
80	18.12.2002	22.06.2006	Conv. Torture Opt. Prot. Prevention
66	10.12.1984	26.06.1987	Conv. Tort. Art. 22 Ind. Com.
63	10.12.1984	26.06.1987	Conv. Tort. Art. 21 Int.-St. Com.
57	21.12.1965	03.12.1982	Convention Racial Discrim. Ind. Com.
51	20.12.2006	23.12.2010	**Convention Enforced Disappearance**
49	16.12.1966	28.03.1979	Civ. Cov. Art. 41 Int.-St. Com.
48	18.12.1990	01.07.2003	**Convention Migrant Workers**
24	19.12.2011	14.04.2014	Conv. Rights Child Opt. Prot. Ind. Com.
21	10.12.2008	05.05.2013	Econ.-Soc. Cov. Opt. Prot. Ind. Com.
	25.11.1981		*Declaration Religious Discrimination*
	20.11.1963		*Declaration Racial Discrimination*
	10.12.1948		*Universal Declaration*

CHAPTER VII
REGIONAL SYSTEMS OF PROTECTION
OF HUMAN RIGHTS[139]

The most developed systems of international human rights protection have been set up on a regional level. It started in the framework of the Council of Europe and was followed by systems of regional protection in the framework of the Organisation of American States and in that of the Organisation of African Unity.

A. HUMAN RIGHTS PROTECTION IN THE FRAMEWORK OF THE COUNCIL OF EUROPE

The "Committee of Movements for European Unity" organised in 1948 in The Hague (Netherlands) a "Congress of Europe". This led to the establishment in 1949 of the Council of Europe and to the adoption of the European Convention on Human Rights in 1950 and the European Social Charter in 1961.

1. THE EUROPEAN CONVENTION ON HUMAN RIGHTS

The European Convention on Human Rights,[140] adopted in the framework of the Council of Europe, was signed in Rome (Italy) on 4 November 1950 and

---

139 Based on Bossuyt, Marc & Wouters, Jan, *Grondlijnen van Internationaal Recht* (Manual of International Law), Antwerp, Intersentia, 2005, 1086 p., at pp. 792–815.

140 Dembour, Marie-Bénédicte, *Who Believes in Human Rights?: Reflections on the European Convention*, Cambridge, Cambridge Univ. Pr., 2006, 340 p.; Dijk, Pieter van, Hoof, Fried van, Rijn, Arjen van & Zwaak, Leo (Eds.), *Theory and Practice of the European Convention on Human Rights*, 4th Ed., Antwerp, Intersentia, 2006, 1190 p.; Loucaides, Loukis, *The European Convention on Human Rights. Collected Essays*, Leiden, Brill, 2007, 287 p.; Janis, Mark, Kay, Richard & Bradley, Anthony, *European Human Rights Law: Text and Materials*, 3rd Ed., Oxford, Oxford Univ. Pr., 2008, 1016 p.; Fitzmaurice, Malgosia & Merkouris, Panos, *The Interpretation and Application of the European Convention of Human Rights. Legal and Practical Implications*, Leiden, Brill, 2012, 303 p.; Harris, David, O'Boyle, Michael, Bates, Edward & Buckley, Carla (Eds.), *Harris, O'Boyle and Warbrick, Law of the European Convention on Human Rights*, 3rd Ed., Oxford, Oxford Univ. Pr., 2014, 1080 p.; Rainey, Bernadette, White, Elizabeth & Ovey, Claire (Eds.), *Jacobs, White & Ovey, The European Convention on Human Rights*, 6th Ed., Oxford, Oxford Univ. Pr., 2014, 728 p.

entered into force on 3 September 1953. The European Convention guarantees most of the civil and political rights enumerated in the Universal Declaration of Human Rights. Some more disputed rights were later included in additional protocols. Some of the articles of the European Convention guaranteeing rights and freedoms contain a second paragraph which allows for restrictions under strict conditions: "in accordance with the law", "necessary in a democratic society", in the interest of legitimate goals and without discrimination. Some other protocols have amended the institutional provisions of the Convention concerning the control mechanisms set up to supervise the respect by the States parties of the normative provisions. Originally, three organs were entrusted with the supervision of the Convention: the European Commission of Human Rights, the European Court of Human Rights and the Committee of Ministers.

The European Commission of Human Rights was competent to receive individual petitions by victims of a violation by a State party, to decide on their admissibility and to place itself at the disposal of the parties with a view to securing a friendly settlement. If no solution was reached, the European Commission drew up a report to be transmitted to the Committee of Ministers in which it stated its opinion as to whether the facts found disclosed a breach by the State concerned of its obligations under the Convention. If the State party concerned had recognised the competence of the European Court, either the European Commission or the State party concerned could refer the question to that Court. If the question was not referred to the Court within a period of three months from the date of the transmission of the report to the Committee of Ministers, then Committee decided by a majority of two-thirds of its members whether there had been a violation of the Convention.

Before the entry in force of Protocol No. 11 on 1 November 1998, the recognition of the competence to examine individual applications and the competence of the European Court of Human Rights were optional. As of the entry in force of that Protocol, the European Commission has been suppressed and the European Court of Human Rights[141] has become a full time organ which is also competent to decide on the admissibility of the applications. The European Court consists of a number of judges equal to that of the States parties. At present, there are 47 judges elected for nine years. They may sit until the age of 70. The Committee of Ministers remains only competent to supervise the execution of the judgments of the European Court (Article 46).

---

[141]   AROLD, Nina-Louisa, *The Legal Culture of the European Court of Human Rights,* Leiden, Brill, 2007, 211 p.; TULKENS, Francoise, KOVLER, Anatoly, SPIELMANN, Dean & CARIOLOU, Leto, *Judge Loukis Loucaides An Alternative View on the Jurisprudence of the European Court of Human Rights – A Collection of Separate Opinions (1998–2007),* Leiden, Brill, 2008, 381 p.; ANAGNOSTOU, Dia & PSYCHOGIOPOULOU, Evangelia, *The European Court of Human Rights and the Rights of Marginalised Individuals and Minorities in National Context,* Leiden, Brill, 2009, 244 p.; HAIDER, Dominik, *The Pilot-Judgment Procedure of the European Court of Human Rights,* Leiden, Brill, 2013, 347 p.

Any State party may refer to the Court any alleged breach of the provisions of the Convention and its Protocols by another State party (Article 33). The Court may also receive applications from any person, non-governmental organisation or group of individuals claiming to be the victim of a violation by one of the States parties of the rights set forth in the European Convention or its Protocols (Article 34). The European Court may only deal with the matter:

- after all domestic remedies have been exhausted and within a period of six months from the date on which the final decision was taken (reduced to four months once the 15th Protocol of 24 June 2013 enters into force);
- when the application is not anonymous;
- when the application is not substantially the same as a matter that has already been examined by the Court and has not already been submitted to another procedure of international investigation or settlement; and
- when the individual application is not incompatible with the provisions of the Convention, not manifestly ill founded, and not an abuse of the right of individual application (Article 35).

To consider cases brought before it, the Court shall sit in a single-judge formation, in committees of three judges, in Chambers of seven judges and in a Grand Chamber of seventeen judges. The Grand Chamber includes the President, the Vice-Presidents, the Presidents of the Chambers and the judge elected in respect of the State party concerned (Article 26).

A single judge may declare inadmissible an individual application where such a decision can be taken without further examination. If not, the application will be forwarded to a committee of three judges or to a Chamber of seven judges (Article 27). A committee of three judges may, by an unanimous vote, declare an application inadmissible where such a decision can be taken without further examination or declare it admissible and render at the same time a judgment on the merits, if the underlying question is already the subject of well-established case law of the Court. Those decisions and judgments are final (Article 28). If no decision is taken by a single judge or no decision taken or no judgment rendered by a committee, a Chamber of seven judges will decide on the admissibility and, separately or not, on the merits of individual applications. Decisions on the admissibility of inter-State applications are taken separately, unless the Court, in exceptional cases, decides otherwise (Article 29).

Where a case pending before a Chamber raises a serious question or where the resolution of a question might have a result inconsistent with a judgment previously delivered by the Court, the Chamber may relinquish jurisdiction in favour of the Grand Chamber of seventeen judges, unless one of the parties to the case objects (Article 30). In exceptional cases, a panel of five judges of the Grand Chamber may accept a request to refer the case to the Grand Chamber submitted by a party to the case within a period of three months from the date of the judgment of the Chamber (Article 43). In all cases before a Chamber or a Grand Chamber, the State party concerned, any other interested State party or any other person invited by the President of the Court, and the Council of Europe High Commissioner for Human Rights may submit written comments and take part in hearings (Article 36). Reasons shall be given for judgments as well as for decisions declaring applications admissible or inadmissible (Article 45). If the Court finds a violation, it shall, if necessary, afford just satisfaction to the injured party (Article 41). Protocol No. 16, adopted on 2 October 2013, allows the highest courts and tribunals of a State party to request the Court to give Advisory Opinions on questions of principle relating to the interpretation or application of the rights and freedoms defined in the Convention or the protocols thereto.

The Rules of the Court contain a Rule 39 which provides that a Chamber or the President of a Section may indicate to the parties any interim measure which they consider should be adopted in the interests of the parties or of the proper conduct of the proceedings. The Convention itself does not contain any provision on interim measures. In its judgment in *Cruz Varas and Others v. Sweden* (Pl. Ct., 20 March 1991) and in its decision in *Čonka and Others v. Belgium* (13 March 2001), the Court considered that such measures were not binding. However, in its Chamber (6 February 2003) and Grand Chamber (4 February 2005) judgments in the case of *Mamatkulov v. Turkey*, the Court decided that its interim measures had become binding and that not complying with an indicated interim measure violates the effective exercise of the right of petition guaranteed by Article 34 of the Convention.[142]

Only a few inter-State applications have been submitted at the time of writing:

- complaints in 1956 and 1957 by Greece against the United Kingdom concerning events in *Cyprus* (discontinued without judgment);
- a complaint in 1960 by Austria against Italy concerning events in *Alto-Adige* (Sud-Tirol) (discontinued without judgment);
- complaints in 1967 and 1968 by Denmark, Norway, Sweden and the Netherlands concerning events in *Greece* under the colonels regime (discontinued without judgment);
- a complaint in 1971 by Ireland against the United Kingdom concerning events in *Northern Ireland* (Plenary Court judgment of 18 January 1978 finding a violation of Article 3);
- complaints in 1974, 1975, 1977 and in 1999 by Cyprus against Turkey concerning events in the Turkish occupied part of *Cyprus* (Grand Chamber judgment of 10 May 2001 finding continuing violations of Articles 2, 3, 5 and 8, and 1 Protocol No. 1 and violations of Articles 3, 6, 8, 9, 10 and 13, and 2 Protocol No. 1; a Grand Chamber judgment of 12 May 2014 awarded

---

142   See also, *infra*, Chapter XI, B, and Chapter XIII, B.

satisfaction of 30 million euros and 60 million euros for non-pecuniary damage);

- a complaint in 1982 by Denmark, Norway, Sweden, the Netherlands and France against Turkey concerning events during the *Turkish military regime* (discontinued without judgment);
- a complaint in 1997 by Denmark against Turkey concerning the ill-treatment of a Danish citizen (admissibility decision of 8 June 1999; struck of the list by Chamber judgment of 5 April 2000);
- complaints in 2007 (no. 1: concerning expulsions of Georgians from Russia; Grand Chamber judgment of 3 July 2014 finding violations of Articles 3, 5.1, 5.4, 13 (in conjunction with 3 and 5.1), 38 and 1 Protocol No. 4), 2008 (no. 2: pending) and 2009 (no. 3: discontinued without judgment) by Georgia against Russia concerning events in *Abkhazia* and *South Ossetia*;
- complaints in 2014 by Ukraine against Russia concerning events in *Crimea* and the *Eastern regions of Ukraine* and the alleged abduction of children (pending).

On the contrary, many thousands of individual applications have been submitted over the years. In the period 1955–1998 (before the Court became a full-time body), 45,000 applications were allocated to a judicial formation. From 1999 on, the number of applications allocated to a judicial formation did rise continuously and, from 2008 on, it surpassed that number on an annual basis reaching more than 65,000 applications in 2013. In the period 1955–1998, the Court delivered 837 judgments. That number was already surpassed on an annual basis in 2001. In the period 2006–2010, the average number of judgments delivered was above 1,500 (with a maximum of 1,625 in 2010). Since then, that average is slightly under 1,000, as the number of judgments delivered annually has decreased continuously to 823 in 2015.

The backlog of individual applications pending before the Court had grown steadily from nearly 100,000 on 1 January 2009 to more than 160,000 on 1 September 2011. However, the entry into force on 1 June 2010 of Protocol No. 14 of 13 May 2004 has instituted a single judge procedure (dealing in 2013 and 2014 with about 80,000 applications each year) which reduced the backlog on 1 January 2016 to less than 65,000 pending applications. Seven States parties[143] total more than three quarters of all pending applications. The number of applications submitted in 2014 (56,200) and 2015 (40,600) was (for the first time since 2003) not higher than the previous year. To deal with all those applications, in particular with those not benefitting from any prioritisation,[144] will take years, if ever.

---

[143] Ukraine: 13,850 (21.4%), Russia: 9,200 (14.2%), Turkey: 8,450 (13%), Italy: 7,550 (11.6%), Hungary: 4,600 (7.1%), Romania: 3,550 (5.5%) and Georgia: 2,150 (3.3%).

[144] Since 2009, the Court has drawn up a number of categories having regard to the importance and the urgency of the issues raised, in deciding the order in which cases are to be dealt with.

2. THE (REVISED) EUROPEAN SOCIAL CHARTER

On 18 October 1961, the European Social Charter was opened for signature in Turin (Italy). The Charter entered into force in February 1965 and has been ratified by 26 Member States of the Council of Europe. Resolved to update and adapt the substantive contents of the Charter in order to take account in particular of the fundamental social changes which have occurred since the text was adopted, the States parties to the European Social Charter adopted on 3 May 1996 the Revised European Social Charter (entered into force on 1 July 1999) which embodied the rights guaranteed by the Charter as amended and by the Additional Protocols of 1988 and which also added new rights.

The European Social Charter[145] mainly contains standards of social rights and social security rights. The Charter is a so-called "*à la carte*" treaty which does not oblige the States parties to accept all articles. They may select the provisions they accept to be bound by. However, in that selection they are not entirely free. Article A of Part III of the Revised Charter imposes the following restrictions:

"1. [... E]ach of the Parties undertakes:
(a) [...]
to consider Part I of this Charter as a declaration of the aims which it will pursue by all appropriate means, as stated in the introductory paragraph of that part;
to consider itself bound by at least six of the following nine articles of Part II of this Charter: Articles 1 [The right to work], 5 [The right to organise], 6 [The right to bargain collectively], 7 [The right of children and young persons to protection], 12 [The right to social security], 13 [The right to social and medical assistance], 16 [The right of the family to social, legal and economic protection], 19 [The right of migrant workers and their families to protection and assistance] and 20 [The right to equal opportunities and equal treatment in matters of employment and occupation without discrimination on the grounds of sex];
to consider itself bound by an additional number of articles or numbered paragraphs of Part II of the Charter which it may select, provided that the total number of articles or numbered paragraphs by which it is bound is not less than sixteen articles or sixty-three numbered paragraphs".

The majority of the States parties accept a number of articles and paragraphs higher than the required minimum.

Compared with the European Convention on Human Rights, the supervisory organs of the Revised European Social Charter have a much more limited role in the protection of the rights contained in that Charter. The supervisory mechanism of the Charter, contained in its Part IV, is comparable to the one of

---

[145] See also BENELHOCINE, Carole, *The European Social Charter*, Strasbourg, Council of Europe, 2012, 137 p.

the International Labour Organisation. The States parties send to the Secretary General of the Council of Europe a report at two-yearly intervals concerning the application of the provisions of the Charter as they have accepted (Article 21). Those reports are examined by a Committee of Independent Experts which shall draw up a report containing its conclusions (Article 24). The Committee consists of at least nine members elected by the Parliamentary Assembly for a period of six years (Article 25). The reports of the States parties and the Committee are submitted to a Governmental Committee, composed of one representative of each State party. The Governmental Committee prepares the decisions of the Committee of Ministers and may submit proposals to it aiming at studies to be carried out on social issues and on articles of the Charter which possibly might be updated (Article 27). The Committee of Ministers shall adopt, by a majority of two-thirds of those voting, a resolution covering the entire cycle and containing individual recommendations to the States parties concerned (Article 28).

On 9 November 1995, an Additional Protocol to the European Social Charter providing for a system of collective complaints was adopted. Complaints alleging unsatisfactory application of the Charter may be submitted by international organisations of employers and trade unions, other international non-governmental organisations and representative national organisations of employers and trade unions.

B. REGIONAL PROTECTION OF HUMAN RIGHTS IN AMERICA AND IN AFRICA

The protection of human rights in the framework of the Organisation of American States and that in the framework of the African Union have several common characteristics.

1. IN THE FRAMEWORK OF THE ORGANISATION OF AMERICAN STATES

In 1948, the Organisation of American States (OAS) adopted in Bogotà (Colombia) the American Declaration of the Rights and Duties of Man. More than twenty years later, on 22 November 1969, the American Convention on Human Rights[146] was adopted in San José (Costa Rica). It entered into force on 18 July 1978. The American Convention contains a great number of rights and freedoms formulated in terms similar to those of the provisions of the Civil Covenant. As of the beginning of 2016, 23 Latin American and Caribbean States

---

146 MEDINA QUIROGA, Cecilia, *The American Convention on Human Rights: Crucial Rights and their Theory and Practice*, 2nd Ed., Antwerp, Intersentia, 2016, 374 p.

are parties to the American Convention.[147] Two States became party to it, but have denounced it: Trinidad and Tobago on 26 May 1998 and Venezuela on 10 September 2012.

The OAS did not adopt a separate convention on economic, social and cultural rights but Article 26 of the American Convention reads as follows:

> "The States Parties undertake to adopt measures, both internally and through international cooperation, especially those of an economic and technical nature, with a view to achieving progressively by legislation or other means, the full realization of the rights implicit in the economic, social, educational, scientific and cultural standards set forth in the Charter of the Organization of American States as amended by the Protocol of Buenos Aires".

On 17 November 1988, the American Convention was completed with the Additional Protocol of San Salvador (El Salvador) on Economic, Social and Cultural Rights, which entered into force on 16 November 1999. The rights contained in that Additional Protocol are analogous to those contained in the European Social Charter. On 8 June 1990, the Protocol of Asunción (Paraguay) on the Abolition of the Death Penalty was adopted. 13 Latin American States are parties to that Protocol, which entered into force on 28 August 1991.

Five other conventions have also been adopted by the General Assembly of the Organisation of American States: the Inter-American Convention to Prevent and Punish Torture at Cartagena de Indias (Colombia) on 9 December 1985 (entered into force on 28 February 1987), the Inter-American Conventions on Forced Disappearance of Persons (entered into force on 28 March 1996) and on The Prevention, Punishment and Eradication of Violence against Women (entered into force on 5 March 1995), both at Belém do Pará (Brazil) on 9 June 1994, the Inter-American Convention on the Elimination of All Forms of Discrimination against Persons with Disabilities at Guatemala City (Guatemala) on 8 June 1999 (entered into force on 14 September 2011) and the Inter-American Convention against All Forms of Discrimination and Intolerance at La Antigua (Guatemala) on 6 June 2013.

In 1959, the Inter-American Commission on Human Rights was established in order to promote the observance and defence of human rights of the American States. The Inter-American Commission, based in Washington DC, is composed of seven members elected for a term of four years, once renewable. The American Convention enlarged the functions and powers of the Inter-American Commission (Articles 34–51) and established the Inter-American

---

147   Eight Member States of the OAS are not parties to the American Convention: Antigua & Barbuda, Bahamas, Belize, Guyana, St Kitts & Nevis, St Lucia, St Vincent & the Grenadines and the USA.

Court of Human Rights[148] (Articles 52–69). That Court, based in San José (Costa Rica) consists of seven judges elected for a term of six years, renewable once. Except Dominica, Grenada and Jamaica, (the other) twenty States parties to the American Convention have declared, under Article 62, that they recognise the jurisdiction of the Inter-American Court to be binding on all matters relating to the interpretation or application of this Convention.

In the American Convention (in contrast to the European Convention), the competence to examine inter-State communications is optional and that to examine individual communications is compulsory. Indeed, any person or group of persons or any non-governmental entity may lodge petitions with the Commission containing denunciations or complaints of the American Convention by a State party (Article 44). Moreover, the States parties may make a declaration recognising the competence of the Inter-American Commission to receive and examine communications in which a State party alleges that another State party has committed a violation of a human right set forth in the American Convention (Article 45). Such a declaration has been made by nine States parties: Argentina, Chile, Colombia, Costa Rica, Ecuador, Jamaica, Nicaragua, Peru and Uruguay.

2. IN THE FRAMEWORK OF THE AFRICAN UNION

On 26 June 1981, the Assembly of Heads of State and Governments of the Organisation of African Unity (OAU, in the meanwhile replaced by the African Union) adopted in Nairobi (Kenya) the African Charter on Human and Peoples' Rights.[149] That Charter entered into force on 21 October 1986 and 53 States (all the Member States of the African Union) are parties to it. The Charter aims at promoting and protecting human and peoples' rights and freedoms, taking into account the importance traditionally attached to these rights and freedoms in Africa.

The Charter establishes an African Commission on Human and Peoples' Rights, consisting of 11 members (Article 31) and based at Banjul (The Gambia). The African Commission started its activities in November 1987. Its most important functions are to promote human and peoples' rights, to ensure the protection of those rights, to interpret all the provisions of the Charter and to perform any other tasks which may be entrusted to it by the

---

[148] PASQUALUCCI, Jo, *The Practice and Procedure of the Inter-American Court of Human Rights*, 2nd Ed., Cambridge, Cambridge Univ. Pr., 2012, 462 p.

[149] NMEHIELLE, Vincent O. Orlu, *The African Human Rights System: Its Laws, Practice, and Institutions*, Leiden, M. Nijhoff, 2001, 443 p.; EVANS, Malcolm & MURRAY, Rachel, *The African Charter on Human and Peoples' Rights. The System in Practice, 1986–2000*, Cambridge, Cambridge Univ. Pr., 2002, 419 p.; OKAFOR, Obiora, *The African Human Rights System, Activist Forces and International Institutions*, Cambridge, Cambridge Univ. Pr., 2007, 352 p.

Assembly of Heads of State and Government (Article 45). The Commission may receive communications by a State Party directed against another State party (Article 47). The Commission may also, if a simple majority of its members so decides, consider "Communications other than those of States Parties" (Article 55). When it appears that one or more communications apparently relate to special cases which reveal "the existence of a series of serious or massive violation of human and peoples' rights", the African Commission shall draw the attention of the Assembly of Heads of State and Government to these special cases (Article 58).

A Protocol to the African Charter on Human and Peoples' Rights on the Establishment of an African Court on Human and Peoples' Rights was adopted on 10 June 1998 at Ouagadougou (Burkina Faso) and entered into force on 25 January 2004. Half of the membership of the African Union (27) has ratified that Protocol. The Court is based at Arusha (Tanzania) and consists of 11 judges elected for six years, renewable once. All judges, except the President, perform their functions on a part-time basis. The Court may receive complaints and/or applications submitted to it either by the African Commission, by State parties to the Protocol or by African inter-governmental organisations. Non-governmental organisations with observer status before the African Commission and individuals from States which have made a declaration accepting the jurisdiction of the Court (Burkina Faso, Ghana, Malawi, Mali, Rwanda, Tanzania and the Republic of Côte d'Ivoire) can also institute cases directly before the Court. The Court delivered its first judgment on 15 December 2009.

A Protocol of the Court of Justice of the African Union was adopted on 11 July 2003 at Maputo (Mozambique). On 1 July 2008, a Protocol on the Statute of the African Court of Justice and Human Rights was adopted at Sharm El-Sheik (Egypt). It will replace the above-mentioned Protocols of 1998 and 2003 and merge both Courts into a single Court: the "African Court of Justice and Human Rights". That African Court will consist of 16 judges elected for a period of six years, renewable once. All judges, except the President and the Vice-President, will perform their functions on a part-time basis. The Court will have a General Affairs Section and a Human Rights Section.

PART TWO
SPECIFIC HUMAN RIGHTS PROTECTION

The second part of this book deals with specific human rights issues and regimes. Some issues are rather procedural such as those dominating the closing of the World Conference against Racism and the question of the internal applicability of the provisions of human rights treaties. More substantive issues are the question of the death penalty and irreducible life sentences, the limits to the jurisdiction of the European Court of Human Rights and the interpretations of that Court attributing positive obligations to the rights and freedoms set forth in the European Convention. Somewhat at the periphery of international human rights protection, a special legal regime is set up for refugees, minorities and victims of armed conflicts.

A. SOME SPECIFIC HUMAN RIGHTS ISSUES

By way of an example showing the importance procedural issues may have in defining international norms and in setting up monitoring bodies, a detailed analysis is given of such a discussion at the final day of the World Conference against Racism of 2001 in Durban (Chapter VIII).

Another issue concerns the internal applicability in domestic law of the provisions of human rights treaties, with particular reference to the European Convention on Human Rights and to the International Covenant on Civil and Political Rights (Chapter IX).

A more substantive issue is the death penalty which has not been prohibited by the main human rights conventions. Progressively, protocols aiming at the abolition of that penalty, additional to the International Covenant on Civil and Political Rights and to the European and the American Conventions on Human Rights, have been adopted. More recently, the European Court of Human Rights of Strasbourg has interpreted Article 3 of the European Convention (prohibiting torture and inhuman punishment) as opposing the imposition of irreducible life sentences both in a domestic context and in the context of extradition requests (Chapter X).

At the European level, the question may be raised whether there are limits to the jurisdiction of the Court of Strasbourg: is the Court competent to continuously impose additional obligations on the States parties to the European Convention which go manifestly beyond the original intentions of its drafters (Chapter XI)?

An analysis will be made of the developments of the case law of the same European Court with respect to positive obligations. Questions will be raised as to the dangers caused by "dynamic" interpretations tending to create new obligations without democratic legitimation (Chapter XII).

CHAPTER VIII

PROCEDURAL ISSUES AT THE DURBAN CONFERENCE AGAINST RACISM[150]

International protection of human rights is first of all a matter of defining international norms and setting up international systems of monitoring respect for those norms. The process of negotiating the adoption of such norms and systems takes place in political fora. Such a process is governed by procedural rules which take a prominent role when political tensions between the negotiators are high. The United Nations Commission on Human Rights, now replaced by the Human Rights Council, even the former Sub-Commission on Human Rights, but foremost the General Assembly, and its Third Committee, and Human Rights World Conferences are such political fora by excellence. By way of an example showing the importance procedural issues may have, a detailed analysis of such discussions at the 2001 World Conference against Racism, Racial Discrimination, Xenophobia and Related Intolerance[151] is given below.

That World Conference took place at Durban (South Africa) from 31 August to 8 September 2001. The Conference was scheduled to come to an end in the evening of 7 September 2001, but as neither the Working Groups nor the Facilitators to whom some particular "difficult issues" had been entrusted could finish their work in time, the Conference lasted one day longer. In the early morning of Saturday 8 September 2001, the two Working Groups, one on the draft declaration and one on the draft programme of action, resumed their work from 7 am to 10 am. Soon after the closure of the Working Groups' last meeting, the Drafting Committee, chaired by Ambassador Ali Khorram

---

150   Based on Bossuyt, Marc, "Procedural Confusion at the Main Committee of the Durban Conference against Racism", *Human Rights Monitor*, 2001/56, pp. 12–15; see also: Bossuyt, Marc, "The Issue of Reparation for Slavery and Colonialism and the Durban World Conference against racism" (with Stef Vandeginste), *Human Rights Law Journal*, 2001, pp. 341–350.

151   The official report of the World Conference against Racism, Racial Discrimination, Xenophobia and Related Intolerance has been published as document A/CONF.189/12 (Part I–III). For the Report of the Main Committee, see *ibid.*, Part II, pp. 25–32. The present analysis is mainly based on the videos of the meetings of the Main Committee which may be consulted on internet: www.un.org/WCAR/webcast/0908/-maincomittee/smil. The text of the Declaration and the Programme of Action is available on www.unhchr.ch/htlm/racism. Durban/htm.

(Islamic Republic of Iran), started with the adoption of its report based on the brief reports transmitted to him by the Chairpersons/Rapporteurs of the two Working Groups.[152] It is important to note that all those organs (the two Working Groups, the Drafting Committee, the Main Committee and the Conference) were plenary organs in which the 171 participating States were represented.

Once the report of the Drafting Committee was adopted, it was presented to the Main Committee. Three so-called difficult issues remained to be solved. Those issues related to (1) the grounds of discrimination, (2) the Middle East, and (3) the Past, which included the questions of slavery and colonialism. They had been entrusted to Facilitators who tried to agree on a consensus language which would be a substitute for the paragraphs in the draft declaration and in the draft programme of action concerning those issues.

Besides the paragraphs relating to the "difficult issues", only a few paragraphs were still ongoing at the level of the Working Groups when they concluded their work.[153] Some of those paragraphs belonged to a small number on which there was no agreement on the question whether they belonged to the category of paragraphs that would be substituted by those on which the Facilitators should try to reach a general agreement. This was particularly the case with preambular paragraph 30[154] and operative paragraph 33[155] of the draft declaration. Those paragraphs related to foreign

---

[152]   The Working Group on the draft declaration was chaired by Professor Marc Bossuyt (Belgium) and the Working Group on the draft programme of action by Ambassador Bonaventure Bowa (Zambia).

[153]   As far as the more than 160 paragraphs of the Durban Declaration are concerned, 15% of those paragraphs were adopted during the second session of the Preparatory Committee, 31% during its third session, 40% by the Working Group in Durban and 13% were the result of the work of the Facilitators to whom the "difficult issues" were entrusted. From the paragraphs not entrusted to them, only four contained language between brackets when the Working Group had to stop its work at 10 am of 8 September.

[154]   The draft preambular paragraph 30 read as follows: "[*Reaffirming* that colonization by settlers and foreign occupation constitute sources, causes and forms of racism, racial discrimination, xenophobia and related intolerance]". An alternative wording had been suggested in the Working Group on the draft declaration on which it had also been impossible to reach a general agreement: "Reaffirming/*Affirming* that [colonization/settlers colonization] of an occupied territory in violation of article 49 of the 4th Geneva Convention of 1949 *creates a situation conducive to* forms of racism, racial discrimination, xenophobia and related intolerance". Those drafts had been taken up for discussion by the Working Group on the draft declaration on the very morning of 8 September, but without success.

[155]   The draft operative paragraph 33 read as follows: "We affirm that a foreign occupation founded on settlements, its laws based on racial discrimination, with the aim of continuing domination of the occupied territory, as well as its practices which consist of reinforcing a total military blockade, isolating towns, cities and villages under occupation from each other, totally contradict the purposes and principles of the Charter of the United Nations and constitutes a serious violation of international human rights and humanitarian law, a new kind of apartheid, a crime against humanity and a serious threat to international peace and security".

occupation in a wording which was considered by some delegations to be generic in language and by others as referring to the situation in the Middle East.

On the assumption that the Facilitators would come up in the Main Committee with wording that would be a substitute for the paragraphs relating to the difficult issues, the only remaining issue was the fate of those few other paragraphs on which the Working Groups had not been able to reach a general agreement. Was it possible, in the final stage of the Conference, to reopen the discussion on those paragraphs or was the only way out the deletion of the ongoing paragraphs or, at least, of all words kept between square brackets?

A. PROCEDURE BEFORE THE MAIN COMMITTEE (FIRST PART)

The first part of the Main Committee consisted of four meetings separated by successive suspensions.

1. THE FIRST MEETING

Among the many interventions made during the first meeting of the first part of the Main Committee, chaired by Ambassador Claudio Moreno (Italy), four delegations enquired on the status of the remaining paragraphs. On questions on this matter put successively by the representatives of Iran, Pakistan and Kenya, the executive secretary of the Conference, Mr Singh, replied that there was no clear answer to those questions and that a referral of those issues to the next session of the Commission on Human Rights could be a way out. Shortly after the arrival at the Main Committee of the President of the Conference, Mrs Nkosazana Dlamini Zuma (South Africa), the representative of the United Arab Emirates expressed his "dismay and shock" that the "generic" paragraphs were not discussed. He considered this to be "unfair and unacceptable". The Chairperson took note of this statement.

Soon afterwards, Mrs Zuma informed the Main Committee of the general agreement reached on the paragraphs concerning the Past and the Middle East. The adoption without a vote of those paragraphs was welcomed by applause. Further interventions on diverse issues were referred by the Chairperson to the plenary. When several delegations insisted on asking for the floor, the Chairperson suspended the meeting.

2.   THE SECOND MEETING

At the resumption of the meeting, the representative of Qatar made a rather long statement on behalf of the Organisation of the Islamic Conference. In this statement, he complained about a distorting and misleading media campaign orchestrated against his group. While welcoming the recognition of the inalienable right of the Palestinian people to the establishment of an independent State, he regretted the failure to condemn the discriminatory policies of Israel.

Immediately afterwards, the representative of Syria requested support for the adoption of the remaining paragraphs relating to the question of foreign occupation. This request was supported by Pakistan and Egypt, while Canada, supported by Belgium, on behalf of the Member States of the European Union, and Australia, rejected any re-negotiation. After the representative of Iran had stated that those "general" paragraphs, which, in his opinion, were discriminated against, should not be again deferred to a later stage, the Chairperson suspended the meeting for an exchange of ideas by the regional coordinators on the continuation of the work.

3.   THE THIRD MEETING

After this second suspension of the meeting, the Chairperson read out the wording on grounds of discrimination,[156] which were then adopted by general agreement. With respect to the other outstanding paragraphs, on the contrary, he announced that, despite a meeting at the highest level, there was no consensus for a political solution and, therefore, he recurred to the advice of the representative of the Legal Counsel.

Twice the representative of the Legal Counsel explained that the Conference could not adopt bracketed text and that the Main Committee could not delete the brackets or retain the language without a decision of the Main Committee, nor maintain the brackets, the consequence being deleting the language, without a decision of the Main Committee. Twice the Chairperson "adopted" the "solution" forwarded by the representative of the Legal Counsel. Twice the

---

[156]   The final wording of this paragraph reads as follows: "*Recognizes* that racism, racial discrimination, xenophobia and related intolerance occur on the grounds of race, colour, descent or national or ethnic origin and that victims suffer multiple or aggravated forms of discrimination based on other related grounds such as sex, language, religion, political or other opinion, social origin, property, birth or other status". This is a substitute for wording that would have enlarged the enumeration of the Universal Declaration of Human Rights with grounds such as gender, disability, age, HIV/AIDS or other health conditions, sexual orientation and work.

representative of Pakistan intervened to enquire whether there was a consensus for deletion or keeping the brackets. Invoking time constraints, the Chairperson adjourned the meeting.

4.   THE FOURTH MEETING

After this third suspension of the meeting, the Chairperson stated that under the ruling of the President of the Conference, he had to resume the meeting of the Main Committee. He stated that the Committee had listened to the advice of the Legal Counsel and had accepted that advice, so that the Committee should address the issue of the paragraphs which were in brackets. He proposed to proceed on the basis that, unless there was a request to discuss those paragraphs, they would be deleted.

The Minister of Foreign Affairs of Syria insisted on reaching a consensus on the paragraphs concerning foreign occupation, in the absence of which he would ask for a vote. Invoking a lack of time and of interpretation facilities, the Chairperson stated that the Committee should have to go straight to a vote.

On behalf of the European Union, the Minister of Justice of Belgium, requested to avoid a vote at all cost and appealed the Committee to concentrate on the text on which there was consensus. The representative of Pakistan also considered that this was not the time for a vote and she proposed that the Drafting Committee should meet for one or two hours to discuss those paragraphs which, as she stated, were never discussed. In support of Pakistan, the representative of Malaysia stated that there would have been no request for a vote if proper consultations had taken place, which was denied by those delegations asking consensus now. He emphasised that the vote had been requested not on the presidential text relating to the Middle East but on the paragraphs proposed by Syria.

When the Chairperson announced that he would adjourn for an exchange of views with the Presidency of the Conference, the representative of Brazil asked the floor to join the appeal made on behalf of the European Union and he stated that, irrespective of the substance of those paragraphs, he had firm instructions to vote against, if they would be put to the vote. After the representative of Canada had also asked not to go to a vote on those paragraphs which had been raised in the Working Groups and in the sessions of the Preparatory Committee and had given rise to strong objections, the Chairperson adjourned the meeting.

B. PROCEDURE BEFORE THE MAIN COMMITTEE (SECOND PART)

After yet another suspension, which lasted more than two hours, the second part of the Main Committee was chaired by one of its vice-chairpersons: Ambassador Alexander Slabi (Czech Republic).

1. THE APPEAL OF MRS ZUMA

At the start of this meeting, the President of the Conference, Mrs Zuma, made, as she said, a last appeal, which was followed by loud applause: "This was not going to be an easy Conference. We are running out of time, but can we, who have worked so hard, at the end not come to any conclusion?". The Chairperson then proposed that everything which had not been accepted, be put aside.

The Minister of Foreign Affairs of Syria, however, referred to new language[157] for preambular paragraph 30 and operative paragraph 33 of the draft declaration, which, according to his words, had been suggested by the President of the Conference. The representative of Pakistan stated that, if "putting aside" would mean that those paragraphs would not be retained in the final document without discussion, she could not accept the proposal of the Chairperson. She affirmed that the European Union had given assurances that those paragraphs should be dealt with once there was a solution on the paragraphs relating to the Middle East.[158] Taking the floor, two more times, she insisted that the Committee should first take a decision on the proposal made by Syria, before dealing with the proposal of the Chairperson to put all non-consensus text aside. The same position was taken by the United Arab Emirates, while Belgium, on behalf of the European Union, supported by the Russian Federation and Brazil, considered that the proposal of the Chairperson should be dealt with first.

After one more intervention by Pakistan and three by Syria, who kept referring to wording offered by the President of the Conference, the Chairman stated that, as during the two-hour break "nothing happened or maybe something happened but the result was nothing", the new text referred to by

---

[157] The wording referred to by the Minister of Foreign Affairs of Syria read as follows:
  - Preambular para. 30 "*Reaffirming* that foreign occupation contrary to international law can result in conditions that give rise to racism, racial discrimination, xenophobia and related intolerance";
  - Operative para. 33: "We reaffirm that foreign occupation contrary to the principles and purposes of the Charter of the United Nations is a threat to international peace and security".

[158] As a matter of fact, those paragraphs belonged precisely to the category of a few paragraphs on which Pakistan, on behalf of the Islamic States, and Canada, on behalf of the Western Group, had been unable to agree as to the question whether they should be substituted or not by the paragraphs on the Middle East.

Syria was not submitted properly. Accordingly, his own proposal was the only one officially raised.

2. THE NO ACTION MOTION

When the Chairperson announced that he intended to make a ruling under Rule 21 of the Rules of Procedure,[159] Brazil asked for the floor on a point of order to make a formal "no action motion", under Rule 44.3 of the Rules of Procedure,[160] on all remaining paragraphs not considered by the Working Groups. The Chairperson interpreted the no action motion of Brazil as a motion of adjournment of the debate under Rule 26 of the Rules of Procedure and announced that he would give the floor to two representatives in favour and two opposing the motion. The first speaker on the issue was the representative of Algeria, who complained about a degree of lightness or frivolity with the Rules of Procedure and requested the Chairperson to explain whether his proposal "which was considered favourably by Syria, was a substitute that would enable the Committee to respond favourably to the appeal of Mrs Zuma".[161] The second speaker was the Minister of Foreign Affairs of Syria who said that one should either accept the proposal referred to as Mrs Zuma's proposal[162] or his original proposal.[163]

The Chairperson interpreted the statements by Algeria and Syria as opposing the motion and asked whether another representative wanted to speak in favour of the motion. The representative of New Zealand spoke in favour of the Brazilian motion. The representative of Iran expressed great frustration at the way the

---

[159] Rule 21: "During the discussion of any matter, a representative of a State may at any time raise a point of order, which shall be immediately decided by the President in accordance with these rules. A representative may appeal against the ruling of the President. The appeal shall be immediately put to the vote, and the President's ruling shall stand unless overruled by a majority of the representatives present and voting. A representative may not, in raising a point of order, speak on the substance of the matter under discussion". The Rules of Procedure of the World Conference appear in document A.CONF.189/2 (14 August 2001).

[160] "A motion requiring that no decision be taken on a proposal shall be put to the vote before a vote is taken on the proposal in question". The text of this third paragraph of Rule 44 is analogous to the well-known Rule 65.2 of the Rules of Procedure of the functional commissions of the Economic and Social Council (E/5975/Rev.1, 1994): "A motion requiring that no decision be taken on a proposal shall have priority over that proposal".

[161] Rule 26: "A representative of any State participating in the Conference may at any time move the adjournment of the debate on the question under discussion. Permission to speak on the motion shall be accorded to only two representatives in favour of and two opposing the adjournment, after which the motion shall, subject to Rule 29, be immediately put to the vote".

[162] From this and the two later interventions made by Algeria, it appears that the proposal referred to by Syria as the President's (Mrs Zuma's informal) proposal was considered by some as a proposal made by the Chairperson of the Main Committee.

[163] *Cf. supra* note 157.

Chairperson conducted the work of the Committee stating that the first proposal came from Syria and should be acted upon first. The Chairman called upon the representative of the Legal Counsel for a clarification of the Rules of Procedure.

3.   THE REPRESENTATIVE OF THE LEGAL COUNSEL

In a rather long intervention, the representative of the Legal Counsel referred first to Rule 44.1, 1st sentence, according to which "[i]f two or more proposals, other than amendments, relate to the same question, they shall, unless the Conference decides otherwise, be voted on in the order in which they were submitted".[164] This would apply to the original Syrian proposal and to the proposal of the Chairperson. However, the Committee was now confronted with a no action motion, in accordance with Rule 44.3, on Syria's proposal having precedence over action on that proposal.[165] According to the representative of the Legal Counsel – and as was stated by the Chairperson – a "no action motion" is to be dealt with in accordance with Rule 26.[166] Accordingly, permission to speak on the motion should be accorded to only two representatives in favour and two opposing, after which the motion should be immediately put to a vote.

The representative of Pakistan did agree with this reading of the Rules of Procedure, but she contested that anyone had spoken in favour or against the Brazilian proposal. The Chairperson replied that Algeria and Syria had not contradicted him when he considered their interventions as opposing the motion. The representative of Algeria reacted very forcefully. He did not allow the Chairperson to interpret his words wrongly and said that he would challenge the Chairperson if he would continue that kind of game. Apparently intimidated by this unusual personal attack, the Chairperson asked whether Brazil insisted on its motion.

Stating that he only wanted to provide an opportunity for a way out, the representative of Brazil withdrew its motion as only one delegation had spoken in favour of it. This withdrawal was met with applause. However, the representative of the Russian Federation intervened immediately to state that he had raised his nameplate at several occasions to give support for the Brazilian motion and the Minister of Justice of Belgium, on behalf of the European Union, reintroduced the Brazilian no action motion.[167]

---

164   The text of this first sentence of the first paragraph is identical to the first sentence of Rule 65.1 of the above-mentioned (*supra* note 160) Rules of Procedure of the functional commissions of ECOSOC.

165   *Cf. supra* note 159.

166   *Cf. supra* note 161.

167   In doing so, Brazil and Belgium applied Rule 31 of the Rules of Procedure: "A proposal or a motion may be withdrawn by its sponsor at any time before voting on it has commenced, provided that it has not been amended. A proposal or a motion thus withdrawn may be reintroduced by any representative".

Consequently, the Chairperson returned back to the procedure provided for in Rule 26: the representative of Argentina, who stated that he also had tried unsuccessfully to ask for the floor to support Brazil, and the representative of the Russian Federation supported the (now) Belgian no action motion, while that motion was opposed by the representative of Syria and, surprisingly, by the representative of South Africa, who stated, under applause, that he could not support postponing discussion on any matter or on this matter in particular.

4. THE VOTE ON THE NO ACTION MOTION

After a request for clarification from the representatives of India and China, met by the Chairperson in reading out Rule 26 once again, the vote – at the request of the representative of Australia, a roll call vote – took place. The result of the vote was 51 votes to 37, with 11 abstentions and astonishingly 70 absent or not participating in the vote.[168] According to Rule 36 of the Rules of Procedure,[169] the Belgian "no action motion", a matter of procedure requiring a simple majority,[170] was adopted. After some brief interventions by a few delegations, mainly explaining their vote, the Chairperson concluded the work of the Main Committee by stating that the texts that had already been adopted went to the plenary.

∗∗∗

The debates at the Main Committee were characterised by a lot of confusion. This was due, at least as far as some of the key players are concerned, to a lack of knowledge of the Rules of Procedures and a lack of experience with procedural

---

[168] Voted in favour: 23 Western States, 12 Latin-American States, 11 Eastern European States, 3 African States (Gabon, Ghana and the Democratic Republic Congo) and 2 Asian States (Fiji and Japan); voted against: 19 Asian States, 14 African States and 4 Caribbean States; abstained: 4 African States (Kenya, Senegal, Seychelles and Togo), 3 Asian States (India, Philippines, Singapore), 3 Eastern European States (Armenia, Azerbaijan and Bosnia-Herzegovina) and 1 Latin-American State (Ecuador). Most impressive was the high number of States absent or not participating in the vote: 30 African States, 14 Asian States, 11 Latin-American or Caribbean States, 11 Eastern European States and even 4 Western States (Andorra, Greece, Iceland and Malta).

[169] Rule 36: "1. Subject to Rule 34 ['The Conference shall exert all possible efforts to ensure that its work and the adoption of its report are accomplished by general agreement'], decisions of the Conference on all matters of substance shall be taken by a two-thirds majority of the representatives present and voting. 2. Unless the Conference decides otherwise and except as otherwise provided, decisions of the Conference on all matters of procedure shall be taken by a simple majority of the representatives present and voting".

[170] The adoption of the Syrian proposals, a matter of substance, would have required a two-third majority.

debates, as well as to a lack of time, a lack of coordination within and among regional groups and a lack of flexibility in the decision-making process within some groups which would have liked a suspension for consultations before any procedural move. All this was aggravated by the physical and mental exhaustion of many delegates at the end of a very tiring conference, by the frustration of several delegations which felt that they had given in too much or obtained too little and by the setting in the Conference room who was unfit for a major procedural battle. The Chair, as well as the members of the Secretariat assisting him, could in many instances neither see the nameplates of the delegations nor distinguish which delegations asked for the floor and in what order. While most of the formal Conference proceedings had taken place within two working groups in which the delegations got used to work with each other during long days and under a stable chairmanship, the final debate took place among actors who were not acquainted with working together.

An analysis of the records reveals an accumulation of misunderstandings, as for instance, between the text of the agreement on the Middle East and on the Past proposed by Mrs Zuma and the bracketed paragraphs proposed by Syria, between the proposal of the Chairperson of the Main Committee (Ambassador Slabi) to delete the bracketed paragraphs and the informal proposal made by the President of the Conference (Mrs Zuma) in replacement of the bracketed paragraphs proposed by Syria, between the said proposal of the Chairperson of the Main Committee and the no action motion proposed by Brazil (and reintroduced by Belgium) and between this no action motion under Rule 43.3 of the Rules of Procedure and a motion of adjournment of the debate under Rule 26 of the Rules of Procedure. There was also confusion as to the – nonetheless clear – intervention of the representative of the Legal Counsel on the need of a decision by the Main Committee in order to delete the brackets or to delete the bracketed text and as to whether the no action motion was related to the bracketed paragraphs proposed by Syria or to all bracketed paragraphs of the draft declaration and the draft programme of action.

While undoubtedly the great majority of the delegations disliked having a vote taken at the end of the Conference, it could not be avoided, due to the insistence of the Minister of Foreign Affairs of Syria. Despite the great number of delegations absent or not participating in the vote or rather *due* to this unusual great number of delegations not present or not voting, the majority was sufficiently great (51 against 37) to discourage any attempt by the minority to press for further votes. This allowed the Chairperson of the Main Committee to put an end to the proceedings of the Main Committee and the President of the Conference could, after a brief suspension, proceed to the adoption of the Declaration and the Programme of Action without a vote.[171] The adoption of

---

[171] The difficulties that have arisen later to the precise location in the Declaration and the Programme of Action of some of the paragraphs of the agreement on the Past, were unrelated

the Declaration and the Programme of Action was followed by a long series of declarations and statements which are reproduced in the Report of the World Conference.[172] The outcome of the Conference lost much of the attention it deserved when three days later (on September 11, 2001) two planes flew into the Twin Towers in New York.

---

to the discussion which had taken place in the Main Committee. Those difficulties could have been avoided, if the paragraphs of the agreement had been sent in the early morning of the last day of the Conference to the two Working Groups. Indeed, both Working Groups hold their last meeting on Saturday 8 September from 7am to 10am. There would have been no ambiguity on the question whether some paragraphs belonged either to the Declaration or to the Programme of action or to both texts, if they had been sent to the Working Groups for inclusion in their respective drafts.

172 See the declarations made by Australia, Belgium, Canada, Chile, Ecuador, Iran, Syria and Switzerland as well as the statements that were intended to be made by Barbados, Guatemala, Japan, Latvia, New Zealand, Trinidad and Tobago, and Turkey before and by Brazil, China, Iraq, Mexico, Qatar, the United Arab Emirates and Venezuela after the adoption of the Declaration and the Programme of Action and the statements made at the closure of the Conference on behalf of the regional groups by Kenya, India, Slovakia, Mexico and Belgium (A/CONF.189/12 (Part II), pp. 38–63).

CHAPTER IX

THE INTERNAL APPLICABILITY OF HUMAN RIGHTS TREATY PROVISIONS[173]

As there is quite a lot of confusion[174] in the terminology dealing with the issue of the internal applicability of human rights treaty provisions, it is necessary at the outset to indicate what meaning is given to the terms used in the present chapter. Indeed, different terms are sometimes used to describe one particular notion and the same term is sometimes used for different notions. To use different terms for different legal situations, corresponding as much as possible to their natural meaning, may contribute to the clarification of the issues at stake.

A. SELF-SUFFICIENT PROVISIONS OF DIRECTLY INCORPORATED TREATIES ARE SELF-EXECUTING

Direct applicability is viewed as a particular form of the internal effects of a treaty. While the international effects of a treaty depend on the validity of that treaty at the international level, its internal effects concern the domestic status of the treaty in national law. The latter depends on the constitutional system of the State party concerned. In general, international law is not even interested in the domestic status of treaty provisions. International law requires that the State parties fulfil their obligations on the international plane without caring about how this is ensured on the domestic level. Only in exceptional cases does a treaty provide for what – and even more exceptionally how – internal effects should be granted to its provisions.

---

[173] Based on a contribution to a colloquium of the Belgian Society of International Law in Antwerp on 7 November 1980: BOSSUYT, Marc, "The direct applicability of international instruments on human rights (with special reference to Belgian and U.S. law)", *Belgian Review of International Law*, 1980/2, pp. 317–343; see also VÁZQUEZ, Carlos Manuel, "The Four Doctrines of Self-Executing Treaties", *American Journal of International Law*, 1995, pp. 695–723, and "Treaties as Law of the Land: The Supremacy Clause and the Judicial Enforcement of Treaties", *Harvard Law Review*, 2008, pp. 599–695.

[174] *Cf.* VÁZQUEZ, *A.J.I.L.*, *supra* note 173, p. 695: "The precise nature of this distinction [between treaties that are 'self-executing' and those that are not] is a matter of some controversy and much confusion"; p. 722: "Much of the problem is the result of sloppy reasoning and careless use of precedent".

For many treaties whose object is confined to purely inter-State relations, there is not any need for its provisions to have internal effects. In the event that the provisions of a treaty by their very object need implementation at the national level, it will be desirable that its provisions have internal effects but that is not necessarily indispensable to avoid violations of the international obligations. As a rule, international law is not concerned as long as the international obligation is respected,[175] regardless of whether this is done on the basis of the treaty provision itself or not. If the existing national legislation contains provisions ensuring the same legal effect as aimed by the treaty provisions, the international obligation may be respected in national law, even if the treaty has no internal effects. Nevertheless, it is obvious that the safest means to guarantee respect for such treaty provisions is to give them internal effects.

To give internal effects to treaty provisions can be done in a direct or in an indirect manner.[176] Treaty provisions are *directly applicable* in national law when, according to the constitutional system of the State party concerned, they can be invoked before the national judicial organs as soon as the international conditions of validity (in most cases ratification and entry into force) and the national conditions (generally parliamentary approval and publication) are fulfilled. The expression "immediate effect" is used when acts of an international organisation, such as regulations of the European Union, have internal effects without requiring the traditional conditions of international law (as ratification) and national law (such as parliamentary approval). In many States, however, treaty provisions can only be invoked before the national judicial organs once the relevant provisions are adopted in a legislative act. To distinguish this situation from the one mentioned above, it seems more appropriate in this case to speak about treaty provisions that are *indirectly applicable* in national law.

However, not all provisions of a treaty incorporated in national law can be applied by a judge. The formulation of the provision has to be sufficiently clear and complete. Whether a treaty provision has such a *self-sufficient* character or not can be verified, independently of the constitutional law provisions determining the incorporation of international law in national law. A treaty provision can only properly be called *self-executing* if it is self-sufficient and if the treaty is incorporated in the national law of the State party. The term "self-executing", which is commonly used in legal terminology, often causes confusion as it is sometimes viewed as being synonymous to "self-sufficient"

---

[175] VÁZQUEZ, *Harvard L.R.*, *supra* note 173, p. 634 "international law is generally concerned with ends and not means."

[176] *Ibid.*, p. 635, note 166: "I use the term 'direct enforcement' to mean enforcement by domestic officials without implementing legislation, and 'indirect enforcement' to mean enforcement by domestic officials only after legislative implementation"; see also *ibid.*, p. 672.

and sometimes as relating to the direct, and even indirect, incorporation of the treaty concerned in national law, while disregarding the requirement of self-sufficiency.[177]

This confusion explains to a large extent the controversy about the question whether the self-executing character of a treaty provision depends either on national or international law.[178] Two requirements have to be fulfilled in order to call a treaty provision "self-executing": (a) the treaty has to be incorporated in national law and (b) the treaty provision has to be self-sufficient. The first requirement (the incorporation) is determined by the constitutional system of the State party concerned. Except in the rare cases that the treaty itself has made the incorporation in national law an international obligation, the great variety of the constitutional rules governing this matter makes it impossible to give an answer to that question that would be valid for all States parties. As for the second requirement (the self-sufficient character) it is possible to give an answer valid for all States parties, since it is a matter of international law.

By its very nature, it is part of the judicial function to determine whether a treaty provision is formulated in a sufficiently clear and complete manner enabling the judge to ensure its application. However, the international judge is seldom empowered to interpret and to apply treaty provisions. When it concerns a treaty which is incorporated in national law, it will be mostly up to the national judge to determine whether the self-sufficient requirement is fulfilled. To determine whether this requirement is fulfilled, the judge has to look into the intention of the States parties as expressed in the text of the provision invoked. Consequently, the ability for a national judge to apply a treaty provision will depend not only on a national law requirement (the constitutional rules regarding the incorporation of international law) but also on a requirement of international law (the wording chosen by the States parties). Particularly, so far as multilateral treaties are concerned, one may not require that it should be the intention of the States parties that the provisions of such treaties should be self-executing in all States parties, since that is out of the question in those States which do not incorporate the treaty in their national law.

---

[177] The statement "Article 6 of the European Convention is self-executing" could be correct for some States parties but not for those where the Convention is not incorporated in the domestic legal order (cf. VÁZQUEZ, A.J.I.L., supra note 173, p. 704: "a treaty can be 'self-executing' in the United States even if it is 'non-self-executing' for other nations by virtue of their constitutions"). The statement "the European Convention is self-executing" could be correct for some provisions of the Convention but not for those which are not formulated in a sufficiently clear and complete manner to be able to be applied by national judges (cf. ibid., p. 709: "it is well accepted that some [p. 722: certain] provisions of a treaty may be self-executing while others are not".

[178] See also RIESENFELD, Stefan, "The Doctrine of Self-Executing Treaties and U.S. v. Postal: Win at Any Price?", American Journal of International Law, 1980, pp. 892–904, esp. pp. 896 and 898.

The internal applicability of a treaty may vary according to the State concerned. That does not lead to a "dangerous variety of the obligations".[179] All States parties assume exactly the same obligation: to respect the normative provisions of the treaty. That obligation is not violated by the mere fact that such a normative provision is not applicable in the national law of the State party concerned, but only if the provision itself is not respected. The inability of certain States to prevent such violations because the treaty is not incorporated in their national law is, however, by no means an excuse for violations of their international obligations. But for States where the treaty is incorporated in their domestic law, it will be easier to prevent in their domestic law violations of their international obligations. In conclusion, a treaty provision is self-executing when the treaty is directly incorporated in the domestic legal order and the treaty provision is self-sufficient.

B. THE INTERNAL APPLICABILITY OF THE EUROPEAN CONVENTION AND THE CIVIL COVENANT

It is worthwhile to examine in more detail the question of the internal applicability with respect of the provisions of the European Convention on Human Rights and the International Covenant on Civil and Political Rights.

1. THE INTERNAL APPLICABILITY OF THE EUROPEAN CONVENTION

In 1965, Thomas Buergenthal[180] defended the opinion according to which a State that does not incorporate the European Convention in its national law would violate its conventional obligations. While certainly desirable, the majority legal opinion favours the view that the European Convention leaves its States parties free to determine the manner in which they will give effect to their conventional obligations.

In its judgment of 18 January 1978 in the case of *Ireland v. the United Kingdom*, §239, the European Court of Human Rights created the impression that it would appear from the *travaux préparatoires* that its authors intended to grant direct applicability to its provisions:

---

[179] *Contra* VERHOEVEN, Joe, "La notion d''applicabilité directe' du droit international", *Belgian Review of International Law*, 1980/2, §15.

[180] BUERGENTHAL, Thomas, "The Effect of the European Convention on Human Rights on the Internal Law of Member States", *International and Comparative Law Quarterly*, Suppl. 11, 1965, pp. 79–106.

"By substituting the words 'shall secure' for the words 'undertake to secure' in the text of Article 1, the drafters of the Convention also intended to make it clear that the rights and freedoms set out in Section I would be directly secured to anyone within the jurisdiction of the Contracting States [...]. That intention finds a particularly faithful reflection in those instances where the Convention has been incorporated in domestic law [...]" (references omitted).

However, by considering the incorporation to be "a particularly faithful reflection", the Court appears to be aware that non-incorporation does not *ipso facto* constitute a violation of the Convention. In any case, a great number of States parties have not incorporated the Convention in their domestic legal order. As a matter of fact, the domestic status of the European Convention in the national law of the States parties varies widely. Rather than holding that the States parties that have not granted internal effects in their national legal order to the provisions of the European Convention violate their international obligations, it appears more correct to assume that the European Convention is one of the many international treaties where the States parties did not make a conventional obligation of the direct applicability of its provisions.

2. THE INTERNAL APPLICABILITY OF THE CIVIL COVENANT

The *travaux préparatoires* of the International Covenant on Civil and Political Rights show that, according to general opinion, "there was no reason to include provisions in the covenant which might interfere with the application of constitutional processes".[181] The Working Group of the Commission on Human Rights dealing with the measures of implementation had noted in 1947 that:

"If the constitutional law of any State concerned permits the immediate application within the legal system of the State of treaties ratified, the Working Group considers that this solution should certainly be adopted, since it is so simple and practical from the point of view of implementation".[182]

In any case, the Working Group was of the opinion that:

"The provisions of the Bill or Convention must be part of the fundamental law of States ratifying it. States, therefore, must take action to ensure that their national laws cover the contents of the Bill, so that no executive or legislative organs or government can over-ride them, and that the judicial organs alone shall be the means whereby the rights of the citizen of States set out in the Bill are protected".[183]

---

181   A/2929, Chapter V, §12.
182   E/6000, Annex C, §24.
183   *Ibid.*, §14.

In 1948, the Drafting Committee agreed – on the proposal of Mrs Franklin Roosevelt (United States), endorsed by Mr Geoffrey Wilson (the United Kingdom) – to point out that, in its view, "the Covenant is not self-operative".[184] In order to place on the same footing the States where a ratified treaty became the highest law of the country and those where the treaty provisions needed to be repeated in a legislative text, in the Commission on Human Rights in 1949 Mrs Roosevelt proposed the inclusion in Article 2 of the Civil Covenant of the following sentence: "The provisions of this Covenant shall not themselves become effective as domestic law".[185]

Several representatives opposed the American proposal. Mr Jose Inglès (Philippines) pointed out that in his country all international treaties and conventions, when ratified, were incorporated without further formalities in domestic law. He observed that, even if that sentence were to be introduced, it would not change the constitutional rule of the Philippines and that the Government of the Philippines was prepared to agree that the Covenant, when ratified, would automatically become a law of its country.[186] According to Mr Charles Malik (Lebanon), the American proposal which eliminated the automatic incorporation of the Covenant in domestic law of States, the constitution of which provided that every treaty became the law of the land, was useless. In his opinion, it was entirely a question of the constitutional law of States and there was no reason why the Covenant should interfere with the application of that law.[187] Mr Loufti (Egypt) also preferred the Philippine amendment to that of the United States because the former did not exclude automatic incorporation of the Covenant in domestic law where permissible under the constitution and, where it was not automatic, provided for such incorporation by means of law or other procedure.[188]

On the basis of the foregoing discussion, the Commission on Human Rights rejected the proposal by nine to one, with four abstentions.[189] It clearly shows that the authors of the Civil Covenant, while not requiring direct applicability of its provisions,[190] did not intend to exclude it in the States parties whose

---

[184]   E/CN.4/AC.1/SR.33, pp. 4 and 6; E/CN.4/AC.1/SR.43, p. 2; E/800, Annex B, p. 15.
[185]   E/CN.4/SR.125, p. 5.
[186]   Ibid., pp. 6–7.
[187]   Ibid., p. 8.
[188]   Ibid., p. 9.
[189]   Ibid., p. 17.
[190]   In its General Comment No. 31 [80] on the Nature of the General Legal Obligation Imposed on States Parties to the (Civil) Covenant, adopted on 29 March 2004, the Human Rights Committee stated: "Article 2 allows a State Party to pursue this in accordance with its own domestic constitutional structure and accordingly *does not require that the Covenant be directly applicable in the courts*, by incorporation of the Covenant into national law. The Committee takes the view, however, that Covenant guarantees may receive enhanced protection in those States where the Covenant is automatically or through specific incorporation part of the domestic legal order" (point 13) (emphasis added).

constitutional system allows direct incorporation of international treaties in domestic law.

C. "SELF-EXECUTING TREATIES" IN US CONSTITUTIONAL LAW

The discussions in the US Senate on four human rights treaties (1979) and the judgment of the US Supreme Court in the case of *Medellín* (2008) are of particular interest for the issue of "self-executing treaties".

1. THE US SENATE HEARINGS ON FOUR HUMAN RIGHTS TREATIES

When on 23 February 1978 the President of the United States Jimmy E. Carter submitted four human rights treaties (both Covenants, the Racial Convention and the American Convention) for advice and consent, he announced his intention to declare at the moment of ratification that those four treaties were non-self-executing. In the subsequent Hearings[191] held before the US Senate in November 1979, Senator J. Javits (NY) took the initiative to request a written reply, *inter alia*, on the following questions:

"1. Are the treaties in and of themselves self-executing?
2. Would the Department of State's proposed non-self-executing declaration render them non-self-executing?

The following analysis of the answers on those questions is limited to the Civil Covenant. The answers on the first question[192] concern a matter of international law relevant for all countries which incorporate the Covenant, while the answers on the second question relate essentially to a question of US constitutional law. The answers are complemented with elements from articles written on the same

---

[191]   *Hearings Before the Committee on Foreign Relations, Unites States Senate*, 96th Cong., 1st Sess., on Ex. C, D, E and F, 95–2. Four Treaties Relating to Human Rights, Washington DC, US Government Printing Office, 1980, 554 p. (hereafter: *Hearings*).

[192]   A better wording of that question would have been: "Do those treaties contain *provisions* which are in and of themselves *self-sufficient*?". Because in the United States, where treaties, once ratified, are incorporated in the domestic legal order, self-sufficient provisions may be considered self-executing, US scholars have the tendency to use the latter term for the former. For that reason, that term is also used in the present chapter when referring to discussions in the US.

issue by Michael Craig,[193] Charles Dearborn,[194] James Skelton[195] and David Weissbrodt.[196]

a.   *The First Question: "Are the Treaties in and of themselves Self-Executing?"*

The Legal Adviser of the State Department, Robert Owen, expressed a negative view: "In our judgment the substantive provisions of the four human rights treaties submitted to the Senate in February are in and of themselves non self-executing". With the exception of Norman Redlich, all other experts (Philip Anderegg, Oscar Garibaldi, Louis Henkin, Harry Inman, Oscar Schachter, Morton Sklar and David Weissbrodt) disagreed with this view.[197] Most experts and writers[198] took as starting point for their analysis the words of Chief Justice Marshall in the case of *Foster v. Neilson*, 27 U.S. (2 Pet.) 253, 314–15 (1829):[199]

> "Our Constitution declares a treaty to be the law of the land. It is, consequently, to be regarded in courts as *equivalent to an act of the legislature*, whenever *it operates of itself without the aid of any legislative provision*" (emphasis added).

The most important criterion in deciding whether or not a treaty provision is self-executing is the wording used in the provision concerned. As the courts do not hesitate to also apply provisions which are not particularly precise, such as "equal protection" and "due process", one should not exaggerate that requirement.[200] It is sufficient that the language used does not prevent the judge from applying it.

---

[193]   CRAIG, Michael, "The International Covenant on Civil and Political Rights and United States Law: Department of State Proposals for Preserving the Status Quo", *Harvard International Law Journal*, 1978, pp. 845–886.

[194]   DEARBORN, Charles, "The Domestic Legal Effect of Declarations that Treaty Provisions are not Self-Executing", *Texas Law Review*, 1979, pp. 233–251.

[195]   SKELTON, James, "The United States Approach to Ratification of the International Covenants on Human Rights", *Houston Journal of International Law*, 1979, pp. 103–125.

[196]   WEISSBRODT, David, "United States Ratification of the Human Rights Covenants", *Minnesota Law Review*, 1978, pp. 179–222.

[197]   *Hearings, supra* note 191, pp. 291, 280, 300, 287, 285, 276, 289 and 286.

[198]   BOSSUYT, *supra* note 173, p. 334, note 87.

[199]   Focussing on the English text of the 1819 Treaty between Spain and the United States ("shall be ratified and confirmed"), the Supreme Court interpreted that treaty as contemplating a future act to be executed by the legislature before it may be applied by the courts (VÁZQUEZ, *A.J.I.L.*, *supra* note 173, p. 701). Fours year later, in *United States v. Percheman* [32 US (7 Pet.) 51, 88–89 (1833)], the same Court, relying on the Spanish text ("*quedarán ratificadas y reconocidas*"), found the same treaty provision self-executing. The Spanish text was understood to mean in English "shall *remain* ratified and confirmed" which does "not necessarily" contemplate implementing legislation (VÁZQUEZ, *Harvard L.R.*, *supra* note 173, p. 644).

[200]   See also VÁZQUEZ, *A.J.I.L.*, *supra* note 173, p. 715: "For example, the 'vagueness' of the Due Process and Equal Protection clauses of the Constitution is not thought to render them judicially unenforceable".

Quite often, reference is made to the intention of the States parties. This does not mean, however, that it should have been their common intention to make from the direct application in the national law of all States parties of the treaty provision concerned an obligation of international law. It is sufficient that it was the intention of the States parties that the provision should be self-executing in the States where the treaty concerned would be incorporated in their national law. As stated by David Weissbrodt:

> "In regard to a multilateral treaty, [...] it is doubtful whether the intent of the parties manifested either at drafting or in ratification should serve as an appropriate standard of evaluation. The interest of merely a few parties to a multilateral treaty should not control its self-executing effect".[201]

The best approach is undoubtedly to deduce the intentions from the wording of the treaty. In particular, as far as the Civil Covenant is concerned, Oscar Schachter considers it "plainly wrong" to infer from Article 2 of that Covenant that its provisions are non-self-executing:

> "How can an obligation to adopt legislative or other measures as may be necessary be read as requiring legislation that is not necessary? When the constitution provides that a treaty shall be the law of the land and when a provision of that treaty can be directly applied by a court, then it is obvious that no legislation is necessary for that purpose".[202]

Consequently, as stated by Oscar Garibaldi:

> "paragraph 2 [of Article 2 of the Civil Covenant] neither mandates nor prohibits the incorporation of the Covenant in municipal law. The matter has been left entirely to each contracting State. The obligation imposed by paragraph 2 [...] is a conditional obligation; it applies only if the legal system does not already contain adequate implementation measures".[203]

b.   The Second Question: "Would the Department of State's Proposed Non-Self-Executing Declaration Render them Non-Self-Executing?"

Most experts were very critical about the proposed declaration which was called "unfortunate",[204] "undesirable",[205] "most unwise",[206] "improper",[207] "distressing"[208] and "troublesome".[209] Several experts (Philip Anderegg, Louis

---

[201]   WEISSBRODT, *supra* note 196, p. 69.
[202]   *Hearings, supra* note 191, pp. 277–278.
[203]   *Ibid.*, pp. 312–313.
[204]   Richard LILLICH, *Hearings, supra* note 191, p. 349, and SKLAR, *ibid.*, p. 262.
[205]   GARIBALDI, *ibid.*, p. 301.
[206]   Thomas BUERGENTHAL, *ibid.*, p. 333.
[207]   WEISSBRODT, *supra* note 196, p. 71.
[208]   SKELTON, *supra* note 195, p. 118.
[209]   *Hearings, supra* note 191, p. 125.

Henkin, Oscar Garibaldi and Oscar Schachter)[210] were afraid that, in case such a declaration were made, the courts would probably give the intended effect to such a declaration. Other experts (Harry Inman, Morton Sklar and David Weissbrodt)[211] disagreed. The Legal Adviser of the State Department, Robert Owen, also was of the opinion that:

> "The non-self-executing declaration proposed by the Department of State and Justice does not automatically render the treaties non-self-executing. [...] In the United States, the final determination as to whether a treaty is self-executing or not is made by the judiciary, and it is the intention of the parties as found by the courts, rather than declarations attached to the resolution of ratification, that would render the human rights treaties non-self-executing".[212]

Indeed, once established that nothing in the Civil Covenant precludes the self-executing character of most of its normative provisions, it is not such a declaration that could prevent it. As stated by Charles Dearborn: "a declaration that is not part of the treaty is merely a Senate resolution and does not bind the courts".[213] Such a declaration is not a reservation, but if the courts were to give it its intended effect, it would be impossible for them to prevent violations of the Covenant and the beneficiaries of the rights would not be obliged to exhaust the local remedies[214] in the event that they would like to submit a communication to the Human Rights Committee under the (First) Optional Protocol. Ultimately, it is the responsibility of the courts and tribunals to decide in the cases submitted to them on the interpretation of the relevant treaty provisions and, in doing so, to examine whether they are self-sufficient – and thus in the United States – self-executing or not.[215]

2. THE US SUPREME COURT JUDGMENT IN THE CASE OF *MEDELLÍN*

While the US Constitution still proclaims that "all Treaties [...] shall be the supreme Law of the Land", the judgment of the US Supreme Court in the case of *Medellín* shows that it is certainly not giving a maximum effect to that constitutional provision. Article VI, cl. 2, of the US Constitution provides that:

---

[210] *Ibid.,* pp. 281, 288, 301 and 278.
[211] *Ibid.,* pp. 285–286, 290 and 286.
[212] *Ibid.,* p. 315.
[213] DEARBORN, *supra* note 194, p. 245.
[214] *Cf.* BUERGENTHAL, *Hearings, supra* note 191, p. 349.
[215] *Cf.* DEARBORN, *supra* note 194, p. 237, and WEISSBRODT, *supra* note 196, p. 67.

"This Constitution, and the Laws of the United States which shall be made in pursuance thereof and *all Treaties* made, or which shall be made, under the Authority of the United States, *shall be the supreme Law of the Land; and the Judges in every State shall be bound thereby,* any Thing in the Constitution or Laws of any State to the Contrary notwithstanding" (emphasis added).

In doing so, the US Constitution reversed the British rule under which "all treaty provisions, no matter how phrased, required implementation by Parliament".[216] As stated by Chief Justice Marshall, "[i]n the United States a different principle is established".[217] This was done in order to

"show the world that we make the faith of treaties a constitutional part of the character of the United States; that we secure [their] performance no longer nominally, for the judges of the United States will be enabled to carry [them] into effect".[218]

The purpose of this so-called "Supremacy Clause" was "to avert violations of treaties attributable to the United States"[219] in the light of "the repeated violations by states of the Treaty of Peace [of 3 September 1783] with Great Britain".[220] As observed by Carlos Manuel Vázquez,[221] the Founders' fear of treaty violations

"was a much greater concern for them than it is for us now. The nation then was comparatively weak; [...]. A constitution written for a hyper power might well make very different arrangements for both treaty making and treaty enforcement".

In its judgment of 31 March 2003 in the case *concerning Avena and Other Mexican Nationals (Mexico v. United States of America)*, the International Court of Justice had found, by 14 to 1, that the United States of America had breached the obligations incumbent upon it under Article 36 (concerning "Communication and contact with nationals of the sending State") of the Vienna Convention on Consular Relations of 24 April 1963, and, unanimously, that:

"should Mexican nationals nonetheless be sentenced to severe penalties, without their rights under Article 36, paragraph 1 *(h),* of the Convention having been respected, the United States of America shall provide, by means of its own choosing, review and reconsideration of the conviction and sentence".

---

216   Vázquez, *Harvard L.R., supra* note 173, p. 621.
217   In *Foster,* p. 314.
218   Vázquez, *Harvard L.R., supra* note 173, p. 617, quoting James Wilson during the debates on the adoption of the Federal Constitution, see *ibid.,* note 68.
219   Vázquez, *A.J.I.L., supra* note 173, p. 699.
220   *Ibid.,* p. 698.
221   Vázquez, *Harvard L.R., supra* note 173, p. 665.

One of those Mexican nationals on death row, José Ernesto Medellín Rojas,[222] relied on Article 94 of the UN Charter to require such a review and reconsideration. That Article 94 reads as follows:

> "Each Member of the United Nations *undertakes to comply* with the decision of the International Court of Justice in any case to which it is party" (emphasis added).

In its judgment of 25 March 2008 in the case of *Medellín v. Texas*, 128 S. Ct. 1346 (2008), the first on "self-executing treaties" 175 years after *Percheman*,[223] the US Supreme Court admitted that "the [ICJ] *Avena* decision [...] constitutes an international law obligation on the part of the United States"[224] but, as summarised by Vázquez,[225] "[n]evertheless it held that the state courts are not required to provide the hearing contemplated by *Avena* because Article 94 is not self-executing". The Supreme Court understood the words "undertakes to comply" in Article 94 of the UN Charter to reflect a need for future action.[226] This is in contrast with international law usage where "an 'undertaking' is well recognized to be a hard, immediate obligation".[227]

The Supreme Court also relied on Article 59 of the Statute of the International Court of Justice, which provides that its decisions have "no binding force except between the parties" and noted that the parties in that case were the United States and Mexico and not Medellín.[228] It is hard not to agree with Vázquez[229] when he writes that *Medellín* has transformed the US Constitution "into one that tells other nations that they must close every imaginable loophole if they expect the United States to comply with its treaties". If the Supreme Court were to apply "equivalent"[230] standards to acts of the legislature, there would not be many such acts enforceable by courts.

---

[222] Convicted in 1997 for rape and murder on 24 June 1993 of two young girls, he was executed on 5 August 2008.

[223] See *supra*, note 199.

[224] *Medellín*, p. 1356.

[225] Vázquez, *Harvard L.R.*, *supra* note 173, p. 647.

[226] *Ibid.*, p. 656.

[227] *Ibid.*, p. 661, quoting in his note 293 the judgment of 26 February 2007 of the International Court of Justice in the case concerning the *Application of the Convention on the Prevention and Punishment of the Crime of Genocide (Bosnia and Herzegovina v. Serbia and Montenegro)*, §162: "The ordinary meaning of the word "undertake" is to give a formal promise, to bind or engage oneself, to give a pledge or promise, to agree, to accept an obligation. It is a word regularly used in treaties setting out the obligations of the Contracting Parties [...] It is not merely hortatory or purposive".

[228] Vázquez, *Harvard L.R.*, *supra* note 173, p. 647.

[229] *Ibid.*, p. 666.

[230] See Chief Justice Marshall in *Foster*, p. 314.

CHAPTER X

THE DEATH PENALTY AND IRREDUCIBLE LIFE SENTENCES

In the framework of the international protection of human rights, an ever more critical approach is adopted with respect to the maximum penalties the State may impose on persons who have committed criminal offences. This has resulted in the abolition of the death penalty as well as, more recently, in the rejection of irreducible life sentences. In 1989 a Second Optional Protocol on the Abolition of the Death Penalty was already adopted in the framework of the United Nations. Moreover, in 2013, the European Court of Human Rights declared that irreducible life sentences are inhuman punishments.

A. THE UN OPTIONAL PROTOCOL ON THE DEATH PENALTY[231]

The initiative to elaborate a Second Optional Protocol to the International Covenant on Civil and Political Rights, aiming at the abolition of the death penalty, was taken in 1980 at the UN General Assembly by Mr Hans-Dietrich Genscher, Minister of Foreign Affairs of the Federal Republic of Germany.[232] That proposal was sent down[233] from the General Assembly to the Sub-Commission on the Prevention of Discrimination and the Protection of Minorities, which in its resolution 1984/7 of 28 August 1984, nominated the present writer as Special Rapporteur to prepare an analysis taking into account the views expressed "in favour or against" that idea.

---

[231] Based on a contribution to the *Essays in Honor of Bill Schabas* entitled "The UN Optional Protocol on the Abolition of the Death Penalty", in *Arcs of Global Justice*, The Hague, 2016 (forthcoming).
[232] GA Decision 35/437 of 15 December 1980 and GA resolution 36/59 of 25 November 1981.
[233] GA Resolution 37/182 of 18 December 1982 and Commission resolution 1984/19 of 6 March 1984.

1.   THE ANALYSIS OF THE SPECIAL RAPPORTEUR

The *travaux préparatoires* of Article 6 of the International Covenant on Civil and Political Rights[234] show that its authors have subjected the death penalty – without prescribing its abolition – to strict conditions: requirements of gravity, legality, non-retroactivity, procedure and conformity with the provisions of the (Civil) Covenant and the Genocide Convention (§2). Moreover, they have encouraged its non-execution by favouring amnesty, pardon or commutation of the sentence (§4), excluding crimes committed by persons below 18 years of age and by pregnant women (§5) and stating that nothing in this article shall be invoked to delay or to prevent its abolition (§6).

Similarly, on 27 July 1982 the Human Rights Committee noted – in its General Comments on Article 6 – that it refers to abolition, considered as progress in the enjoyment of the right to life, in terms which strongly suggest that it is desirable. Moreover, already in its resolution 2857 (XXVI) of 20 December 1971, the General Assembly had affirmed that the main objective to be pursued is that of progressively restricting the number of offences for which capital punishment may be imposed, with a view to the desirability of abolishing this punishment in all countries.

At the time of drafting of the Second Optional Protocol, only the American Convention on Human Rights (22 November 1969) contained in Article 4.3 a prohibition to re-establish the death penalty, once it was abolished. The African Charter on Human Rights and People's Rights (26 June 1981) does not contain any specific provision on the death penalty.[235] And even the European Convention on Human Rights (4 November 1950) did not prohibit the death penalty when stating in Article 2.1, 2nd sentence, that:

> "No one shall be deprived of his life intentionally save in the execution of a sentence of a court following his conviction of a crime for which this penalty is provided by law".

---

[234]   See also Bossuyt, Marc, "The death penalty in the *'travaux préparatoires'* of the International Covenant on Civil and Political Rights", in Association de consultants internationaux en droits de l'homme, *Essais sur le concept de "droit de vivre" (en mémoire de Yougindra Khushalani)*, Brussels, Bruylant, 1988, pp. 251–265; Schabas, William, "Article 6" and "Deuxième Protocole facultatif", in Decaux, *supra* note 60, pp. 179–199 and 869–882.

[235]   However, a Protocol to the African Charter on the Rights of Women in Africa (11 July 2003) provides in its Article 4.2(j) that the States parties shall take appropriate and effective measures to "ensure that, in those countries where the death penalty still exists, not to carry out death sentences on pregnant or nursing women". Moreover, a Continental Conference on the Death Penalty, held in Benin on 2–4 July 2014, called upon all African Union Member States to support the adoption of a Protocol to the African Charter on the abolition of the death penalty in Africa. See also Chenwi, Lilian, *Towards the Abolition of the Death Penalty in Africa. A Human Rights Perspective*, Pretoria University Law Press, 2007, 239 p.

However, Protocol No. 6 of the European Convention on Human Rights concerning the abolition of the death penalty (28 April 1983)[236] provides in Article 1 that:

"The death penalty shall be abolished. No one shall be condemned to such penalty or executed."

That obligation is limited to times of peace, since Article 2 of that Protocol provides that:

"A State may make provision in its law for the death penalty in respect of acts committed in time of war or of imminent threat of war".[237]

2. THE DRAFTING OF THE SECOND OPTIONAL PROTOCOL

In comparison with that initial draft,[238] the draft[239] elaborated by the Special Rapporteur was completed with five preambular paragraphs. Article 1 was drafted in two paragraphs: (a) the wordings of the first paragraph ("No one within the jurisdiction of a State party to the present Optional Protocol shall be executed") are sufficient clear and complete in order to confer to everyone within the jurisdiction of a State party an individual right derived from that protocol, at least in the States parties where the constitutional system allows for direct application of treaty provisions in their national legislation; and (b) the second paragraph ("Each State party shall take all necessary measures to abolish the death penalty within its jurisdiction") requests States parties, if necessary, to take legislative measures to abolish the death penalty.

Referring to a number of States that had abolished the death penalty for ordinary crimes while keeping it for crimes of a military nature or committed in exceptional circumstances, such as in time of war, and to Protocol No. 6 to the European Convention which was only adopted in 1983, among others, by five of the seven authors of the initial draft, the Special Rapporteur provided for an exception for "a most serious crime of a military nature committed during wartime". That exception, which has to take the form of a reservation, is subject to two strict conditions: (a) a communication at the time of ratification or accession of the relevant provisions of legislation applicable in wartime; and (b) a notification of the beginning and end of a state of war. It was considered

---

236   It entered into force on 1 March 1985 and 46 States are now parties to it. The Russian Federation has signed this protocol but has not ratified it.
237   See Bossuyt, Marc, "International Protocols aiming at the Abolition of the Death Penalty", *Revue internationale de droit pénal*, 1987, pp. 371–385.
238   A/C.3/35/L.75, Annex, submitted at the 35th session of the General Assembly in 1980 by Austria, Costa Rica, the Dominican Republic, the Federal Republic of Germany, Italy, Portugal and Sweden.
239   E/CN.4/Sub.2/1987/20, Annex I.

utopic to believe that States would be willing to accept obligations in the framework of the United Nations sensibly larger than those they were willing to accept – at that moment[240] – in a regional framework. That only a few States parties[241] have taken advantage of that possibility may be explained by the very strict conditions imposed by Article 2. It undoubtedly contributed to facilitate the adoption of the Second Optional Protocol at a moment that the total abolition of the death penalty had not yet been accomplished in a large number of countries.

In his conclusions, the Special Rapporteur observed that there appeared a confusion between, on the one hand, the possibility for a given State to abolish *hic et nunc* the death penalty and, on the other hand, the desirability of adopting a Second Optional Protocol aiming at that abolition. He failed to see any valid reason why States not yet in a position to do so should try to put obstacles in the way of the initiative of those States desirous to undertake that international commitment.

3. THE ADOPTION OF THE SECOND OPTIONAL PROTOCOL

By its resolution 1988/22 of 1 September 1988, adopted without a vote, the Sub-Commission transmitted the draft Second Optional Protocol to the Commission on Human Rights, which decided, in its resolution 1989/25 adopted on 6 March 1989 without a vote,[242] to transmit the draft to the General Assembly, via the Economic and Social Council. In its final phase, it was not possible to maintain the consensus.[243] The draft was adopted, without any modification, first by the Third Committee on 26 November 1989 by 55 votes to 28, with 45 abstentions, and then by the General Assembly itself in its resolution 44/128 of 15 December

---

240 Only much later (on 3 May 2002), Protocol No. 13 to the European Convention "concerning the abolition of the death penalty in all circumstances" was adopted. It entered into force on 1 July 2003 and 43 States are parties to it. Azerbaijan and the Russian Federation did not sign that Protocol. Armenia and Poland did sign it, but did not ratify it. On 6 August 1990, a Protocol to the American Convention on Human Rights to abolish the death penalty was already adopted, to which 13 States are parties. That Protocol allows for no reservations but the States parties may, under conditions similar to those of the Second Optional Protocol, declare that "they reserve the right to apply the death penalty *in wartime* in accordance with international law, *for extremely serious crimes of a military nature*" (emphasis added). Only Brazil and Chile made such a declaration.

241 This is the case of Spain (11 April 1991), Malta (29 December 1994), Greece (5 May 1997), Azerbaijan (22 January 1999), Cyprus (10 September 1999) and Brazil (25 September 2009). The reservation was withdrawn by Spain (13 January 1998), Malta (15 June 2000) and Cyprus (20 June 2003). Germany, France, Finland, the Netherlands and Sweden objected to the initial reservation of Azerbaijan which modified it on 28 September 2000.

242 That resolution was presented by the representative of the Federal Republic of Germany and only the representative of Japan made a declaration after its adoption.

243 The transmission to the General Assembly of the draft Second Optional Protocol, by decision 1989/139 of 19 May 1989 of the Economic and Social Council, was decided by 28 votes (including the United States of America) to 4 (Saudi Arabia, Iran, Libya and Oman), with 17 abstentions (including Japan).

1989 by 59 votes to 26, with 48 abstentions.[244] The total of States opposing or abstaining (74) was higher than the number of the States voting in favour (59). That could have made the draft very vulnerable in case a procedural motion requesting the postponement of the vote had been submitted. The success of the final outcome was made possible by the political climate of the moment which was exceptionally favourable to human rights (hardly one month after the fall of the Berlin wall), and by the endeavours of the Federal Republic of Germany which had campaigned intensively in the capitals. Already on 11 July 1991, the Second Optional Protocol entered into force after its ratification by ten States.

∗∗∗

In conclusion,[245] the question of the usefulness of an international instrument such as the Second Optional Protocol may be raised. It is obvious that any State may abolish the death penalty without becoming a party to the Second Optional Protocol. Nevertheless, that Protocol fulfils two important functions. The first function is to constitute a legally binding international engagement consisting of three elements: (1) not to apply the death penalty; (2) to suppress the death penalty in the penal codes; and (3) not to re-establish the death penalty. By giving this triple engagement the form of an obligation in international law vis-à-vis other States assuming the same international legal obligation, it becomes more solid. The second function is to serve as an attraction pole for other States who have not yet undertaken such an engagement to do so, creating thus a link of solidarity between States having a high conception of the right to life and of human dignity. The ever-increasing number[246] of States parties to the Second Optional Protocol (81 as of 15 December 2014, 25 years after its adoption)[247] demonstrate that it fulfils those functions successfully.

---

244 The majority of the States belonging to the Group of the Western European States and Others (with the exception of the abstention of Israel and Turkey and the negative vote of the USA), the majority of the States belonging to the Group of the Latin American and Caribbean States (20 votes in favour with 10 abstentions) and – quite remarkable – the majority of the States belonging to the Group of Eastern European States (9 in favour, including the USSR confirming in doing so its new policy of *glasnost* and *perestroika*, with the abstention of Romania only) voted in favour, while the majority of the African States abstained (2 votes to 8, with 23 abstentions) and the majority of the Asian States (7 votes to 17, including China and Japan, with 12 abstentions) opposed the adoption of the Second Optional Protocol.

245 On the death penalty in international law, see SCHABAS, William, *The Abolition of the Death Penalty in International Law*, 3rd Ed., Cambridge, Cambridge Univ. Pr., 2002, 506 p.

246 During the years 1990–1995, the number of States parties increased on average by ten every two years and since 1997 by ten every three years. Most recently, the following States became parties to that protocol: Kyrgyzstan in 2010, Benin and Mongolia in 2012, Bolivia, Guinea-Bissau and Latvia in 2013 and Gabon, El Salvador and Poland in 2014.

247 There are 28 States belonging to the Group of Western States and Others, 20 belonging to the Group of Eastern European States, 15 belonging to the Group of Latin American and Caribbean States, 11 belonging to the African Group and 7 belonging to the Asian Group.

If there is one important question[248] in every discussion concerning the death penalty, it is how it is possible that some believe that they have to express the high value they attach to respect of life by coldly executing those that have impaired the life of others. How can they not understand that associating themselves – be it as an executioner, a judge, a legislator or simply as a citizen supporting the death penalty – with the execution of a human being impairs their own human dignity?

B. THE EUROPEAN COURT OF HUMAN RIGHTS AND IRREDUCIBLE LIFE SENTENCES[249]

In accordance with the judgment of the European Court of Human Rights (hereinafter: the Court) in the case of *Soering v. the United Kingdom* (Pl. Ct., 7 July 1989), Member States of the Council of Europe do not extradite persons, whatever the charges they face, to any country if they run the risk of being subjected to the death penalty. The (Plenary) Court decided that the extradition of Soering, a German national who had killed the parents of his girlfriend in Virginia where he would run a real risk of spending years on death row, would violate Article 3 of the European Convention, which provides that "[n]o one shall be subjected to torture or to inhuman or degrading treatment or punishment".

1. DECISIONS OF NO VIOLATION OF ARTICLE 3 OF THE EUROPEAN CONVENTION

In inadmissibility decisions[250] taken in 2001–2003, the Court did not rule out the possibility that also the imposition of an irreducible life sentence might raise an issue under Article 3 of the Convention. The first case in which the

---

[248] The *Study on the question of the death penalty in Africa* (Banjul, 58 p.) by the Working Group on the Death Penalty, adopted by the African Commission on Human and People's Rights in October/November 2011 (www.achpr.org/files/news/2012/04/d46/study_question_deathpenalty_africa_2012_eng.pdf), contains a list of arguments against the death penalty which can be summarised as follows: it is cruel and morally unjustifiable, irreversible and not amendable to rectification, illogical (requiring the State to commit homicide), an affront to human dignity and inconsistent with the right to life as the most important of all human rights, unnecessary and expendable (crime rates no higher where capital punishment is abolished), not a deterrent (people do not expect to be caught), simplistic (the theory of an eye for an eye expresses an emotional impulse inappropriate in a more mature society).

[249] Based on a contribution at Seminars on the Abolition of the Death Penalty in Paramaribo (Suriname), 2–6 February 2015; see also Bossuyt, Marc, "The European Court of Human Rights and irreducible life sentences. The *Trabelsi v. Belgium* judgment of 4 September 2014", *Human Rights Law Journal*, 2014, pp. 269–276.

[250] ECtHR, *Nivette* (dec. 3 July 2001) and *Einhorn* (dec. 16 October 2001) *v. France* and *Stanford* (dec. 12 September 2002) and *Wynne* (dec. 22 May 2003) *v. the United Kingdom*.

Grand Chamber of the Court dealt with the issue of irreducible life sentences was *Kafkaris v. Cyprus* (GC, 12 February 2008). In that judgment concerning a domestic context, the (Grand Chamber of the) Court, by ten votes to seven, did not find a violation of Article 3 of the Convention. Nor did the (Chamber of the) Court in three judgments of 2012 against the United Kingdom (two concerning extradition requests by the United States and one concerning a domestic context) find such a violation.

In its judgment in *Harkins and Edwards v. the United Kingdom* (17 January 2012), the Court considered that, as far as both applicants, a British and a US national, were concerned, a mandatory or a discretionary sentence of life imprisonment without parole would not be "grossly disproportionate". Moreover, they had not yet been convicted and it was not certain that, even if the point at which their continued incarceration would no longer serve any purpose were ever reached, the state governors would refuse to commute their sentence.

In its judgment in *Babar Ahmad and Others v. the United Kingdom* (10 April 2012) concerning four British nationals as well as an Egyptian and a Saudi Arabian national, indicted on various charges of terrorism, the Court also did not find a violation of Article 3 of the Convention as a result of conditions at ADX Florence (a so-called "supermax" prison in Colorado) or the length of their possible sentences, if they were extradited to the United States.

In another judgment (*Vinter and Others v. the United Kingdom*, 17 January 2012) concerning a domestic context (three British nationals, serving mandatory sentences of life imprisonment), the (Chamber of the) Court, by four votes to three, considered that, when the sentence is "discretionary", "an Article 3 issue cannot arise at the moment when it is imposed" (§92) and that, even when it is "mandatory", it is not "*per se* incompatible with the Convention" (§93). The (majority of the Chamber of the) Court was satisfied that the incarceration of Vinter, who has only been serving his sentence for three years, as well as the continued incarceration of Bamber and Moore, serves "the legitimate penological purposes of punishment and deterrence". The latter two applicants, who had served respectively 26 and 16 years in prison, had been effectively re-sentenced in 2009 by the High Court which gave "relevant, sufficient and convincing reasons for its decision" (§95).

The minority judges of the (Chamber of the) Court, on the contrary, concluded that:

> "there was a procedural infringement [of Article 3 of the Convention] by reason of the absence of some mechanism that would remove the hopelessness inherent in a sentence of life imprisonment from which, independently of the circumstances, there is no possibility whatsoever of release while the prisoners is still well enough to have any sort of life outside prison".

In their opinion,

> "there should already be in place [right from the beginning] a suitable [review] mechanism in the domestic system [... affording] a measure of hope to the convicted person".

That judgment did not become final as it was referred to the Grand Chamber.

2. VIOLATIONS IN A DOMESTIC CONTEXT

By taking sides with the minority of the Chamber judgment in the case of *Vinter and Others*, the Grand Chamber judgment of 9 July 2013 in that case became the first in which the Court, by 16 to one,[251] found a violation of Article 3 of the Convention because the applicants were sentenced to an irreducible life sentence.[252] According to the (Grand Chamber of the) Court, a life sentence should be "*de jure* and *de facto* reducible" (§108) and the life prisoner should have, "a prospect of release"[253] and "a possibility of review" (§110):

> "which allows the domestic authorities to consider whether any changes in the life prisoner are so significant, and such progress towards rehabilitation has been made in the course of the sentence, as to mean that continued detention can no longer be justified on legitimate penological grounds" (§119).

A crucial element in this judgment is that the life prisoner should know, "at the moment of the imposition of the life sentence" (§122),[254] when such a review will

---

251   In his dissenting opinion, Judge Mark Villiger (Liechtenstein) stated that the Court did not do justice to "the cardinal importance of [Article 3] within the Convention": "[N]owhere [... the] 'standards' and 'requirements' [of Article 3 are] explained, analysed and applied. [... The judgment provides] for a generalised interpretation of Article 3 [, while it] would normally require an individualised assessment of each applicant's situation. [... B]y taking a prospective view of the prisoners' situation – extending to many decades ahead in the prisoners' lives (and also after the Court's examination of the present case) – the judgment provides for an abstract assessment [...]. How can the Court know what will happen in ten, twenty or thirty years?".

252   On this judgment, see DE RUE, Maïté, "Les peines de perpétuité réelles sont contraires à la dignité humaine: la Cour européenne des droits de l'homme consacre un droit à l'espoir pour tous les condamnés (Cour eur. dr. h., Gde Ch., *Vinter e.a. c. Royaume-Uni*, 9 juillet 2013)", *Revue trimestrielle des droits de l'homme*, 2014, pp. 667–687.

253   In her concurring opinion, Judge Ann Power-Forde (Ireland) stated that she voted with the majority, while sharing many of the views expressed by Judge Villiger, since the Court confirmed that Article 3 encompasses "the right to hope [...] an important and constitutive aspect of the human person".

254   In his concurring opinion, Judge Paul Mahoney (the United Kingdom) stated that "the abhorrence of torture and of inhuman and degrading punishment or treatment in a democratic society is such that it requires [...] measures foreseeably entailing potential violations in the future, so as to prevent such future violations occurring" (§5). It is this

take place. That review should be no later than 25 years[255] after the imposition of the life sentence (§120) and be conducted preferably "within a wholly judicial framework" (§124).

In two Chamber judgments[256] posterior to the Grand Chamber judgment in *Vinter and Others* (GC, 9 July 2013), the Court found a violation of Article 3 of the Convention as to the imposition of a life sentence without possibility of conditional liberation. Neither the possibility of liberation on humanitarian grounds or of an amnesty law, nor the institution of presidential clemency, did prevent the qualification of their penalty as irreducible.

3. VIOLATION IN AN EXTRADITION CONTEXT

The (Chamber) judgment in *Trabelsi v. Belgium* (4 September 2014) is the first in which the Court found a violation of Article 3 of the Convention in the extradition of an applicant upon whom an irreducible life sentence is liable to be imposed. That judgment became final on 16 February 2015 when the panel rejected the request of the Belgian Government to refer the case to the Grand Chamber.

Arrested in Belgium on 14 September 2001, the applicant, a Tunisian national, was sentenced to ten years' imprisonment on 30 September 2003, upheld by the Brussels Court of Appeal on 9 June 2004, for attempting to blow up the Kleine Brogel Belgian army base (§§8–9). On 24 June 2012 (§55), after the completion of his sentence, including nine months imposed upon him in 2007 (§11), he was taken into custody pending extradition at the request of the United States where he was charged with

> "A. Conspiracy to kill United States nationals outside of the United States [... while in Germany, and elsewhere in Europe, and in Afghanistan, and ...] B. Conspiracy and attempt to use of weapons of mass destruction, [... both offences carrying a maximum term of life imprisonment]" (§15).

On 12 November 2008, the US authorities assured the Belgian Government that he would not be prosecuted before a military commission and that he would be

---

"preventive requirement [of the prohibition on irreducible life sentences, 'inherent in Article 3'] that should logically come into play at the moment of sentencing and not later" (§7).

[255] The Court observes that a large majority of Contracting States guarantees, if they impose life sentences, a review of those sentences, usually after 25 years' imprisonment (§117), and that Article 110(3) of the Rome Statute of the International Criminal Court provides for review of a life sentence after 25 years (§118). That paragraph 3 reads as follows: "When the person has served two thirds of the sentence, or 25 years in the case of life imprisonment, the Court shall review the sentence to determine whether it should be reduced. Such a review shall not be conducted before that time".

[256] *Öcalan v. Turkey (No. 2)*, 18 March 2014, and *László Magyar v. Hungary*, 20 May 2014.

detained in a civilian facility (§17). On 11 November 2009, the US Department of Justice added:

> "If, however, Trabelsi is sentenced to life, he would not be eligible for any reduction in his sentence. Finally, Trabelsi can apply for a Presidential pardon or sentence commutation. [...] However, this is only a theoretical possibility in Trabelsi's case. We are not aware of any terrorism defendant ever having successfully applied for a Presidential pardon or sentence commutation" (§22).

On 23 December 2009, the applicant lodged an application with the European Court.

With the Indictments Division of the Court of Appeal of Brussels having on 10 June 2010 issued a favourable opinion on the applicant's extradition, specifying a number of conditions (§26), the US authorities confirmed on 10 August 2010 that he was not liable to the death penalty, that he would not be extradited to any third country, that the maximum life sentence was not mandatory and that the US legislation provided for several means of reducing life sentences (§27).

On 23 November 2011, the Minister for Justice adopted a ministerial decree granting the applicant's extradition to the US Government.[257] On 6 December 2011, the day of the notification of that decree to the applicant, he lodged a request with the Court for the indication of an interim measure, pursuant to its Rule 39.[258] The Court acceded to that request the same day (§§38–39). On 23 September 2013, the application for judicial review of the ministerial decree was dismissed by the *Conseil d'Etat*. Ten days later, on 3 October 2013, and despite the interim measure ordered by the Court, the applicant was extradited to the United States.[259]

In its judgment of 4 September 2014, the (Chamber of the) Court reiterates (§§117–119) that:

> "it is acutely conscious of the difficulties faced by States in protecting their populations against terrorist violence, which constitutes, in itself, a grave threat to human rights. It is therefore careful not to underestimate the extent of the danger

---

[257] It was noted in the decree that "no re-extradition to the Tunisian Republic [was] possible" and that "[t]he constituent elements of the respective US and Belgian offences, their scope and the place(s) and time(s) of their commission [did] not match up" (§31).

[258] Rule 39.1: "The Chamber or, where appropriate, the President of the Section or a duty judge appointed pursuant to paragraph 4 of this Rule may, at the request of a party or of any other person concerned, or of their own motion, indicate to the parties any interim measure which they consider should be adopted in the interests of the parties or of the proper conduct of the proceedings".

[259] On this case (up to the moment of the extradition of the applicant), see Watthée, Sandrine, "L'affaire *Trabelsi*, ou comment la lutte contre le terrorisme prend le pas sur le respect par la Belgique de ses obligations conventionnelles", *Journal des Tribunaux*, 2013, pp. 727–729; on the judgment of 4 September 2014, see the same author in *Journal des Tribunaux*, 2014, pp. 660–662, where she notes the "alarming way" in which the number of interim measures not respected by Member States is increasing.

represented by terrorism and the threat it poses to society [...]. It considers it legitimate, in the face of such a threat, for Contracting States to take a firm stand against those who contribute to terrorist acts"[260]

and that:

"[By assessing] the situation in the requesting country in terms of the requirements of Article 3 [... it does not ...] involve making the Convention an instrument governing the actions of States not Parties to it or requiring Contracting States to impose standards on such States".[261]

While inferring from the diplomatic note of the US authorities of 10 August 2010 that "there are several possibilities for reducing" a life sentence (§134), but noting that they have "at no point provided an assurance that the applicant would be spared a life sentence", the Court considers that their explanations are "very general and vague and cannot be deemed sufficiently precise" (§135).[262]

The Court concludes that:

"none of the procedures provided for amounts to a review mechanism requiring the national authorities to ascertain, on the basis of objective, pre-established criteria of which the prisoner had precise cognisance at the time of imposition of the life sentence, whether, while serving his sentence, the prisoner has changed and progressed to such an extent that continued detention can no longer be justified on legitimate penological grounds (§137)".

Noting that the respondent State "deliberately and irreversibly lowered the protection of the rights set out in Article 3 of the Convention" (§150), that "it was not for the Belgian State [...] to substitute its own appraisal for the Court's assessment" (§151) and that "the Government's actions have made it more

---

260 Referring to *Othman (Abu Qatada) v. the United Kingdom* (17 January 2012), §183.
261 Referring to *Soering*, §86, and *Al-Skeini and Others v. the United Kingdom*, GC, 7 July 2011, §141.
262 Judge Ganna Yudkivska (Ukraine) only concurred in that judgment, "albeit with serious hesitations", because of the "regrettably uncertainty" transpiring from the letter of 11 November 2009 which contained the "unfortunate passage" that a Presidential pardon remains "only a theoretical possibility in Trabelsi's case". The reasoning of the judgment appears to her "rather elusive": requiring that a "potential" whole life prisoner (the applicant not yet being convicted) should be "entitled to know that such a penalty is reducible already *as of the moment of facing charges,* represents "too remote and abstract assessment". Moreover, in her opinion, such a procedural requirement can hardly be deemed to comply with the Court's position that "the Convention does not purport to be a means of requiring the Contracting States to impose Convention standards on other States": "we cannot impose on the rest of the world the evolution of European standards and the European concept of integration [into the society] as the key aim of incarceration". She also disagrees with the majority view that the explanations provided are "very general and vague". Because, in any case, "[n]o one can predict what will happen in twenty-five or thirty years", she finds those explanations "to be adequate in the circumstances of the present case".

difficult for the applicant to exercise his right of petition" (§153), the Court also held that the respondent State, by not complying with the indicated interim measure, had failed in its obligations under Article 34 of the Convention. The Court awarded the applicant 60,000 euros in respect of non-pecuniary damage and 30,000 euros in respect of costs and expenses.[263]

***

Whatever may be the criticism concerning those judgments of the Court,[264] they show that it is not sufficient to replace the death penalty with irreducible life sentences in order to satisfy the requirements of a present-day interpretation of international human rights conventions or to prevent the rejection of extradition requests. In any case, it is preferably that, when the death penalty is replaced with life sentences, it should be accompanied by a review mechanism after a period of time that may vary between a minimum of 15 and a maximum of 25 years. It may also be recommended to entrust the judiciary with such a mechanism, at least at the appeals level. It is up to independent judges to take such decisions at last instance.

Moreover, the criteria for determining whether a person sentenced to life imprisonment will or will not benefit from a measure of liberation, and eventually under which conditions, should be specified. Among those criteria thought may be given to the reparation of the victims and their family members, the perception of guilt of the actor of the crime, his behaviour in prison, the risks of recidivism and the possibility of reintegration into society. It can hardly be denied that only such a mechanism, which should have retroactive effect for persons previously sentenced, can give those sentenced to life imprisonment the "right to hope [...] which is an important and constitutive aspect of the human person"[265] and would correspond to the "fundamental values of democratic societies".[266]

---

[263] A total of about US $114,000.

[264] See the dissenting opinion of Judge Villiger, *supra* note 251, the separate opinion of Judge Yudkivska, *supra* note 262, and BOSSUYT, *supra* note 249, pp. 275–276: "The Court might wonder whether the mechanical combination of continually lowering the threshold of Article 3 of the Convention and/or enlarging its scope of application with the imposition of extraterritorial effects of such interpretations and applications on States parties will not lead to results that sooner or later reach the borderlines of what can be considered reasonable".

[265] See the separate opinion of Judge Power-Forde, *supra* note 253.

[266] *Selmouni v. France*, GC, 28 July 1999, §101.

CHAPTER XI

LIMITS TO THE JURISDICTION OF THE COURT OF STRASBOURG?[267]

At the opening of the judicial year 2007 of the European Court of Human Rights, Judge Françoise Tulkens (later Vice-President of the Court) made a presentation in which she formulated the following relevant questions:

> "Can international treaties be interpreted in such a way as to impose more obligations on States than they are prepared to accept? More specifically, to what extent does the sovereignty principle admit of an interpretation that goes beyond the original intention of the treaty and modifies the substance of the obligations to which the States initially committed themselves?"[268]

At the seminar organised on the occasion of the opening of the judicial year 2011 of the Court, Judge Tulkens repeated the same questions and one of the speakers at that seminar,[269] Baroness Hale of Richmond, Justice at the Supreme Court of the United Kingdom, tried to reply.

A. "THERE MUST BE SOME LIMITS"

In another speech,[270] delivered at the Barnard's Inn Reading on 16 June 2011, Baroness Hale of Richmond, referring to *Tyrer v. the United Kingdom*,

---

[267] Based on a contribution to a colloquium at the University of Leuven on 2 September 2011; see also: Bossuyt, Marc, "Des limites à la juridiction de la Cour de Strasbourg?", in *L'homme et le droit (en hommage au Professeur Jean-François Flauss)*, Paris, Pedone, 2014, pp. 117–127.

[268] Tulkens, Françoise, "The European Convention on Human Rights between International Law and Constitutional Law", *Dialogue between Judges 2007*, European Court of Human Rights, Council of Europe, Strasbourg, 2007, pp. 14–15, and background paper to the Seminar "What are the limits to the evolutive interpretation of the Convention?", *Dialogue between Judges 2011*, European Court of Human Rights, Council of Europe, Strasbourg, 28 January 2011, §19.

[269] Intervention of Baroness Hale of Richmond, *ibid.*, pp. 11–19.

[270] www.gresham.ac.uk/lectures-and-events/beanstalk-or-living-instrument-how-tall-can-the-european-convention-on-human-rights-grow, also published under the title "Common Law and Convention Law: The Limits to Interpretation", *European Human Rights Law Review*, 2011, pp. 534–543.

25 April 1978, §31 ("the Convention is a living instrument[271] which [...] must be interpreted in the light of present day conditions"),[272] observed:

> "A tree has a life of its own, but it can only grow and develop within its natural limits [273]. It is not an unstoppable beanstalk grown from a magic bean. At a time when many are worried about how far the ECHR may develop beyond the original expectations of its framers, it seems reasonable to ask whether there are any natural limits to its growth and what those might be".[274]

She believes that some things are better left to Parliament because (a) courts cannot engage in empirical research or conduct opinion polls, (b) courts cannot devise whole new legislative schemes[275] and (c) some things *ought* to be decided by a democratically elected Parliament rather than by the courts.[276] As far as the interpretation of statutes is concerned, she recognises that:

> "trying to divine what Parliament really meant [...] is mostly an illusion, because on most points [...] Parliament did not have any intention at all. It had never been thought of".[277]

She recalled, however, that Sir Gerald Fitzmaurice argued forcibly in *Golder v. the United Kingdom* (Pl. Ct., 21 February 1975) that:

---

271   See also ENGLISH, Rosalind, *UK Human Rights Blog*, 6 July 2010: for some the notion of a "living document" is "a Trojan horse for judicial activism, giving Strasbourg judges the liberty to find what they want to find in the interstices of Convention rights" and "the exercise of determining the meaning of a provision by diligent attention to its history [...] is the very thing that gives the adjudication its authority, because that is where transparency lies. It prevents judges, national or international, finding that words, in Humpty Dumpty terms, mean what they like to think they mean".

272   See also BOSSUYT, *supra* note 54, p. 328: "[T]here is a tremendous difference between adopting a present-day interpretation of civil rights in order to condemn judicial corporal punishment of children (as in *Tyrer v. the United Kingdom*, 25 April 1978), or the distinction between legitimate and illegitimate children (as in *Marckx v. Belgium*, Pl. Ct., 13 June 1979), or the absence of indispensable legal assistance in a civil procedure (as in *Airey v. Ireland*, 9 October 1979), and the extension of the jurisdiction of the Court to the field of social security by relying on a property protection provision. It is not simply a widening of the margin of interpretation of the Court, but *it is a suppression of any non-self-imposed limitation to its jurisdiction*" (emphasis added).

273   Paraphrasing Lord Sankey in *Edwards v. Attorney-General*, [1930] AC 124, at 136, on the Canadian Constitution (Hale, *Dialogue between judges 2011*, p. 13).

274   HALE, *supra* note 269, p. 535 (the quoted text is not present in *Dialogue between judges 2011*).

275   An example of a judgment having created major difficulties (and expenses) is *Salduz v. Turkey*, GC, 27 November 2008. On *Salduz*, see MYJER, Egbert, "One *Salduz* a year is enough. 20 Associative Thoughts on Judge Rozakis, Judicial Activism and the *Salduz* Judgment", in *The European Convention on Human Rights, a living instrument (Essays in Honour of Christos L. Rozakis)*, Louvain-La-Neuve, Bruylant, 2011, pp. 419–430.

276   HALE, *supra* note 269, p. 535.

277   *Ibid.*, p. 536.

"judge-made law might be acceptable in domestic adjudication, but not in international adjudication which depends upon the agreement between states".[278]

Baroness Hale identifies at least four different ways in which the Convention jurisprudence has developed beyond the expectations of the original parties:

(1) The autonomous concepts:[279] there is no problem when the language of the Convention is applied

"to situations which may not have been contemplated by the original framers, but which are entirely capable of being covered by the language used and are consistent which its underlying principles and purpose".

However, the concept of a "civil right",[280] for example, has been developed in a way that has, in her view, now reached its natural limits:

"claims for services, which require a high degree of discretionary judgment on the part of officials, are not readily susceptible to court-like adjudication on the merits".

(2) The implication of rights: some decisions[281] are

"examples of an evolution in the Court's jurisprudence which, however admirable it may be from some points of view, does risk going further than anything the member States committed themselves to at the time. They raise the question: should one of the limiting principles be what the States Parties might reasonably have considered that they were committing themselves to when they ratified the treaty, albeit one which committed them to a 'living instrument'?"[282]

Even if Parliament must have known that the Convention was a living instrument which could develop beyond its original intentions,

---

278   *Ibid.*, p. 537: quoting Lord Bingham ("a strong supporter of the Convention and of the values it represents") (in *Brown v. Stott* [2003] 1 AC 686, at p. 703) who also emphasised that States parties "have included the terms which they wished to include on which they were able to agree, omitting other terms which they did not wish to include or on which they were not able to agree". On p. 537 the quotation continues as follows: "the risk is to be averted that the contracting parties may, by judicial interpretation, become bound by obligations which they did not expressly accept and might not have been willing to accept".

279   Hale, *supra* note 269, pp. 538–539.

280   The autonomous meaning in the Convention led the Court to widen the notion of "civil rights" in Article 6.1 of the Convention in order "to enlarge its jurisdiction to a number of fields which were never intended to be covered by the Court" (Bossuyt, *supra* note 54, p. 327 and note 64: "Also according to Frédéric Sudre, [...] (*Revue française de droit administratif*, 1997, p. 975) the concept of a 'pecuniary right' has been used by the Court to enlarge without limits ('*démesurément*') the concept of 'civil rights and obligations'").

281   Reference is made to the judgments *McCann and Others v. the United Kingdom*, GC, 27 September 1995, *Šilih v. Slovenia*, GC, 9 April 2009, and *Varnava and Others v. Turkey*, GC, 18 September 2009.

282   *Dialogue between judges 2011*, p. 15.

"those developments should be foreseeable, for otherwise states might be landed with obligations which they would not have signed up had they known".[283]

(3) The development of positive obligations:

"The more controversial area is the development of substantive positive obligations – for the State actually to provide some benefit which it could not otherwise be obliged or wish to provide. Are we seeing the glimmerings of the evolution of socio-legal rights?"[284]

As far as housing is concerned, for example, it is

"hard to strike a fair balance between the interests of other, unidentified people who really need the home in question and the particular person before the court [Are we beginning to see] the emergence of socio-economic rights [... a]nd is that a good thing or a bad thing?".[285]

(4) The narrowing of the margin of interpretation: Baroness Hale refers to Lord Bingham[286] who relied upon

"the degree of respect to be shown to the considered judgment of a democratic assembly [...] The democratic process is liable to be subverted if [...] opponents of the Act achieve through the courts what they could not achieve in Parliament".[287]

(5) Conclusion:[288] the limits to the growth of a living tree are

"not set by the literal meaning of the words used, [not] by the intentions of the drafters [and not even by what they] definitely did not intend. [...] *But there must be some limits.*[289] [...T]he development should be a predictable one".

Developments of the jurisprudence should (a) not contradict the express language of the Convention; (b) be consistent with the established principles of the Convention jurisprudence and (c) with the standards set in other international instruments; (d) reflect the common European understanding; and (e) seek to strike a fair balance, between the universal values of freedom and equality embodied in the Convention, and the particular choices made by democratically elected Parliament of Member States. Baroness Hale fears that otherwise the judgments of the Court

---

283   HALE, *supra* note 269, p. 540.
284   *Dialogue between judges 2011*, p. 16.
285   HALE, *supra* note 269, p. 542.
286   In the *Hunting Act Case: R (Countryside Alliance) v. Attorney General* [2007] UKHL 52, [2008] 1 AC 719.
287   *Dialogue between judges 2011*, p. 17.
288   HALE, *supra* note 269, p. 543.
289   Emphasis added.

"and those of the national courts which follow them, will increasingly be defied by our governments and Parliaments. This is a very rare phenomenon at present and long may it remain so".[290]

B. CRITICISM OF THE ROLE OF THE EUROPEAN COURT

The reference to the "common European understanding" should be considered with caution. National legislation should not be considered as violating fundamental rights depending on a comparative law study which reveals the existence or not of analogous provisions in many other States parties, but by an examination in its own right with reference to the Convention. The finding of a violation should neither depend on the expected absence of resistance from the governments of the States parties.[291] Those are policy considerations and the protection of human rights is entrusted by the policy makers to judges precisely in order to have such decisions based on legal (and not on policy) considerations.

As far as economic and social rights are concerned, the Court itself seems to be conscious that the Contracting States enjoy a "wide" or a "broad" margin of appreciation.[292] Could it not be for the same reason that they have included the protection of property only in an Additional Protocol and foremost that they have preferred not to subject social rights to the same system of jurisdictional control as civil rights and fundamental freedoms? The Court is faced with the following alternative: either it will stick to this prudent approach and the question may be raised whether it was really worthwhile to extend its jurisdiction to the extremely vast field of social and economic rights or – and this would give rise to even greater concern (certainly as far as its workload is concerned) – it is only a style formula which will not be maintained once its dynamism will lead it progressively to an ever stricter control of the infinite variety of all kind of distinctions that various Contracting States have introduced in their economic and social legislation.[293]

A striking example of disregard for the intentions of the States parties, expressed at the time of the drafting of the Convention as well as more recently

---

[290]   In his intervention at the same Seminar, Professor Jan Helgesen, First Vice-President of the Venice Commission, observed: "we have left the governments behind, we have lost them. [...] There is a lack of trust between many governments and the international supervisory bodies" (*Dialogue between judges 2011*, p. 25).

[291]   See *infra* note 305.

[292]   *Stec and Others v. the United Kingdom* (merits), GC, 12 April 2006, §52, and *Andrejeva v. Latvia*, GC, 18 February 2009, §89.

[293]   Translated from BOSSUYT, Marc, "L'extension de la compétence de la Cour de Strasbourg aux prestations sociales", *Revue de droit monégasque*, 2009–2010, p. 125. In recent case law concerning Article 1 of Protocol No. 1, the Court is reinforcing claims for social benefits, even non-contributory, rather than the protection of effectively acquired goods (*ibid.*, note 86).

by rejecting the inclusion of a provision on binding interim measures in an additional protocol, is the judgment of the Grand Chamber of the Court of 4 February 2005 in the case of *Mamatkulov and Askarov v. Turkey*, in which it decided that interim measures[294] have become binding and that a failure to comply with such measures is a violation of the right of individual application guaranteed in Article 34 of the Convention (§§128–129). The Court disregarded – as emphasised in the joint partly dissenting opinion (§§14–23)[295] of judges Lucius Caflisch (on behalf of Liechtenstein), Riza Türmen (Turkey) and Anatoly Kovler (Russian Federation) – "the text of the treaty; teleological interpretation; the subsequent practice of the Contracting Parties; the preparatory work; and relevant rules of international law" (§13), and, in doing so, *"ceases to interpret and assumes legislative functions"* (§16).[296]

As stated by the Court in its *Annual Report 2007*, the examination of the requests of interim measures requires "a great deal of work, usually in great haste". Since then, the Court has been confronted with an exponential growth of requests of interim measures: 112 in 2006, 883 in 2007, 2,871 in 2008, 2,638 in 2009 and 4,786 in 2010. In a declaration of 11 February 2011, the President of the Court expressed concern about the "alarming rise" in the number of requests for interim measures in view of "the need to process these applications as a matter of urgency, and given the limited human resources available". Yet the Court "knew or ought to have known" that this would be the unavoidable effect

---

[294] On those measures, see KRENC, Frédéric (Dir.), *Les mesures provisoires devant la Cour européenne des droits de l'homme. Un référé à Strasbourg*, Brussels, Larcier, 2011, 152 p.

[295] The dissenting judges relied on four sets of arguments:

(a) *The Court's case law* (§§5–7)
There has not been "any change since since *Čonka* which would justify the Court on a re-examination of its case-law reaching a diametrically opposite conclusion. [...T]he Court should [...] not depart, without good reason, from its own precedents".

(b) *The case law of the ICJ: LaGrand* (§§8–12)
"[T]he ICJ was called upon to interpret a provision *of its own constitutive treaty"*, while, "[b]y contrast, *no such provision* can be found in the European Convention [... T]here is a wide difference between the mere *interpretation* of a treaty and its *amendment*, between the exercise of judicial functions and international law-making".

(c) *The European Convention in the light of the canons of treaty interpretation* (§§13–21)
"[The States Parties] had no intention whatsoever of asserting a duty to comply with interim measures indicated by the Court on the sole strength of its Rules of Procedure it would enact; nor did they have any intention of doing so later on, as is shown [...] by the non-acceptance of proposals to introduce in a protocol a provision on the binding character of interim measures".

(d) *The relevant rules of international law* (§§22–23)
"There must [...] be a *customary rule* allowing international courts and tribunals [...] to enact Rules of Procedure, a rule which may include the power to *formulate* interim measures, [but which does not] include the power to *prescribe* such measures".

(e) *Conclusion* (§§24–25)
"[T]he matter examined here is one of *legislation* rather than of *judicial action*. [...] To conclude that this Court is empowered, *de lege lata*, to issue binding provisional measures is *ultra vires*".

[296] BOSSUYT, *supra* note 54, p. 328, note 73.

of its Grand Chamber judgment *Mamatkulov and Askarov* (§334). The interim measures taken by the Court, "mostly in sensitive cases concerning the rights of aliens and the right of asylum" (*Annual Report 2008*), are a source of concern to the Governments of the States parties to the Convention.

At its High Level Conference in Izmir on 26 and 27 April 2011, the Committee of Ministers of the Council of Europe expressed concern that

> "the number of interim measures requested in accordance with Rule 39 of the Rules of the Court has greatly increased, thus further increasing the workload of the Court",

recalled that

> "the Court is not an immigration Appeals Tribunal or a Court of fourth instance",

and invited

> "the Court when examining cases related to asylum and immigration, to assess and take full account of the effectiveness of domestic procedures and, where these procedures are seen to operate fairly and with respect for human rights, to avoid intervening except in the most exceptional circumstances".

Such a rebuke to the Court by the Committee of Ministers, albeit expressed in diplomatic words, is exceptional and should be taken seriously.[297] The binding force given to interim measures did increase the number of those applications drastically. As a consequence, the Court got more and more involved with applications by asylum seekers and, with respect to those applications, it fulfils a great variety of functions. In a great number of those cases, interim measures were granted and the Court moreover gives priority to the treatment of those applications.

C. A MORE APPROPRIATE ROLE FOR THE COURT OF STRASBOURG

At a time when the Court was confronted with a considerable backlog (more than 160,000 pending applications at the end of August 2011), some reflections were formulated on the proper role of the European Court of Strasbourg:

> "[I]s it realistic to expect that the European Court of Human Rights will have the capacity to perform within a reasonable time,
> – sometimes as a supreme judge of appeal or cassation on all legal procedures (on the basis of its interpretation of Article 6, §1, of the Convention), and

---

[297] *Cf.* Bossuyt, Marc, "Belgium Condemned for Inhuman or Degrading Treatment Due to Violations by Greece of EU Asylum Law", *European Human Rights Law Review*, 2011, pp. 582–597.

- sometimes as a constitutional court (of appeal in the countries having a constitutional court and of first and last instance in the others) of all domestic laws and regulations,
- or even in response to emergency interlocutory applications (on the basis of its judgment in the case of *Matmatkulov and Askarov*),
- and all this with respect to all individual rights (on the basis of its interpretation of Article 1 of Protocol No. 1 in its judgment on the admissibility of the case of *Stec and others* or on the basis of Protocol No. 12) of the several hundreds of millions of individuals living, whatever their nationality, in the (since the accession of Montenegro on 11 May 2007, now) 47 States parties to the European Convention?".[298]

"National courts are not supposed to be capable to cumulate all those different functions. Is that different for the European Court?".[299]

A more appropriate role of the Court can be envisaged as follows:

"[I]t is up to the Court, when it deals with individual applications, to control the compatibility of legislative norms with the normative provisions of the Convention. In doing so, it may also control judgments of supreme courts of the judicial and of the administrative order on the same compatibility. As a matter of principle, this does not apply to the judgments of courts and tribunals of inferior levels, as the obligation to exhaust local remedies requires that those judgments are first attacked before the highest national jurisdictions, unless such a remedy would not be effective.

A supreme jurisdiction, such as a court of cassation, does not examine the facts of a case but limits itself to verify the lawfulness of the judgments attacked, including their compatibility with the Convention. The first mission of an international court, such as the Court of Strasbourg, is without any doubt to control the conformity, with the norms of the Convention, of the legislation of the States parties and of the cases dealt with by the highest national jurisdictions. It is doubtful that the Court itself should establish the reality of the facts, if it does not want to substitute itself for the specialized domestic instances and lose sight of the subsidiary nature of its control. This is, however, what the Court is doing when it tries to evaluate the risks a foreigner is facing in case of expulsion to his country of origin. This exercise is even more delicate as, in general, the Court is not determining what has happened but is speculating on what could happen, a role which is normally not entrusted to judges.

The Court remains within its proper role when it considers that certain procedures or practices do not offer sufficient guarantees that the national instances fulfill their tasks correctly. On the other hand, to substitute themselves for the competent domestic instances in evaluating the credibility of the asylum seekers as well as the sometimes quite volatile political situation in countries nonparties to the Convention is certainly not the natural mission of judges, nor *a fortiori* of

---

[298] Bossuyt, *supra* note 54, p. 331.
[299] Bossuyt, Marc, "Judges on Thin Ice: The European Court on Human Rights and the Treatment of Asylum Seekers", *Inter-American and European Human Rights Journal*, 2010, pp. 3–48, at p. 47.

international judges, and is far away from the realities of the treatment of asylum applications in the field".[300]

As far as the introductory questions of Judge Tulkens are concerned, one should keep in mind that:

> "[P]rovisions of a treaty are only binding because they result from the common expression of the will of States. Treaties are only binding because – and to the extent that – States have expressed their will to be bound by them. [...] That is the reason why international judicial organs – even more than national judicial organs – should exercise their competence with caution and circumspection, with restraint and reservation".[301]

Certainly, there are lot of cases in which reasonable persons may disagree on whether the Court did or did not overstep the borders of its jurisdiction, but it would be good if the Court would at least recognise that:

> "To disregard, willingly and knowingly,[302] the intentions of the authors of a treaty amounts to a limitation of State sovereignty without democratic legitimacy".[303]

Whatever non-international lawyers may say, the Convention is an international treaty[304] and not a Constitution and, even more obvious, the European Court is an international and not a constitutional court. Consequently, the European Court does not have the same liberty as a constitutional court which is composed of nationals of the country and which is much more familiar with the economic, social, political and legal context in which the national legislation was adopted.[305]

---

[300]   *Ibid.*, pp. 47–48.

[301]   Bossuyt, *supra* note 54, p. 330.

[302]   As far as interpretation is concerned, there are three different schools: the "founding fathers school", the "ordinary meaning of the words school" and the "aims and objects school". Article 31.1 of the Vienna Convention on the Law of Treaties ("A treaty shall be interpreted in *good faith* in accordance with the ordinary meaning to be given to the terms of the treaty in their context and in the light of its object and purpose") does not give priority to one of those schools but combines them in a masterly manner. But "[t]he many maxims and phrases [.] are merely *prima facie* guides to the intention of the parties and must always give way to contrary evidence of the intention of the parties in a particular case" (Lord McNair, *The Law of Treaties*, Oxford, Clarendon, 1986, pp. 364–366). The cardinal principle in the interpretation of treaties (of international law in general), the principle of "good faith", does not allow for an interpretation that "willingly and knowingly" disregards the intention of the parties (*cf.* Bossuyt & Wouters, *supra* note 139, pp. 75–82).

[303]   Bossuyt, *supra* note 54, p. 330.

[304]   It is because the Convention is a treaty that its provisions are legally binding.

[305]   That is also why one day the Constitutional Court of Italy may declare that there should be no crucifixes in schools in Italy, but it is not up to the European Court to do so (and to award the applicant, the mother of the two boys of 11 and 13 years old, 5,000 euros in respect of non-pecuniary damage because the Italian Government had not expressed its "readiness to review the provisions governing the presence of crucifixes in classrooms"). See *Lautsi and and Others v. Italy* (GC, 18 March 2011), which reversed, by 15 votes to 2, *Lautsi v. Italy* (3 November 2009), adopted by 7 votes to 0. According to the *Education Law Blog* (29 March 2011), "*Lautsi* might be considered as an example of what a sufficiently robust response to

Moreover, in the event that a constitutional court oversteps the limits of its jurisdiction, the democratically elected assemblies can intervene to call it to order by modifying the Constitution. However difficult that may be, it is easier to reach the required majority within one State than to obtain the agreement of 47 States parties in amending an international treaty, certainly a treaty such as the European Convention. It is not because the States parties have agreed to entrust a Court to make binding judgments on the interpretation of the Convention provisions that the Court is free to adopt whatever interpretation it feels desirable to ensure "the further realisation of human rights and fundamental freedoms".[306]

Ignoring the intentions of the States parties "is likely to undermine confidence in international law and in its primacy".[307] Why should States ratify treaties on human rights and agree to be bound to give the provisions of treaties priority over their national law, if a court composed of "unelected foreign individuals" may disregard their intentions as well as the text agreed upon, in order to impose upon those States more obligations than they have accepted? It is not in the protection of human rights that the Court is going too far, but in ever widening its jurisdiction by closing its eyes to the provisions of the Convention on which its jurisdiction is based. The Court is not going too far by interpreting the rights guaranteed by the Convention in a "practical and effective" manner and "in the light of present-day conditions",[308] as long as it remains within the borders of its jurisdiction. The rule of law – and ultimately the protection of human rights – would not be served if the Court itself would not respect the rules of law that apply to its own functioning. There are limits on the jurisdiction of the European Court of Human Rights and those limits cannot only be self-imposed. To pretend otherwise would not be compatible with the fundamental principles of a democratic society governed by the rule of law.

Consequently, it is difficult to answer the questions raised at the beginning of the present chapter other than in the negative: no, the principle of good faith does not allow an international court to interpret the international treaty for which it is competent in a way as to impose more obligations on the States parties than they have accepted; no, the sovereignty principle does not admit of an interpretation that manifestly goes beyond the intention of the treaty and substantially modifies the obligations to which the States committed themselves.

---

errant holdings of the Strasbourg Court can achieve: in the face of unified opposition from the Italian Government and senior judiciary the Grand Chamber arguably had no option but to retreat from the position adopted by the Second Section". In the case before the Grand Chamber, the Governments of Armenia, Bulgaria, Cyprus, Romania, the Russian Federation, Greece, Lithuania, Malta, Monaco and San Marino did also intervene. In his concurring opinion (§1.4) attached to the Grand Chamber judgment, Judge Giovanni Bonello (Malta) referred to "a court in a glass box a thousand kilometres away" which had been "engaged to veto overnight what [had] survived countless generations".

[306] Preamble of the Convention.
[307] BOSSUYT, *supra* note 54, p. 330.
[308] *Tyrer v. the United Kingdom*, 25 April 1978, §31.

CHAPTER XII

THE COURT OF STRASBOURG
AND POSITIVE OBLIGATIONS[309]

An analysis of the developments of the case law of the European Court of Human Rights progressively attributing positive obligations to all rights and freedoms set forth in the European Convention will be followed by drawing attention to some of the dangers raised by such interpretations.

A. THE CREATION OF POSITIVE OBLIGATIONS

In their classic meaning, civil rights and fundamental freedoms entail negative obligations for the State. The State is prohibited from torturing someone, holding someone in slavery or discriminating in the enjoyment of the rights and freedoms set forth in the Convention, arbitrarily depriving someone from his life and freedom, interfering in someone's right to respect for privacy, to freedom of thought, of expression, of assembly and association, etc.[310] Only a few provisions explicitly impose positive obligations on the States parties.

Nevertheless, already in its judgment of 23 July 1968 on the merits of its third case (the *Belgian linguistic* case), the European Court of Human Rights stated – contrary to the Commission – that, despite the negative formulation of the right to education in Article 2 of the (First) Additional Protocol to the European Convention on Human Rights ("No person shall be denied the right to education"), "it cannot be concluded from this that the State has no positive obligation to ensure the respect for such a right".[311] This was strongly criticised

---

309 Based on a contribution (with Willem Verrijdt) to a symposium at the Central University Budapest on 27 October 2013; see also Bossuyt, Marc, "Is the European Court of Human Rights on a slippery slope?", in Spyridon Flogaitis, Tom Zwart & Julie Fraser, *The European Court of Human Rights and its discontents: Turning criticism into strength*, Cheltenham, Edward Elgar, 2013, 217 p., at pp. 27–36; *id.*, "Judicial Activism in Strasbourg", in Karel Wellens, *International Law in Silver Perspective. Challenges Ahead*, Leiden, Brill/ Nijhoff, 2015, 206 p., at pp. 31–56.

310 See also Bossuyt, *supra* note 2, pp. 359–373, *supra* note 51 (H.R.J.), pp. 783–820, and *supra* note 58 (Mahoney & Mahoney), pp. 51–55.

311 ECtHR, Case *"relating to certain aspects of the laws on the use of languages in Belgium" v. Belgium* (merits), Pl. Ct., 23 July 1968, The Law, I, B, §3.

by Judge Terje Wold (Norway), who considered that inserting a positive obligation into that Article 2 was "not a valid interpretation". According to Judge Wold, it would be embarking on "a very dangerous road"[312] to admit that the regulation of human rights "may vary in time and place according to the needs and resources of the community". In his view, "the human rights granted are absolute rights" which must be the same for everyone, since "everyone" is "every person on the earth". Once a freedom is protected by law against interference by the state, it is a "right". That does not imply, contrary to what was stated by the Court, that it implies positive obligations. As emphasised by Judge Wold, "[i]mposing a negative obligation upon the State is important and has a full meaning".

The Court relied on the use of the term "right" to attribute positive obligations to the right to education. However, once a freedom is protected by law against interference by the State, it is a "right" and, contrary to what was stated by the Court, that does not necessarily imply positive obligations. Further criticism of the Court's approach was expressed by Judge Sir Gerald Fitzmaurice (the United Kingdom),[313] particularly in his elaborate separate opinion (34 p.) to the judgment *Golder v. the United Kingdom* (Pl. Ct., 21 February 1975). In that judgment, the Court decided that the right of access to a court is "inherent in the right stated by Article 6 of the Convention" (§36). In his opinion (§32), Sir Gerald Fitzmaurice did stress that:

> "There is a considerable difference between the case of 'law giver's law edicted in the exercise of sovereign power, and law based on convention, itself the outcome of a process of agreement, and limited to what has been agreed, or can properly be assumed to have been agreed".

In another important judgment (*Marckx v. Belgium*, Pl. Ct., 13 June 1979), the Court attributed positive obligations to Article 8 of the Convention. In that judgment, the Court stated that the right to respect for family life "does not merely compel the State to abstain" from arbitrary interference by the public authorities: "in addition to this primarily negative undertaking, there may be positive obligations inherent in an effective 'respect' for family life".

In a comment published in 1980 in the *Belgian Review of International Law*, it was stated that the Court had transformed a civil right into a social right

---

[312] In my PhD thesis defended in 1975 (*L'interdiction de la discrimination dans le droit international des droits de l'homme,* Brussels, Bruylant, 1976, 262 p.), doubts were expressed that this "positive" interpretation corresponded to the will of the States parties and it was stated that, in doing so, the Court took a path with "incalculable" dangers (*ibid.* p. 217).

[313] See also MERRILS, John Graham, *Judge Sir Gerald Fizmaurice and the Discipline of International Law,* The Hague, Kluwer, 1998, 340 p.; FITZMAURICE, Sir Gerald, "Some Reflections on the European Convention on Human Rights – and on Human Rights", in Rudolf BERNHARDT ET AL., *Völkerrecht als Rechtsordnung Internationale Gerichtsbarkeit Menschenrechte (Festschrift für Hermann Mosler)*, Berlin, Springer Verlag, 1983, pp. 203–219.

requiring an active intervention by the legislator[314] and that, by neglecting the distinction between classical freedoms and social rights, the Court did risk exceeding its competence, which may not be done by way of interpretation. It was also observed that the method of interpretation of the Court would cause the legal counsel of the applicants quite a lot of pleasant surprises.[315] Needless to say, for counsel of the defendant governments those surprises are, on the contrary, particularly unpleasant.

Four months later, in another important judgment (*Airey v. Ireland*, 9 October 1979), the Court declared with respect to Article 6 of the Convention that "the fulfilment of a duty under the Convention on occasion necessitates some positive action on the part of the State". According to the Court, also in civil litigation, Article 6 of the Convention does "compel the State to provide for the assistance of a lawyer when such assistance proves indispensable for an effective access to court".

Today, the Court has attributed positive obligations to virtually all Convention rights.[316] At the time of the earlier judgments, the positive obligations were generally confined to the obligation to take legislative measures which did not entail considerable expenses. This did change,[317] when the Court decided in its judgment in *Gaygusuz v. Austria* (16 September 1996)[318] that emergency assistance in case of unemployment which was linked to the payment of contributions was a pecuniary right for the purposes of Article 1 of Protocol No. 1 (Protection of property). The situation became worse when the Court, in its judgment in *Koua Poirrez v. France* (30 September 2003), decided that even a non-contributory social benefit for disabled adults must be considered to be a

---

314   See BOSSUYT, Marc, "L'arrêt *Marckx* de la Cour européenne des droits de l'homme", *Belgian International Law Review*, 1980, pp. 53–81, at p. 68. The author assented (*ibid.*, p. 67) with the dissenting opinions of Sir Gerald in the cases of *National Union of Belgian Police* (Pl. Ct., 27 October 1975) (see *id.*, *supra* note 1, pp. 233–240), and *Marckx* (Pl. Ct., 13 June 1979) *v. Belgium* (as did also François RIGAUX, "La loi condamnée. À propos de l'arrêt du 13 juin 1979 de la Cour européenne des droits de l'homme", *Journal des Tribunaux*, 1979, pp. 513–524), but not with his dissenting opinions in the cases of *Golder* (Pl. Ct., 21 February 1975), *Tyrer* (25 April 1975) and *Ireland* (Pl. Ct., 18 January 1978) *v. the United Kingdom*.

315   *Ibid.*, p. 79.

316   On the concept of positive obligations, see DUMONT, Hugues & HACHEZ, Isabelle, "Les obligations positives déduites du droit international des droits de l'homme: dans quelles limites?", in Yves CARTUYVELS ET AL., *Les droits de l'homme, bouclier ou épée du droit pénal?*, Brussels, Bruylant, 2007, pp. 45–73; HAJIYEV, Khanlar, "The evolution of positive obligations under the European Convention on Human Rights by the European Court of Human Rights", in *The European Convention on Human Rights, a living instrument (Essays in Honour of Christos L. Rozakis)*, Brussels, Bruylant, 2011, pp. 207–218; XENOS, Dimitris, *The Positive Obligations of the State Under the European Convention of Human Rights*, Abingdon, Routledge, 2012, 272 p.

317   BOSSUYT, *supra* note 54, pp. 321–324.

318   On the (rather limited) effects of that judgment, see DEMBOUR, Marie-Bénédicte, "*Gaygusuz* revisited: The Limits of the European Court of Human Rights' Equality Agenda", *Human Rights Law Review*, 2012, pp. 689–721.

pecuniary right. This interpretation was confirmed by the Grand Chamber of the Court in its decision on admissibility in *Stec and Others v. the United Kingdom* of 6 July 2005. In that decision, the Court declared itself competent to examine the applications of Ms Stec and others complaining about discrimination based on gender concerning the pension schemes in the United Kingdom. This positive interpretation of the right to property is designed to enlarge the jurisdiction of the Court to social rights, including social security regulations, in order to overcome the limitation on the rights and freedoms set forth in the Convention contained in the prohibition of discrimination provided for in Article 14 of the Convention.

It is true that the Court has recognised that in the field of social and economic rights the States parties enjoy a "wide" or a "broad" margin of appreciation.[319] As long as the Court sticks to this prudent approach, it may be questioned whether this praetorian extension of the Court's jurisdiction was worthwhile. But how long will it take before the so-called "dynamic" interpretation of the Court will lead to a stricter control of the infinite variety of distinctions that States parties have introduced in their economic and social legislation?[320]

Another important judgment on positive obligations is *Hatton and Others v. the United Kingdom* (2 October 2001) concerning complaints of an increase in the level of noise caused at the applicants' homes by aircraft using Heathrow airport. In that judgment, the (Chamber of the) Court stated that:

> "the applicants' complaints fall to be analysed in terms of a positive duty on the State to take reasonable and appropriate measures to secure the applicants' rights under Article 8 §1 of the Convention".

In the opinion of the Court, the Government had

> "failed to strike a fair balance between the United Kingdom's economic well-being and the applicants' effective enjoyment of their right to respect for their homes and their private and family lives".

It seems rather inappropriate if judges were to determine where airports should be located and which lanes should be used by aircrafts to land or to take off with the only terms of reference being a provision stating that "[e]veryone has the right to respect for his private and family life". Fortunately, that judgment was overturned on 8 July 2003 by the Grand Chamber of the Court, which decided that the authorities "had not overstepped their margin of appreciation".

---

[319] *Stec and and Others v. the United Kingdom* (merits), GC, 12 April 2006, §52, and *Andrejeva v. Latvia*, GC, 18 February 2009, §89.

[320] BOSSUYT, *supra* note 293, p. 125.

Also concerning Article 8 of the Convention, the Court found a violation of that article in its judgment in *Georgel and Georgeta Stoicescu v. Romania* (26 July 2011) because the Government had not provided

"any indication as to the concrete measures taken by the authorities [... to address] the serious problem of public health and threat to the physical integrity of the population represented by a large number of stray dogs [in Bucharest]" (§61),[321]

and in its judgment in *Di Sarno and Others v. Italy* (10 January 2012) because the Government had failed to take appropriate measures to ensure the normal functioning of collecting, treating and eliminating garbage in Somma Vesuviana.[322]

The Court justifies such extensions to positive obligations mainly by quoting its judgment *Tyrer v. the United Kingdom* (25 April 1978) in which it stated that:

"the Convention is a living instrument which [...] must be interpreted in the light of present-day conditions" (§31)

and its judgment *Airey v. Ireland* (9 October 1979) in which it stated that:

"[t]he Convention is intended to guarantee not rights that are theoretical or illusory but rights that are practical and effective" (§24).

According to Lord Hofmann (Leonard)[323] the concept of a "living instrument" is

"the banner under which the Strasbourg court has assumed power to legislate what they consider to be required by 'European public order'".[324]

---

321   In his dissenting opinion Judge Luis López Guerra (Spain) considered that the assessment of the Court was "the result of an undue extension of the concept of positive obligations". He does not deem it warranted "to demand that authorities adopt all necessary measures to protect all people from all forms of danger in general. The public powers are required to meet practically unlimited needs with inevitably limited means. They must provide vital services such as clean water, sewer systems, waste disposal, health care, traffic safety and public safety, among many others. And the numbers of victims of the faulty delivery of those services may be considerable. But it is the competent authorities of each country and not this Court who must establish priorities and determine preferences when allocating efforts and resources".

322   In his dissenting opinion, Judge András Sajó (Hungary) considered that persons, working in that village but not residing there, had not shown that the presence of garbage had affected their private life and their home.

323   (Lord) HOFMANN, Leonard, "The Universality of Human Rights" (Judicial Studies Board Annual Lecture, 19 March 2009), *Law Quarterly Review*, 2009, pp. 416–432, at §27.

324   For further criticism of the Court, see EDELMANN, Bernard, "La Cour européenne des droits de l'homme: une juridiction tyrannique", *Recueil Dalloz*, 2008, pp. 1946–1953; FLAUSS, Jean-François, "Actualité de la Convention européenne des droits de l'homme", *Actualité Juridique Droit Administratif*, 2009, pp. 872–884, GANNAGE, Léna, "A propos de l''absolutisme' des droits fondamentaux", in *Vers des nouveaux équilibres entre ordres juridiques: liber amicorum Hélène Gaudemet-Tallon*, Dalloz, Paris, 2008, pp. 265–284; LEQUETTE, Yves, "Des juges littéralement irresponsables", in Loïc CADIET, Pierre CALLE, Thierry LE BARS & Pierre MAYER (Eds.), *Mélanges dédiés à la mémoire du doyen Jacques Héron*, Paris, LGDJ, 2008, pp. 309–330.

The "living instrument" doctrine is not without value for normative provisions of the Convention such as "discrimination", "torture", "family life", etc. which should not be interpreted as they were understood in 1950. But the Court does not take sufficiently into account the fact that its dynamic interpretation of the normative provisions of the Convention may not exceed the limits of its jurisdiction. This happens when the Court transforms – by way of interpretation – a civil right into a social right. Indeed, a civil rights loses its very nature if the positive obligations attributed to it entail expenditures which many States cannot afford and which require choices to be made and priorities to be established at the expense of other rights or other categories of persons. In doing so, the Court disregards the intentions of the authors of its constitutive treaty in a manner which is incompatible with the principle of good faith, the cardinal principle of any legal interpretation. Moreover, this amounts to a limitation of State sovereignty without democratic legitimation.[325]

B. THE DANGERS OF THE CREATION OF POSITIVE OBLIGATIONS

A first casualty of the positive obligations doctrine is democracy itself. It is up to the national constitutions to determine which organs are granted which powers. In conformity with the separation of powers principle, it is up to political organs to create the rules and to the judiciary to apply them. The Court is entitled to interpret the rules, not to extend its own competences by creating new rules. According to the text of the Convention, the power of the national legislators is limited by essentially negative obligations. There is no clear basis in the Convention empowering the Court to impose upon the States parties positive obligations that may not be assumed – in good faith – to be inherent to or implied by the rights and freedoms set forth in the Convention, without the intervention of parliament.

Moreover, the concept of positive obligations is open-ended. The Court does not indicate what the limits of those positive obligations are. With respect to the negative obligations, several articles of the Convention provide, in their second paragraph, for the possibility of restricting those negative obligations of the State on the condition that they are "prescribed by law", "necessary in a democratic society", taken in the interest of a number of goals specifically mentioned in the relevant paragraph, and all this in a non-discriminatory way. It is not feasible

---

For a more lenient approach, see GERARDS, Janneke, "The Prism of Fundamental Rights", *European Constitutional Law Review*, 2012, pp. 173–202; CHRISTOFFERSEN, Jonas & MADSEN, Mikael Rask, *The European Court of Human Rights between Law and Politics*, Oxford, Oxford Univ. Press, 2013, 256 p.

[325] BOSSUYT, *supra* note 54, p. 330.

to apply the same conditions to positive obligations: for example a State cannot be required to demonstrate the necessity in a democratic society to restrict a particular rather than another social right to all or to certain categories of persons. In the event of scarcity of resources, it is up to the political authorities of the State to set up priorities as far as the rights, their beneficiaries and the timetable of their realisation is concerned, without having to justify that a particular restriction rather than another is "necessary in a democratic society".

The Court has appropriated for itself the power to judge to what extent it may impose positive obligations on the States parties. In view of the very broad interpretation the Court gives to the rights set forth in the Convention, the material scope of those rights is hardly a limit at all.[326] The attribution of positive obligations has also resulted in the multiplication of cases of conflicts between human rights, giving the opportunity to the Court to further expand its powers by balancing the one right against the other.

Secondly, it is not only problematic that those positive obligations are created by a court, but even more so that they are created by an international court. A national constitutional court functions within the framework of the national constitution and is composed of nationals of the State, which are familiar with the economic, social, cultural and political environment of the national community upon which the constitutional court exercises its jurisdiction. An international court is composed in its overwhelming majority by non-nationals who are much less familiar with the national environment in which the decisions it controls are taken.

Moreover, at any time, the competent political authorities can amend the laws and even the constitution when the interpretation of domestic courts goes beyond what is considered appropriate. As an amendment of the European Convention requires 47 ratifications, it is practically impossible for the States parties to counter the Court's judicial activism. The knowledge that the jurisdiction of the Court is based on an agreement given by the States parties in the form of an international treaty, should induce the Court to exercise its jurisdiction with great restraint rather than continuously trying to extend it beyond the limits expressed by the negative formulation of the rights set forth in the Convention.

As long as the Court applies the rights and freedoms of the Convention in the light of their negative formulation, the lack of familiarity of foreign judges with the national environment of the State parties concerned is generally not problematic. However, when attributing to those rights positive obligations which may entail considerable expenses, the Court needs an overall view of the factual and legal situation in the country concerned, taking into account the whole of the national context, including the other interests of the State and of

---

[326] XENOS, *supra* note 316, p. 4.

other citizens and groups and not in the least the budgetary implications of its judgments.

Thirdly, the extension of the Court's jurisdiction to economic and social rights leads to the development of a purely regional human rights standard, unattainable by many countries, and depriving human rights of their universality, which is one of the strengths of the traditional concept of human rights. Indeed, as the realisation of those social rights depends on the availability of resources in the State concerned, there is no universal standard, not even a common regional standard among States parties, in view of the great disparity in economic development even among Member States of the Council of Europe.[327]

Fourthly, the extension of the Court's jurisdiction to economic and social rights also enlarges the applicability of the prohibition of discrimination guaranteed in Article 14 of the Convention. The general prohibition of discrimination provided for in Protocol No. 12 has only been the subject of ratification by a minority of the Member States of the Council of Europe.[328] This number will not increase rapidly if States become aware of the fact that the application of the prohibition of discrimination to economic and social rights amounts to relinquishing a considerable degree of sovereignty from the national legislators to the international judge, much more than is the case with respect to civil rights and fundamental freedoms.

This is particularly the case since the Court, when examining differences of treatment, attaches great weight to the element of proportionality. In a *Festschrift* published in 2010 – in honour of the former German Judge at the Strasbourg Court, Renate Jaeger – Paul Mahoney, former Registrar and at present the British judge at the Strasbourg Court, expressed his worries over the "interventionist tendency whereby the principle of proportionality becomes merely the means by which a small group of international judges substitute their own personal view as to the desirability of the regulatory policy chosen for that of the democratic institutions of the country, judicial as well as executive and legislative".[329]

Fifthly, The reliance of the Court on EU regulations and directives, as in its *M.S.S.* judgment,[330] to define the extent of the positive obligations the States are supposed to have assumed by becoming parties to the Convention is highly questionable. The obligations accepted by the States parties to the Convention are minimum obligations: according to the preamble of the Convention,

---

[327] BOSSUYT, *supra* note 54, p. 329.
[328] This Protocol No. 12 has only been ratified by 18 of the 47 Member States of the Council of Europe: 11 Eastern European (Albania, Armenia, Bosnia and Herzegovina, Croatia, Georgia, Montenegro, Romania, Serbia, Slovenia, Former Yugoslav Republic of Macedonia, Ukraine) and 7 Western European (Andorra, Cyprus, Finland, Luxembourg, Netherlands, San Marino, Spain) Members of the Council of Europe.
[329] MAHONEY, Paul, "Reconciling Universality of Human Rights and Local Democracy – the European Experience", in *Grundrechte un Solidarität. Durchsetzung und Verfahren (Festschrift für Renate Jaeger)*, Kehl-am-Rhein, N.P. Engel Verlag, 2010, pp. 147–161, at p. 158.
[330] See *infra*, Chapter XIII, B, 1.

the governments signatory thereto were resolved to take the "first steps" for the collective enforcement of "certain" of the rights stated in the Universal Declaration.

In any case, the Court cannot rely on those regulations and directives to interpret the Convention with respect to the 19 States parties which are not Members of the European Union. And the Court may neither interpret the extent of the obligations applicable to the 28 Member States of the European Union differently from those applicable to the 19 other States parties to the Convention. Finally, it is not up to the Court in Strasbourg – but to the Court of Justice in Luxembourg – to interpret the extent of the EU regulations and directives and to impose sanctions when they are not respected.

***

As mentioned in the previous chapter,[331] Baroness Hale of Richmond, Justice at the Supreme Court of the United Kingdom, considered in important speeches delivered in 2011 the development of positive obligations as "the more controversial area" of the case law of the Court and she concluded: "there must be some limits". The problem is, however, that the only limitations to its jurisdiction that the Court seems to accept are self-imposed limitations.[332] It would help if the Court were to state clearly that it cannot extend its jurisdiction "to the creation of rights not enumerated in the Convention, however, expedient or even desirable such new rights might be".[333] In particular, when reaching the limits of its jurisdiction, the Court should exercise its competence "with caution and circumspection, with restraint and reservation".[334]

---

[331] See *supra*, Chapter XI, A.
[332] BOSSUYT, *supra* note 54, p. 328.
[333] Dissenting opinion of Judge Egbert Myjer (Netherlands) in *Munoz Diaz v. Spain*, 8 December 2009.
[334] BOSSUYT, *supra* note 54, p. 330.

B. SOME SPECIFIC HUMAN RIGHTS REGIMES

Some specific human rights regimes are set up for refugees (Chapter XIII), minorities (Chapter XIV) and victims of armed conflicts (Chapter XV). While not at the centre of general human rights protection, they nevertheless deserve special attention.

CHAPTER XIII

THE PROTECTION OF REFUGEES IN INTERNATIONAL LAW[335]

The Universal Declaration of Human Rights of 10 December 1948 contains an Article 14.1 on asylum:

> "Everyone has the right to seek and to enjoy in other countries asylum from persecution".

However, none of the human rights conventions, neither at the universal nor at the regional level, mention a right to asylum. Even the Geneva Convention Relating to the Status of Refugees of 28 July 1951 does not guarantee a right to asylum.[336]

A. THE GENEVA CONVENTION RELATING TO THE STATUS OF REFUGEES

In the Geneva Convention Relating to the Status of Refugees of 28 July 1951, which entered into force on 22 April 1954, the concept of "refugee" is defined in its Article 1, A, (2), al. 1, as follows:

> "any person who [...] owing to well-founded fear of being persecuted for reasons of race, religion, nationality, membership of a particular social group or political opinion, is outside the country of his nationality and is unable or, owing to such fear, is unwilling to avail himself of the protection of that country".

---

[335] Based on a lecture given at the *Palais des Académies* in Brussels on 1 June 2015: Bossuyt, Marc, "The European Union Confronted with an Asylum Crisis in the Mediterranean: Reflections on Refugees and Human Rights Issues", *European Journal of Human Rights*, 2015/5, pp. 581–605; see also *id.*, *Strasbourg et les demandeurs d'asile: des juges sur un terrain glissant*, Brussels, Bruylant, 2010, 189 p.; *id.*, *supra* note 299; *id.*, "The Court of Strasbourg acting as an Asylum Court", *European Constitutional Law Review*, 2012, pp. 203–245.

[336] In customary international law, the right of asylum, as is the case of the right of diplomatic protection, is the right of a State to grant it, not the right of an individual to obtain it.

A Protocol to that Convention, taken note of by the UN General Assembly on 16 December 1966, removed the geographic and temporal limits of the Convention (events occurring in Europe and before 1 January 1951).

According to its Article 1, F, the provisions of that Convention shall not apply to any person with respect to whom there are serious reasons for considering that:

"(a) he has committed a crime against peace, a war crime, or a crime against humanity, as defined in the international instruments drawn up to make provision in respect of such crimes;

(b) he has committed a serious non-political crime outside the country of refuge prior to his admission to that country as a refugee;

(c) he has been guilty of acts contrary to the purposes and principles of the United Nations".

It is up to the States parties to the Geneva Convention to recognise the status of refugee of persons claiming that status by applying for asylum in one of those States. Such recognition is declaratory and not constitutive in nature:

"A person is a refugee within the meaning of the 1951 Convention as soon as he fulfils the criteria contained in the definition. This would necessarily occur prior to the time at which his refugee status is formally determined. Recognition of his refugee status does not therefore make him a refugee but declares him to be one. He does not become a refugee because of recognition, but is recognized because he is a refugee".[337]

The States parties to that Geneva Convention have not undertaken the obligation to grant asylum to refugees requesting international protection but only the obligation to respect the prohibition of *"refoulement"* contained in its Article 33.1:

"No Contracting State shall expel or return ('*refouler*') a refugee in any manner whatsoever to the frontiers of territories where his life or freedom would be threatened on account of his race, religion, nationality, membership of a particular social group or political opinion".

According to Article 33.2 of the Geneva Convention, however, the benefit of that provision will not be granted to:

"a refugee whom there are reasonable grounds for regarding as a danger to the security of the country in which he is, or who, having been convicted by a final judgment of a particularly serious crime, constitutes a danger to the community of that country".

---

[337] Office of the United Nations High Commissioner for Refugees, *Handbook on Procedures and Criteria for Determining Refugee Status under the 1951 Convention and the 1967 Protocol relating to the Status of Refugees*, Geneva, 1992, no. 28.

The Geneva Convention does not require a jurisdictional – and *a fortiori* not a judicial – procedure to determine the status of refugee. In its conclusions no. 8 (XXVIII) of 12 October 1977, the Executive Committee of the UNHCR has recommended the following:

> "[...] (e) [...] (vi) If the applicant is not recognized, he should be given a reasonable time to appeal for a formal reconsideration of the decision, either to the same or to a different authority, whether administrative or judicial, according to the prevailing stem".

There should be a possibility of appeal, either administrative or judicial, or at least a review by the authority having taken the initial decision. The Geneva Convention does not impose other minimum requirements with respect to the asylum procedure. However, the asylum procedure in the Member States of the Council of Europe became ever more complex due to the "dynamic" interpretation of the European Convention on Human Rights by the European Court of Human Rights and, moreover, in the Member States of the European Union, due to the adoption of Regulations and Directives in the framework of the Common European Asylum System.

B. THE EUROPEAN CONVENTION AND REFUGEES AND ASYLUM SEEKERS

Since 1991, the European Court has developed an impressive case law concerning asylum seekers, mainly with reference to Articles 3 and 13 of the European Convention.

1. CASE LAW WITH RESPECT TO ARTICLE 3 OF THE EUROPEAN CONVENTION

On the basis of the absolute character of Article 3 of the European Convention prohibiting torture and inhuman or degrading treatment or punishment, the Court considers that this provision obliges the States parties to refrain from any act by which a person could become the victim of such treatment or punishment in another State.

In the case of *Amekrane v. the United Kingdom*, the European Commission of Human Rights declared admissible, on 11 October 1973, the application of the German widow of the Moroccan Lt-Col. Mohamed Amekrane who had fled to Gibraltar after the attack of the airplane of King Hassan II by Moroccan air fighters on 16 August 1972. The next day, he was sent back to Morocco where he was executed on 13 January 1973. On 19 July 1974, the European Commission adopted a friendly settlement in this case taking note that the United Kingdom had accepted to pay *ex gratia* £37,500 to his widow. On 7 July 1989, the (Plenary) Court delivered, in the case of *Soering v. the United Kingdom*,[338] its first judgment in which it hold a State Party indirectly responsible for inhuman treatment the applicant was risking in case he would be extradited to a non-State party (*i.c.* the United States of America).

The first judgment of the Court concerning an asylum seeker was delivered on 20 March 1991 in the case of *Cruz Varas and Others v. Sweden*. The (Plenary) Court hold, by 18 votes to one, that the expulsion of the applicants to Chile had not violated Article 3 of the Convention and, by ten votes to nine, that Sweden had not hindered the effective exercise of the right to petition by not complying with the Commission's request not to expel the applicants. The Grand Chamber judgment in *Chahal v. the United Kingdom* of 15 November 1996 was the first in which the Court found, by 12 votes to seven, that there would be an (indirect) violation of Article 3 of the Convention in the event of the decision being implemented to deport the applicant, "well known in India to support the cause of Sikh separatism".

The Court only found such violations in three other judgments[339] before its Grand Chamber judgment of 4 February 2005 in the case of *Mamatkulov and Askarov v. Turkey*. In that judgment, the Court found, by 14 votes to three, no violation in the extradition of the applicants to Uzbekistan, but hold, by 14 votes to three, that Turkey had hindered the effective exercise of the right of application by not complying with the Court's interim measure.[340] In the opinion of the three judges[341] dissenting on the latter issue, the Court had not interpreted but amended the Convention. Year on year, the number of interim measures requested by applicants increased.[342] The percentage of the requests granted by the presidents of the different sections of the Court increased even more. In a declaration of 11 February 2011, the President of the Court expressed his concern about the "alarming rise" in the number of requests for interim measures. At the Izmir Conference in April 2011, the Member States of the Council of Europe recalled that "the Court is not an immigration Appeals Tribunal or a Court of fourth instance". From then on, the number of those requests and the percentage[343] of interim measures granted decreased.

---

[338] See *supra*, Chapter X, B.

[339] *Ahmed v. Austria* (17 December 1996), *D. v. the United Kingdom* (2 May 1997) and *Jabari v. Turkey* (11 July 2000).

[340] On that case, see Bossuyt, *supra* note 299, pp. 14–21.

[341] Lucius Caflisch (Liechtenstein), Riza Türmen (Turkey) and Anatoly Kovler (Russia) (see *supra*, Chapter XI, B).

[342] *Ibid.*

[343] From 38% (1,443) in 2010 to 5% (103) in 2012, 6% (108) in 2013, 11% (216, including 110 concerning the crisis in Ukraine) in 2014, and 11% (161) in 2015.

As a consequence of the high number of such requests by asylum seekers granted, the number of judgments of the Court on applications submitted by asylum seekers also considerably increased as well as, in particular, the number of indirect violations of Article 3 of the Convention found by the Court in case of the extradition or the expulsion of an asylum seeker. Since *Mamatkulov and Askarov*, the Court found (as at February 2015) more than 100 such violations.[344] Those violations were not only *indirect* but most of them were also *potential*, as the extradition or the expulsion had not yet taken place but would violate Article 3 if they would be implemented. Instead of evaluating facts that did happen in States parties to the Convention, the Court speculates about events that could happen in non-States parties to the Convention. And even when it appears that the applicant has not been ill-treated after returning to his country, the State party is condemned because it could have happened.

In addition, starting with its judgment *Dougoz v. Greece* (6 March 2001), the Court also found (up to the end of February 2015) 37 direct violations of Article 3 of the Convention in the way asylum seekers were treated in a State party to the Convention. Not less than 24 of those judgments concern Greece. The other States parties concerned are Belgium (four), Russia and Turkey (three each), France, Malta and Romania (one each). It is also the way asylum seekers are treated in Greece which led to the Grand Chamber judgment *M.S.S. v. Belgium and Greece* (GC, 21 January 2011).[345]

That judgment is the first[346] concerning asylum seekers in which the Court found an EU Member State (Belgium) indirectly responsible for returning an asylum seeker to another EU Member State (Greece), because the conditions of his detention and his living conditions in that country were considered

---

344   38 of those judgments concern extraditions or expulsions by Russia to Uzbekistan (22), to Tajikistan (9), to Kyrgyzstan (4) or to Turkmenistan (3). The other judgments concern extraditions or expulsions by France and Italy (12 each), Turkey (10), Sweden (6), Belgium, Netherlands, Ukraine and the United Kingdom (3 each), Austria, Bosnia-Herzegovina, Bulgaria and Greece (2 each) and Belgium and Greece, Finland, Georgia and Russia and Slovakia (1 each) to the following States non-parties to the Convention: Tunisia (13), Iran (9), Algeria and the Democratic Republic of Congo (3 each), Somalia (2,5), Syria, Sri Lanka, Kazakhstan, Libya and Sudan (2 each), Eritrea (1,5), Afghanistan, Belarus, Bhutan, Chad, Egypt, Morocco, Pakistan and the USA (1 each). The following judgments having found an indirect violation concerning an expulsion or extradition to a State party to the Convention, namely to Russia (*Shamaev and* Others v. Georgia (12 April 2005), *I.K. v. Austria* (28 March 2013), *I. v. Sweden* (5 September 2013), *M.G. v. Bulgaria* (23 March 2014) and *M.V. and M.T. v. France* (4 September 2014)), to Greece (*M.S.S. v. Belgium* (GC, 21 January 2011) and *Sharifi and Others v. Italy* (21 October 2014)) and to Italy (*Tarakhel v. Switzerland* (GC, 4 November 2014)).

345   For more elaborate comments, see Bossuyt, Marc, "Belgium Condemned for Inhuman or Degrading Treatment Due to Violations by Greece of EU Asylum Law", *European Human Rights Law Review*, 2011, pp. 582–597.

346   The first judgment concerning asylum seekers in which the Court found a State party (Georgia) indirectly responsible for extraditing an asylum seeker to another State party (Russia) was: *Shamayev and Others v. Georgia and Russia*, 12 April 2005.

unacceptable. Based on the EU Dublin Regulation,[347] Belgium had transferred to Greece an Afghan interpreter who had paid his smuggler US \$12,000 for travelling to that country. By prohibiting asylum seekers who have entered the Schengen area in Greece to be transferred to that country, the Court undermines the EU's Dublin Regulation, a central piece of the Common European Asylum System.[348] In this case, the Court condemned Greece, directly responsible for the violation of Article 3, to pay 1,000 euros to the applicant, while Belgium, which was only indirectly responsible, had to pay 24,900 euros.

Other developments in this judgment that raise concern are:

(1) The continuous lowering of the threshold of Article 3: not every ill-treatment amounts to torture, or even to inhuman or degrading treatment; a particular level of severity (the threshold) has to be attained. In the first judgments, finding that the conditions of retention of an asylum seeker violated Article 3, the conditions considered "unacceptable" lasted for several months.[349] However, in *M.S.S.* such conditions lasted only four days. This seems to hardly be compatible with the absolute character of the prohibition of torture which allows no exception, no restriction and no derogation "not even in time of war or other public emergency threatening the life of the nation".

(2) The expansion of the list of "particularly vulnerable groups",[350] such as "Roma" in *Oršuš and Others v. Croatia* (GC, 16 March 2010) and "mentally disabled persons" in *Alajos Kiss v. Hungary* (20 May 2010), with asylum seekers, a self-elected category, since every foreigner who decides to apply for asylum is an asylum seeker, regardless of his personal condition or his motives for applying. In doing so, the Court is shifting from protecting civil rights of the universal human being towards protecting social rights

---

[347] See *infra*, sub C, 1, a..

[348] See *infra*, sub C. The situation was made worse by the endorsement of this view by the Court of Justice of the European Union in its judgment of 21 December 2011 in the cases C-411/10 and C-493/10 (see DE BAERE, Geert, "The Court of Luxembourg acting as an Asylum Court", in André ALEN, Veronique JOOSTEN, Riet LEYSEN & Willem VERRIJDT, *Liberae Cogitationes (Liber amicorum Marc Bossuyt)*, Antwerp, Intersentia, 2013, pp. 107–124, at p. 117: "By adopting and endorsing the ECtHR's analysis, the ECJ profoundly unsettled the principle of mutual confidence that underlies the CEAS and, by extension, the entire edifice of European integration". The Court has further undermined the Dublin regulation in its Chamber judgment *Sharifi and Others v. Greece and Italy* of 21 October 2014 and its Grand Chamber judgment *Tarakhel v. Switzerland* of 4 November 2014. If the application of that regulation may have led to unacceptable living conditions for asylum seekers in some States parties to the European Convention, its non-application has led to such conditions in many more States parties to the European Convention (see BOSSUYT, *supra* note 335, pp. 603–604). When the conditions in a State party to the European Convention – and *a fortiori* in a State Member of the European Union – violate Article 3 of that Convention, the complaint should be examined with respect to that State party (such as Greece and Italy) and not with respect to another State party (such as Belgium and Switzerland) (*ibid.*, p. 597).

[349] e.g. 17 months in *Dougoz v. Greece* (6 March 2001).

[350] See also BOSSUYT, Marc, "Categorical Rights and Vulnerable Groups: Moving Away from the Universal Human Being", *The George Washington International Law Review*, 2016, pp. 101–127.

of specific categories of persons with particular needs. According to the Court, persons belonging to one of those categories are entitled to an active intervention of the State beyond the level required for other persons with respect to civil rights and fundamental freedoms.

(3) The extension of the applicability of Article 3 to the living conditions of asylum seekers. As an obligation not to do something, the absolute prohibition of torture has to be and *can* be respected regardless of the available resources. The Court, however, has transformed that civil right *par excellence* into an obligation to provide social benefits to asylum seekers which requires considerable expenditures. Since the resources available for social benefits are not unlimited, this implies that, despite the deep financial crisis in Greece, that country should, according to the Court, give priority to the needs of asylum seekers. Not fulfilling those needs, contrary to what is the case with other needs, would violate the absolute prohibition of Article 3 of the Convention.

Moreover, in its Grand Chamber judgment in *Hirsi Jamaa and Others v. Italy* of 23 February 2012, the Court declared the maritime external borders of all Member States of the Council of Europe wide open for anyone applying for asylum. In that judgment, the Court found a violation of Article 3 of the Convention by Italy and it awarded 15,000 euros in respect of non-pecuniary damage to 11 Eritreans and 13 Somalis each, who had tried to reach Lampedusa by boat, but were sent back to Libya by the Italian Coastguard. That judgment did not discourage migrants from undertaking such a perilous journey at the risk of their lives and it raises a number of intriguing questions relevant to the mission of Frontex (the EU agency managing European border control).

2. CASE LAW WITH RESPECT OF ARTICLE 13 OF THE EUROPEAN CONVENTION

Already in its judgment of 28 May 1985 in the case of *Abdulaziz, Cabales and Balkandali v. the United Kingdom*, the (Plenary) Court has emphasised that:

> "as a matter of well-established international law and subject to its treaty obligations, a State has the right to control the entry of non-nationals into its territory".

However, Article 6.1 of the European Convention which requires "a fair and public hearing within a reasonable time by an independent and impartial tribunal" is not applicable to asylum applications because, as stated by the European Commission in its inadmissibility decision of 16 October 1986 in the case of *Shankerath Lukka v. the United Kingdom*, the proceedings by which political asylum is refused do not involve the determination of the applicant's civil rights and obligations as they are of "an administrative, discretionary nature".

In its Grand Chamber judgment of 5 October 2000 in the case of *Maaouia v. France*, the Court also concluded, by 15 votes to 2, that:

> "decisions regarding the entry, stay and deportation of aliens do not concern the determination of an applicant's civil rights or obligations or of a criminal charge against him, within the meaning of Article 6 §1 of the Convention".

The Court came to this conclusion, after having noted that the provisions of Protocol No. 7, adopted on 22 November 1984, show that the States parties were aware that Article 6.1 did not apply to procedures for the expulsion of aliens and wished to take special measures in that sphere.

On the contrary, when the applicant has an arguable claim of a violation of Article 3 of the Convention, even when the treatment in violation of that Article would be inflicted by another State than the State party concerned, the right to an effective remedy, as guaranteed by Article 13 of the Convention, is applicable:

> "Everyone whose rights and freedoms as set forth in this Convention are violated shall have an effective remedy before a national authority notwithstanding that the violation has been committed by persons acting in an official capacity".

An essential difference with Article 6.1 of the Convention is that this "effective remedy" must not be provided by a jurisdiction. The Court has nevertheless interpreted Article 13 of the Convention in a manner which imposes ever more demanding requirements on the asylum procedures.

In its judgment of 20 March 1991 in the case of *Cruz Varas and Others v. Sweden*, the (Plenary) Court considered that "substantial grounds" had not been shown for believing that the applicant's expulsion would expose him to "a real risk" of being subjected to inhuman or degrading treatment on his return to Chile (§82). In its Chamber judgment of 30 October 1991 in the case of *Vilvarajah and Others v. the United Kingdom*, the Court, after having noted that "a mere possibility of ill-treatment [...] is not in itself sufficient to give rise to a breach of Article 3", stated with reference to Article 13 that it requires:

> "the provision of a domestic remedy allowing the 'national authority' both to deal with the substance of the relevant convention complaint and to grant appropriate relief [...]. However, Article 13 does not go so far as to require any particular form of remedy, Contracting States being afforded a margin of discretion in conforming to their obligations under this provision. Nor does the effectiveness of a remedy for the purposes of Article 13 depend on the certainty of a favourable outcome for the applicant [...]" (§122).

In its Grand Chamber judgment of 15 November 1996 in the case of *Chahal v. the United Kingdom*, the Court stated explicitly that the "effective remedy" should not necessarily be provided by a "judicial authority":

"the notion of an effective remedy under Article 13 requires independent scrutiny of the claim that there exist substantial grounds for fearing a real risk of treatment contrary to Article 3 [... §151]. Such scrutiny need not be provided by a judicial authority but, if it is not, the powers and guarantees which it affords are relevant in determining whether the remedy before it is effective [...]" (§152).[351]

In its Chamber judgment of 5 February 2002 in the case of *Čonka v. Belgium*, the Court stated:

"the notion of an effective remedy under Article 13 requires that the remedy may prevent the execution of measures that are contrary to the Convention and whose effects are potentially irreversible [...]. Consequently, it is inconsistent with Article 13 for such measures to be executed before the national authorities have examined whether they are compatible with the Convention" (§79).

As the recourse to the *Conseil d'Etat* had no suspensive effect, "not even for a minimum reasonable period to enable the *Conseil d'Etat* to decide the application", the Court held, by four votes to three, that there had been a violation of Article 13 of the Convention.

This was amplified by the Court in its Chamber judgment of 26 April 2007 in the case of *Gebremedhin [Gaberamadhien] v. France*, where it stated that:

"Article 13 requires that the person concerned should have access to a remedy with automatic suspensive effect" (§66).

In its Chamber judgment of 27 February 2014 in the case of *S.J. v. Belgium*,[352] the Court stated that a remedy is only effective when it is both suspensive and allowing for an effective examination of the arguments concerning a possible violation of Article 3 of the Convention (§106).

As far as the EU Member States are concerned, the requirements imposed upon them by the Court are surpassed by the guarantees contained in Article 47 of the Charter of Fundamental Rights[353] of the European Union

---

351   In its Chamber judgment of 11 July 2000 in the case of *Jabari v. Turkey*, the Court added that: "the notion of an effective remedy under Article 13 requires independent and rigorous scrutiny of a claim that there exist substantial grounds for fearing a risk of treatment contrary to Article 3" (§50).

352   That Chamber judgment has been referred to the Grand Chamber which decided to strike the case out of its list on 19 March 2015, after having taken note of the friendly settlement arrived at by the parties in this case.

353   The Charter, adopted in Nice (France) by the European Council on 7 December 2000, became legally binding on the EU institutions and on the national authorities of the Member States when they implement EU law, with the entry into force on 1 December 2009 of the Treaty of

which provides a right "to an effective remedy and to *a fair trial*" and adds that "[e]veryone whose rights and freedoms guaranteed by the law of the Union are violated has the right to an effective remedy *before a tribunal*" (emphasis added).

C. THE COMMON EUROPEAN ASYLUM SYSTEM

Article 18 of the Charter of Fundamental Rights also provides that:

> "The right to asylum shall be guaranteed with due respect for the rules of the Geneva Convention of 28 July 1951 and the Protocol of 31 January 1967 relating to the status of refugees and in accordance with the Treaty establishing the European Community".

Since 1999, the European Union has been working to create a Common European Asylum System (CEAS) setting out a legislative framework providing for common standards and closer cooperation to ensure that asylum seekers are treated equally in the EU Member States. The main instruments[354] of that System are two Regulations and three Directives.

1. THE ASYLUM REGULATIONS[355]

The relevant regulations are the Dublin Regulation and the Eurodac Regulation.

a.   The Dublin Regulation

The Dublin Regulation[356] III of 26 June 2013 "establishing the criteria and mechanisms for determining the Member State responsible for examining an application for international protection lodged in one of the Member States by a

---

Lisbon (Portugal) of 13 December 2007 "amending the Treaty on European Union and the Treaty establishing the European Community".

[354]   The explanations given on the CEAS Regulations and Directives are drawn from a brochure of the European Commission (http://ec.europa.eu/dgs/home-affairs/e-library/docs/ceas-fact-sheets/ceas-_factsheet_en.pdf).

[355]   According to Article 288 of the Treaty on the Functioning of the European Union (TFEU), formerly Article 249 of the Treaty establishing the European Community (TEC), "A regulation shall have general application. It shall be binding in its entirety and directly applicable in all Member States".

[356]   Regulation (EU) No. 604/2013 of the European Parliament and of the Council replacing from 1 January 2014 on Council Regulation (EC) No. 343/2003 [Dublin II Regulation] of 18 February 2003 "establishing the criteria and mechanisms for determining the Member State responsible for examining an asylum application lodged in one of the Member States by a third-country national", which had replaced the Dublin I Convention of 15 June 1990.

third-country national or a stateless person" enhances the protection of asylum seekers during the process of establishing the State responsible for examining the application and clarifies the rules governing the relations between States; it creates a system to detect early problems in national asylum or reception systems and address their root causes before they develop into fully fledged crises.

b. The Eurodac Regulation

The Eurodac Regulation[357] of 26 June 2013 "establishing the criteria and mechanisms for determining the Member State responsible for examining an application for international protection lodged in one of the Member States by a third-country national or a stateless person and on requests for the comparison with Eurodac data by Member States' law enforcement authorities and Europol for law enforcement purposes, and amending Regulation (EU) No 1077/2011 establishing a European Agency for the operational management of large-scale IT systems in the area of freedom, security and justice" will allow law enforcement access to the EU database of the fingerprints of asylum seekers under strictly limited circumstances in order to prevent, detect or investigate the most serious crimes, such as murder and terrorism.

2. THE ASYLUM DIRECTIVES[358]

There are asylum directives concerning the standards for the qualification as beneficiaries of international protection and for the reception of applicants for international protection and concerning common procedures for granting and withdrawing international protection.

a. The Qualification Directive

The Qualification Directive[359] of 13 December 2011 "on standards for the qualification of third-country nationals or stateless persons as beneficiaries of

---

[357] Regulation (EU) No. 603/2013 of the European Parliament and of the Council replacing from 20 July 2015 on Council Regulation (EC) No 2725/2000 of 11 December 2000 "concerning the establishment of 'Eurodac' for the comparison of fingerprints for the effective application of the Dublin Convention".

[358] According to the above-mentioned Article 288 TFEU, "[a] directive shall be binding, as to the result to be achieved, upon each Member State to which it is addressed, but shall leave to the national authorities the choice of form and methods".

[359] Directive 2011/95/EU of the European Parliament and of the Council replacing from 21 December 2013 on Council Directive 2004/83/EC of 29 April 2004 "on minimum standards for the qualification and status of third-country nationals or stateless persons as refugees or as persons who otherwise need international protection and the content of the protection granted".

international protection, for a uniform status for refugees or for persons eligible for subsidiary protection, and for the content of the protection granted" intends to clarify the grounds for granting international protection and to improve the access to rights and integration measures for beneficiaries of international protection. In Article 15, the Directive extends the obligations of the EU Member States by providing *subsidiary protection* to persons

> "facing a real risk of suffering serious harm [consisting of] the death penalty or execution [or of] torture or inhuman or degrading treatment or punishment [or of] serious and individual threat to a civilian's life or person by reason of indiscriminate violence in situations of *international or internal armed conflict*" (emphasis added).

b. The Reception Conditions Directive

The Reception Conditions Directive[360] of 26 June 2013 "laying down standards for the reception of applicants for international protection" ensures that there are humane material reception conditions (such as housing) for asylum seekers across the EU and that the fundamental rights of the concerned persons are fully respected; it also ensures that detention is only applied as a measure of last resort.

c. The Asylum Procedure Directive

The Asylum Procedure Directive[361] 26 June 2013 "on common procedures for granting and withdrawing international protection" aims at fairer, quicker and better quality asylum decisions; asylum seekers with special needs will receive the necessary support to explain their claim and in particular there will be greater protection of unaccompanied minors and victims of torture.

As far as the right to an effective remedy is concerned, Article 46 of that revised Asylum Procedure Directive provides that "Member States shall ensure that applicants have the right to an effective remedy before a court or tribunal" against a decision taken on their application for international protection.[362] Moreover,

---

[360] Directive 2013/33/EU of the European Parliament and of the Council replacing from 21 July 2015 on Council Directive 2003/9/EC of 27 January 2003 "laying down minimum standards for the reception of asylum seekers".

[361] Directive 2013/32/EU of the European Parliament and of the Council replacing from 21 July 2015 on Council Directive 2005/85/EC of 1 December 2005 "on minimum standards on procedures in Member States for granting and withdrawing refugee status".

[362] The decisions concerned are those considering applications (i) unfounded or (ii) inadmissible because (a) another Member State has granted international protection; (b) a country which is not a Member State is considered as a first country of asylum or (c) a country which is not a Member State is considered as a safe third country; (d) the application is a subsequent application where no new elements or findings have arisen or (e) the application is lodged by a dependant without facts justifying a separate application (Art. 33.2); (iii) taken at the border

"Member States shall ensure that an effective remedy provides for a full and *ex nunc* examination of both facts and points of law" (Art. 46.3)

and

"shall allow applicants to remain in the territory until the time limit within which to exercise their right to an effective remedy has expired and, when such a right has been exercised within the time limit, pending the outcome of the remedy (Art. 46.5).

However, for a number of decisions "a court or a tribunal shall have the power to rule whether or not the applicant may remain on the territory of the Member State" (Art. 46.6). The European involvement in the asylum procedure has led to anything but simplification and is not designed to cope with the huge numbers of applications several Member States of the European Union are confronted with, nor does it succeed in any way to diminish the attraction of the countries of destination preferred by asylum seekers.

***

Too often, confusion is entertained between refugees, asylum seekers, migrants and aliens staying irregularly on the territory of the country concerned. While orderly migration is beneficial and refugees in the sense of the Geneva Convention deserve international protection, illegal migration has to be fought by the international community as a whole. It cannot be sustained that anybody who prefers to live in another country should be able to do so without being authorised by that country. In a global world, migrant crises cannot be overcome without the cooperation of all concerned, be it countries of origin, transit or destination. Absence of such a cooperation leads to multiple adverse consequences, such as refugees not obtaining the protection they are entitled to, freedom of movement of persons unduly restricted, legal migration severely curtailed, decline of the budgets for development cooperation diverted to accommodate asylum seekers and increased risks of resurgence of xenophobia, islamophobia, racism and racial discrimination.

---

or in the transit zone of a Member State (Art. 43.1); (iv) (a) not to conduct an examination because a competent authority has established that the applicants have entered illegally into the territory of the Member State from a safe third country (Art. 39); (b) not to reopen the examination of an application after its discontinuation, when an applicant explicitly or implicitly withdraws his application (Artt. 27 and 28); (c) to withdraw international protection (Art. 45).

CHAPTER XIV
THE PROTECTION OF MINORITIES IN INTERNATIONAL LAW[363]

In the absence of a definition of the concept of minority, the protection of minorities, while presenting some links with the protection of human rights, hardly surpasses the prohibition of discrimination of persons on the ground of their belonging to a minority. Despite several attempts, it has not been possible, neither in the framework of the United Nations, nor in the framework of the Council of Europe, to formulate in a legally binding instrument a definition of that concept.

A. THE CONCEPT OF MINORITY IN THE FRAMEWORK OF THE UNITED NATIONS

Article 27 of the International Covenant on Civil and Political Rights (1966) reads as follows:

> "In States in which ethnic, religious or linguistic minorities exist, persons belonging to such minorities shall not be denied the right, in community with the other members of their group, to enjoy their own culture, to profess and practise their own religion, or to use their own language".

---

[363] Based on a contribution at the Colloquium of the French Society of International Law on 9–11 June 2011 at Poitiers: BOSSUYT, Marc, "Nationalité et minorités en droit international", in S.F.D.I., *Droit international et nationalité*, Paris, Pedone, 2012, pp. 145–163; see also BOSSUYT, Marc, "La définition du concept de 'minorités' en droit international" in Francis DELPÉRÉE & László TROCSANYI (Dir.), *L'unité et la diversité de l'Europe: les droits des minorités (Les exemples belge et hongrois)*, Brussels, Bruylant, 2003, pp. 21–35; KOVACS, Peter, *International Law and Minority Protection. Rights of Minorities or Law of Minorities?*, Budapest, Akademiai Kiado, 2000, 174 p.; KOVACS, Peter, (Ed.), *Minorités et droit international, Studia Iuris Gentium Miskolcinensia*, vol. III, Miskolc, 2008, 117 p.; WELLER, Marc (Ed.), *Universal Minority Rights: A Commentary on the Jurisprudence of International Courts and Treaty Bodies*, Oxford, Oxford Univ. Pr., 2008, 576 p.; HENRARD, Kristin & DUNBAR, Robert, *Synergies in minority protection: European and international law perspectives*, Cambridge, Cambridge Univ. Pr., 2008, 462 p.; HENRARD, Kristin & DUNBAR, Robert, *Synergies in Minority Protection European and International Law Perspectives*, Cambridge, Cambridge Univ. Pr., 2009, 476 p.

However, neither that Covenant nor Article 14 of the European Convention on Human Rights (1950)[364] contain a definition of the concept of "minority".

It is only in 1979 that in the framework of the United Nations a first attempt to define that concept was undertaken by Professor Francesco Capotorti (Italy), Special Rapporteur of the Sub-Commission on the Prevention of Discrimination and on the Protection of Minorities, in his report on minorities:[365]

"A group numerically inferior to the rest of the population of a State, in a non-dominant position, whose members – being nationals of the State – possess ethnic, religious or linguistic characteristics differing from those of the rest of the population and show, if only implicitly, a sense of solidarity, directed towards preserving their culture, traditions, religion or language."

From 1980 to 1984, the study of a draft declaration on the right of minorities was entrusted by the Commission on Human Rights to a Working Group. In its resolution 1984/62 the Commission requested the Sub-Commission to draft a text defining the term "minority". In 1985 a member of the Sub-Commission, Judge Jules Deschênes (Canada), presented a definition largely analogous to that proposed by Professor Francesco Capotorti:

"A group of citizens of a State, constituting a numerical minority and in a non-dominant position in that State, endowed with ethnic, religious, or linguistic characteristics which differ from those of the majority of the population, having a sense of solidarity with one another, motivated, if only implicitly, by a collective will to survive and whose aim is to achieve equality with the majority in fact and in law".[366]

The two definitions have many common elements: numerically inferior, non-dominant position, ethnic, religious or linguistic characteristics, nationals or citizens of the State, a sense of solidarity and the collective will to survive and to preserve their identity. However, the Declaration on the Rights of Persons Belonging to National or Ethnic, Religious and Linguistic Minorities,[367] adopted on 18 December 1992 by the General Assembly of the United Nations, does not contain a definition.

---

[364] Besides the 12 grounds of discrimination mentioned in Article 2 of the Universal Declaration ("race, colour, sex, language, religion, political or other opinion, national or social origin, property, birth or other status"), Article 14 of the European Convention also mentions a 13th ground ("association with a national minority").

[365] E/CN.4/Sub.2/384 and Add. 1–7.

[366] Adopted on 8 April 1994; E/CN.4/Sub.2/1985/57, p. 85.

[367] This Declaration recognises, in its Article 2.1, to persons belonging to national or ethnic, religious and linguistic minorities "the right to enjoy their own culture, to profess and practise their own religion, and to use their own language, in private and in public, freely and without interference or any form of discrimination".

Nevertheless, the Human Rights Committee has considered in its General Comment No. 23[368] (adopted on 8 April 1994) concerning Article 27 of the Civil Covenant that, though expressed in negative terms, it requires positive measures of protection not only against the acts of the State party itself but also against the acts of other persons within the State party (§6.1). Despite the consensus[369] in the two definitions adopted within the Sub-Commission that Committee considers that the terms used in Article 27 also indicate that the individuals designed to be protected need not be citizens of the State party (§5.1) and that they need not be permanent residents (§5.2).

If Article 27 contains essentially a negative obligation in the sense that the Governments may not interfere in the culture, religion and language of the minority groups, a definition is not very important. Indeed, as far as civil rights and fundamental freedoms are concerned which require essentially an abstention by the States parties of not interfering in the enjoyment of those rights and freedoms, it does not matter very much whether a person belongs or does not belong to a minority.

Everyone is entitled to the enjoyment of those rights and freedoms and nobody, regardless of whether he does or does not belong to a minority, may be arbitrarily deprived of the enjoyment of one of those rights or freedoms. In that sense, whether or not one is a citizen has little importance with respect to Article 27 of the Civil Covenant. That issue is much more delicate when Article 27 of the Civil Covenant is interpreted as requiring the States parties to take positive measures which would also be beneficial to non-citizens.

The definition of the concept of minority acquires a crucial importance when it is necessary to determine which persons – because they belong to a minority – are entitled to particular measures enabling them to preserve and develop their specific identity. At that moment, the protection of minorities goes far beyond the prohibition of discrimination in the enjoyment of civil rights everyone is entitled to. In that situation, persons belonging to minorities may claim from the State to which jurisdiction they belong particular endeavours which may constitute a considerable burden for the budget of the State party concerned.

---

[368] CCPR/C/21/Rev.1/Add.5.

[369] In a particularly interesting contribution on that Article 27 of the Civil Covenant ("Protection of Minorities under Article 27 of the International Covenant on Civil and Political Rights", in *Völkerrecht als rechtsordnung Internationale Gerichtsbarkeit Menschenrechte (Festschrift für Hermann Mosler)*, Berlin, Springer, 1983, pp. 849–979), Professor Christian Tomuschat, then a member of the Human Rights Committee, also noted that the negative formulation of Article 27 ("shall not be denied") had been chosen deliberately and that enlarging the scope of Article 27 by imposing positive obligations could compromise its value and entail a total loss of credibility.

B. THE CONCEPT OF MINORITY IN THE FRAMEWORK OF THE COUNCIL OF EUROPE

Contrary to the other human rights conventions, the European Convention on Human Rights has added the "association with a national minority" to the grounds mentioned in its Article 14 prohibiting discrimination in the rights and freedoms set forth in that Convention, without providing any specific right to persons belonging to a national minority.

In 1992, however, the Committee of Ministers of the Council of Europe entrusted the Steering Committee for Human Rights and its Committee of Experts for the Protection of National Minorities to study the possibility of formulating specific norms concerning the protection of national minorities. Recommendation 1201 (1993), adopted on 1 February 1993 by the Parliamentary Assembly of the Council of Europe, contains the following definition of a "national minority":

> "a group of persons in a state who:
> a. reside on the territory of that state and are citizens thereof;
> b. maintain longstanding, firm and lasting ties with that state;
> c. display distinctive ethnic, cultural, religious or linguistic characteristics;
> d. are sufficiently representative, although smaller in number than the rest of the population of that state or of a region of that state;
> e. are motivated by a concern to preserve together that which constitutes their common identity, including their culture, their traditions, their religion or their language".

That definition refers to persons who are citizens of the State concerned and maintain longstanding, firm and lasting ties with that State. In its report to the Committee of Ministers of 8 September 1993, the Steering Committee for Human Rights, presenting various legal standards which might be adopted in this area, nevertheless noted that there was no consensus on the interpretation of the term "national minorities". Nor does the Framework Convention for the Protection of National Minorities, adopted by the Committee of Ministers of the Council of Europe on 10 November 1994, contain a definition of the notion of "national minority".

In the Commentary on the provisions of that Framework Convention, it is noted, with respect to the Preamble, that the reference to United Nations conventions and declarations does not extend to any definition of a national minority which may be contained in these texts. With respect to Article 1 of the Framework Convention, it is also noted in the Commentary that it is specified that the protection of national minorities which "forms an integral part of the protection of human rights" does not confer any competence to interpret the present Framework Convention on the organs established by the European Convention on Human Rights.

Several reservations and declarations accompanying the ratification of the Framework Convention do clarify the intentions of the States parties. Germany, Poland and Slovenia refer explicitly to the absence in the Framework Convention of a definition of the notion of national minorities. Germany infers from that absence that it is up to the individual Contracting Parties to determine the groups to which it shall apply after ratification. Germany, Austria, Poland and Switzerland state explicitly that the Framework Convention applies to persons having the nationality of the State party concerned. *Austria* adds that those groups live and have traditionally have had their home in parts of its territory and *Germany* states that the Framework Convention will be applied to members of the ethnic groups traditionally resident on its territory.

Switzerland declares that the provisions of the Framework Convention governing the use of the languages in relations between individuals and administrative authorities are applicable "without prejudice to the principles observed by the Confederation and the cantons in the determination of the official languages". *Belgium* also declared, when it signed the Framework Convention on 31 July 2001, that it "applies without prejudice to the constitutional provisions guarantees or principles and without prejudice to the legislative rules which currently govern the use of languages". Belgium added that "the notion of national minority will be defined by the inter-ministerial conference of foreign policy". In the absence of an agreement within that conference, there is no such definition and no ratification by Belgium of the Framework Convention.[370]

Some States parties (Denmark, Germany, the Netherlands, the Former Yugoslav Republic of Macedonia, Slovenia and Sweden) list the minorities on which the Framework Convention is applicable in their respective territories.[371] It must also be noted that three States parties, *Liechtenstein*, *Luxembourg* and

---

[370] On the Belgian declaration, see also (a) the views of the Working Group of the Venice Commission, consisting of Franz Matscher (Austria), Georgio Malinverni (Switzerland), Pieter van Dijk (Netherlands) and Sergio Bartole (Italy), contained in a report adopted on 9 March 2002; (b) the report (Doc. 9395 revised) of 18 April 2002 on "The Protection of Minorities in Belgium" by Mrs Lily Nabholz-Haidegger (Switzerland), Rapporteur of the Committee on Legal Affairs and Human Rights of the Parliamentary Assembly of the Council of Europe; and (c) the Resolution 1301 (2002) on the protection of minorities adopted on 26 September 2002 by the Parliamentary Assembly of the Council of Europe.

[371] Those minorities are: in *Denmark*, the German minority in South Jutland of the Kingdom of Denmark; in *Germany*, the Danes of German citizenship, the members of the Sorbian people with German citizenship, the Frisians of German citizenship and the Sinti and Roma of German citizenship; in the *Netherlands*, the Frisians; in the *former Yugoslav Republic of Macedonia*, the citizens of that Republic who live within its borders and who are part of the Albanian people, Turkish people, Vlach people, Serbian people, Roma people and Bosniac people; in *Slovenia*, the autochthonous Italian and Hungarian National Minorities and the members of the Roma community who live in the Republic of Slovenia; and in *Sweden*, the Sami, Swedish Finns, Tornedalers, Roma and Jews.

Malta, declared that there is no "national minority" on their territories. No objection has been raised with respect to those reservations and declarations.

It is only with respect to States that have subscribed to an international treaty containing a general definition of the notion of minority that persons belonging to a minority corresponding to that definition can invoke a right to benefits guaranteed by that convention. The absence of such a definition does not result from a regrettable oversight or negligence. The reason for this absence is obvious: up to now, States have refused to subscribe to such a definition both in a universal and in a regional context.

A general and abstract definition in international law is probably not even possible (nor maybe desirable) as is the case with the definition of a "people" entitled to the right of self-determination.[372] States are not willing to entrust an international instance with the competence of determining which group of persons must be recognised as a minority entailing the legal obligation for the State to provide them with specific benefits.

States are very reluctant to leave to other States, to an international organisation or even to an international court the power to determine which groups should be entitled to the protection minorities may claim. The recognition of minorities depends on their historic, sociological, economic and even political context characterising the particular group. More particularly, the recognition of a group as minority depends to large extent on the historic context explaining the origin of that particular group and the socio-economic context determining the place of that group in the society.

The historic origin of a particular group takes a prominent place when dealing with minority issues. A minority established for centuries in a given territory but in a minority position due to border changes or military conquests is in a better position to claim measures of protection than the descendants of the former occupying power or persons that preferred to assimilate the culture of such powers. It is not without importance to know whether their minority position results from changes that happened independently of their free will or as a result of initiatives they have freely undertaken themselves. A State may require from those establishing themselves on its territory to respect the culture of its population of origin and take the necessary measures to protect the identity of that population. The dominant position that a given group may occupy depends on the socio-economic conditions characterising them and which determine its needs of protection more than the number of its members.

---

[372] States were not willing to subscribe to a definition of a people which would entail that any group corresponding to the constitutive elements of that definition, could base itself on it to have its rights of self-determination recognised. The international community is not yet ready, e.g., to recognise the competence of the International Court of Justice to determine whether a group of persons corresponds to the definition of a people which would obtain *ipso facto* the right to proclaim its independence in a manner that would be legally binding upon every State.

A dominant majority will need measures of protection analogous to those that minorities are entitled to.

In the absence of a legally binding definition of the notion of minority or rather in the face of the persistent refusal of States to accept such a definition, one has to be satisfied with the recognition of minorities by the State concerned. Such recognition may take place unilaterally, bilaterally or multilaterally. The system of minority protection in the framework of the League of Nations was an example of multilateral recognition of certain minorities in certain countries. Some States have concluded bilateral agreements recognising certain minorities in their respective countries.

However, it is unilateral recognition that most States prefer. Hence the importance of the declarations made by certain States parties to the Framework Convention specifying the minorities to whom that instrument applies within their territory. Generally, those declarations are based on provisions in their domestic legal order – and most frequently in their constitution itself – recognising the existence on their territory of certain minorities. It is only to the extent that those minorities are recognised that they may invoke the rights guaranteed by such treaties.

***

In the classic definition, minorities are persons that are citizens of the State where they live. At present, there is no international obligation for a State to recognise a group of persons as minorities. It would be very difficult to determine the conditions, numbers and the like that should be fulfilled in order to qualify for recognition as a minority. On the one hand, it is obvious that nobody may be deprived of a human right or a fundamental freedom because he belongs to a minority. On the other hand, a State is not under the obligation to provide specific rights to certain persons belonging to a group not recognised as a minority. There is a wide variety of factual situations often determined by history which mean that the same measures may have very different consequences when taken by a State rather by another State. Measures causing no problems when taken by a specific State may provoke strong tensions when another State takes exactly the same measures. For the same reason, there are few rules in international law regulating the question of the attribution of the nationality of a particular State to persons belonging to minorities.

As a matter of principle, it is up to each State to determine freely the rules governing the attribution of its nationality. On the basis of the Convention of 30 August 1961 on the reduction of statelessness, a State may not arbitrarily deprive a person – and *a fortiori* groups of persons – of his (or their) nationality. There is at most the prohibition, based on the general principle of law prohibiting arbitrary treatment of persons, to attribute nationality to persons in an arbitrary manner. When a State, however, decides to attribute its nationality to persons belonging to a specific minority, this is not necessarily arbitrary but maybe the result of a carefully reflected evaluation. Should a State that attributes its nationality to persons belonging to a specific minority, also attribute it – under the same conditions – to persons belonging to another minority? It does not seem to be so. There is a general principle of law based on human dignity according to which all human beings are equal in law, but there is no such a principle which requires the equal treatment of all minorities, regardless of their specific characteristics. Quite the contrary. Minorities may differ in many respects: their origin, their importance, the numbers of persons belonging to the minority, their historical links with the host country and with neighbouring countries, their position of dominance or their status of vulnerability, their criterion of differentiation from the majority population, etc. In the absence of a legally binding definition of the notion of minority, it is up to the host State to recognise multilaterally, bilaterally or unilaterally a certain group of persons as constituting or not a minority.

The principle of the free determination by each State of the regulations attributing it nationality is, however, tempered by rules of *soft law*. Such rules are promoted by instances such as the Organisation for Security and Cooperation in Europe, the Parliamentary Assembly of the Council of Europe or the Venice Commission recommending States to exercise their competences in this matter with caution and moderation, taking into account the effects such measures may have on other States and particularly on neighbouring States. While some of those principles (not exercising its jurisdiction on the territory of another State without its consent and not undermining the territorial integrity of other States) may be considered to be rules of positive law, others (such as not to attribute its nationality in a massive manner and acting to maintain friendly relations with other States and in particular with neighbouring States) are no more than recommendations.

CHAPTER XV

THE PROTECTION OF VICTIMS
OF ARMED CONFLICTS[373]

Contrary to the *jus ad bellum* which deals with the right of waging war and with the restrictions and conditions applicable to that right, the *jus in bello* aims at limiting as much as possible the injuries caused by war. The term most frequently used to refer to that branch of international law is "international humanitarian law", though the term "humanitarian international law" would be more correct. Traditionally, a distinction is made between, on the one hand, the law of The Hague regulating the means of warfare and, on the other hand, the law of Geneva aiming at protecting certain persons and property during war time.

A. THE LAW OF THE HAGUE

The law of The Hague concerns the means of warfare by defining the techniques that may be used and the weapons that are authorised in armed conflicts. The relations between belligerent and neutral States are also governed by the law of The Hague. Several documents are at the origin of the law of The Hague adopted at Conferences in that city in 1899 and 1907.

The so-called "Lieber Instructions" represent the first attempt to codify the laws of war. Those "Instructions for the Government of Armies of the United States in the Field" were prepared during the American Civil War by Professor Francis Lieber and promulgated by US President Abraham Lincoln on 24 April 1863.[374] "Although only binding on the forces of the United States, they correspond", as stated by Dietrich Schindler and Jiri Toman, "to a great extent to the laws and customs of war existing at that time".[375]

The Declaration of St Petersburg of 11 December 1868 "renouncing the use, in time of war, of explosive projectiles under 400 grammes weight" prohibited

---

373 Based on BOSSUYT & WOUTERS, *supra* note 139, pp. 536–562.
374 LIEBER, Francis & HARTIGAN, Richard (Ed.), *Lieber's Code and the law of war*, Chicago, Precedent, 1983, 157 p.
375 SCHINDLER, Dietrich & TOMAN, Jiri, *The Laws of Armed Conflicts*, Leiden, Sijthoff, 1973, p. 3.

the use of small explosive or incendiary projectiles. The Declaration reflects a compromise aimed at reconciling *"the necessities of war with the laws of humanity"*. The need for that conciliation is explained in the preamble of the Declaration as follows:

> "Considering
> That the progress of civilisation should have the effect of alleviating as much as possible the calamities of war;
> That the only legitimate object which states should endeavour to accomplish during war is to weaken the military forces of the enemy;
> That for this purpose it is sufficient to disable the greatest possible number of men;
> That this object would be exceeded by the employment of arms which uselessly aggravate the sufferings of disabled men, or render their death inevitable;
> That the employment of such arms would, therefore, be contrary to the laws of humanity".

The Declaration of Brussels concerning the laws and customs of war was adopted on 27 August 1874 by the delegates of 15 European States convened on the initiative of Czar Alexander II of Russia. The Declaration which was inspired by the Lieber Instructions, reaffirms the principles recognised in the Declaration of St Petersburg. On 9 September 1880, the Institute of International Law (a scientific association founded in 1873 in Ghent, Belgium) adopted the Manual of Oxford on the laws of war on land. Together with the Brussels Declaration, the Oxford Manual formed the basis of the two Hague Conventions adopted in 1899 and 1907.

1. THE HAGUE PEACE CONFERENCES (1899 AND 1907)

The first Hague Peace Conference, convened in 1899, again at the initiative of the Russian Czar, adopted several treaties and declarations. Convention II of 29 July 1899 with respect to the laws and customs of war on land imposes limitations on the methods of warfare and regulates the status of combatants, the treatment of prisoners of war and the authority of the occupant. Important rules are the following:

- "The right of belligerents to adopt means of injuring the enemy is not limited" (Art. 22).
- "[... I]t is specially prohibited [...] (e) To employ arms, projectiles, or material of a nature to cause superfluous [1907: unnecessary] injury" (Art. 23, e).
- "The attack or bombardment [1907: by whatever means] of towns, villages, habitations or buildings which are not defended, is prohibited" (Art. 25).

At the initiative of the Russian delegate von Martens a clause (the so-called "Martens Clause", was inserted in the preamble of Convention II:

"the High Contracting Parties think it right to declare that in cases not included in the Regulations adopted by them, populations and belligerents remain under the protection and empire of the principles of international law, as they result from the usages established between civilized nations, from the laws of humanity, and the requirements of the public conscience".

During the Second Hague Peace Conference that Conference adopted on 18 October 1907 several new conventions, among them Convention IV respecting the laws and customs of war and Convention V respecting the rights and duties of neutral powers and persons in case of war on land. Several other conventions were related to war at sea (status of enemy merchant ships, conversion of merchant ships into warships, the laying of automatic submarine contact mines, the bombardment by naval forces in time of war, etc.).

2. THE CHARACTERISTICS OF THE LAW OF THE HAGUE

The law of The Hague is only applicable to international armed conflicts between States. The conventions of the law of The Hague contain the so-called *si omnes* clause, according to which those conventions had to be respected only if all parties in the conflict concerned were parties to those conventions. Nowadays, most provisions of the law of The Hague reflect customary international law binding on all States. Moreover, later humanitarian law conventions provide that they are always applicable to all States parties regardless of whether another State party in the conflict concerned is party to those conventions.

The law of The Hague has been complemented by specific treaties:

- the Protocol of Geneva of 17 June 1925 for the prohibition of *the use* in war of asphyxiating, *poisonous* or other *gases*, and of *bacteriological* methods of warfare;
- the Hague Convention of 14 May 1954 for the protection of *cultural property* in the event of armed conflict, under the auspices of UNESCO, as well as a First Protocol adopted on the same date. A Second Protocol to that Convention was adopted on 26 March 1999;
- the Convention of 10 April 1972 on the Prohibition of the Development, *Production* and Stockpiling of *Bacteriological* (Biological) and Toxin Weapons and on their Destruction (London, Moscow and Washington);
- the ENMOD Convention on the Prohibition of Military or any Hostile Use of *Environmental Modification* Techniques, adopted by the UN General Assembly on 10 December 1976;
- the Convention of 10 October 1980 on prohibitions or restrictions on the use of certain *conventional weapons* which may be deemed to be excessively injurious or to have indiscriminate effects. That Convention, usually referred to as

the "Convention on Certain Conventional Weapons" or as the "Inhumane Weapons Convention", concerns only conventional weapons, leaving aside weapons of mass destruction. It was amended on 21 December 2001.

Moreover, five Protocols relate to that Convention.
Three of them were also adopted on 10 October 1980:

1) Protocol I on non-detectable fragments (prohibiting weapons the primary effect of which is to injure by fragments which in the human body escape detection by X-rays),
2) Protocol II on prohibitions or restrictions on the use of mines, booby-traps and other devices (this Protocol has been amended on 3 May 1996 to make it applicable to non-international conflicts), and
3) Protocol III on prohibitions or restrictions on the use of incendiary weapons.

Protocol IV on blinding laser weapons was adopted on 13 October 1995 and Protocol V on explosive remnants of war was adopted on 28 November 2003.

– the Paris Convention of 13 January 1993 on the prohibition of the development, *production*, stockpiling and use of *chemical weapons* and on their destruction;
– the Ottawa Convention of 18 September 1997 on the Prohibition of the Use, Stockpiling, Production and Transfer of *Anti-Personnel Mines* and on their Destruction (referred to as the "Anti-Personnel Mine Ban Convention");
– the Dublin Convention of 30 May 2008 on *Cluster Munitions*;
– the *Arms Trade* Treaty adopted by the UN General Assembly on 2 April 2013.

In its Advisory Opinion of 8 July 1996 on "*the legality of the threat or use of nuclear weapons*", the International Court of Justice did not find "a conventional rule of general scope, nor a customary rule specifically proscribing the threat or use of nuclear weapons *per se* [...]" (§74). According to the Court (§78), there can be nevertheless no doubt as to the applicability to nuclear weapons of the two cardinal principles of humanitarian law:

(a) the principle of the distinction between combatants and non-combatants aimed at the protection of the civilian population and civilian objects; and
(b) the principle of the prohibition to cause unnecessary suffering to combatants which implies that States do not have unlimited freedom of choice of means in the weapons they use (§78).

The Court concluded that:

"methods and means of warfare, which would preclude any distinction between civilian and military targets, or which would result in unnecessary suffering to combatants are prohibited. In view of the unique characteristics of nuclear weapons, to which the Court has referred above, the use of such weapons in fact seems *scarcely reconcilable* with respect for such requirements. Nevertheless, the Court considers that it does *not* have sufficient elements to enable it to conclude with certainty that the use of nuclear weapons would *necessarily be at variance* with the principles and rules of law applicable in armed conflict in any circumstance" (§95) (emphasis added).

B. THE LAW OF GENEVA

The law of Geneva concerns the protection of persons not, or not anymore, directly involved in an armed conflict but who are, or may become, victims of such a conflict. This part of humanitarian international law contains general rules for the protection of wounded and sick military, prisoners of war and civilian population. Certain categories, such as women, children and journalists enjoy specific protection. The initiative for more humanity in warfare was taken by Henry Dunant, a businessman from Geneva, who published in 1862 *Un souvenir de Solferino*. In that book, he gives an eyewitness account of the battle on 28 June 1859 in Solferino (North Italy) where, after a combat between Austrian and French troops, thousands of wounded were left unattended. The public outcry about this situation and the cruelties committed during the Crimean war in 1854–1856 led to the establishment of the Red Cross organisations.

1. THE RED CROSS

In 1863, Henry Dunant and four other Swiss nationals established the *Comité international de secours aux militaires blessés*. In 1880 that Committee was succeeded by the International Committee of the Red Cross (ICRC) (*Comité International de la Croix-Rouge*, CICR). The ICRC, consisting exclusively of (maximum) 25 Swiss citizens, is a *curiosum* in international law. It has private law personality according to the civil law of the Canton of Geneva, but international functions are entrusted to it.

The ICRC gives assistance in the establishment of national Red Cross – and Red Crescent – associations and supports them. The establishment of the first national Red Cross association on 4 February 1864 in Brussels was followed by several others. At present, there is a network of 189 national Red Cross or Red Crescent associations. They are assembled in the International Federation of Red Cross Associations. That Federation assists the national associations with financial expertise and coordinates operations in which various national associations participate. The Red Cross movement operates on three levels: the ICRC, the International Federation and the national associations. Each has its own characteristics and activities but all must respect the seven fundamental principles of the Red Cross: humanity, impartiality, neutrality, independence, voluntary service, unity and universality. In 1901, Henry Dunant received the Nobel Peace Prize for his work.

2.   THE GENEVA CONVENTIONS

Before elaborating on the main normative provisions of the law of Geneva, mention should be made of the evolution of that law in the successive Geneva Conventions of 1864, 1929 and 1949 up to the Additional Protocols of 1977.

a.   The Conventions (1864, 1929, 1949) and the Protocols (1977)

On 22 August 1864, at the end of a first diplomatic conference convened in Geneva by the Swiss Government, a Convention for the amelioration of the condition of the wounded in armies in the field was adopted. After the Second World War two new Conventions were adopted in Geneva on 27 July 1929: a Convention for the amelioration of the condition of the wounded and sick in armies in the field and a Convention relative to the treatment of prisoners of war.

After the Second World War, a diplomatic conference adopted on 12 August 1949 in Geneva four conventions replacing the Geneva Conventions of 1929:

- Convention I for the amelioration of the condition of the wounded and sick in armed forces in the field (GC I);
- Convention II for the amelioration of the wounded, sick and shipwrecked members of armed forces at sea (GC II);
- Convention III relative to the treatment of prisoners (GC III);
- Convention IV relative to the protection of civilian persons in time of war (GC IV).

For the first time, a convention (GC IV) was adopted which provides for the protection of civilian persons in time of war:

> "Persons protected by the Convention are those who, at a given moment and in any manner whatsoever, find themselves, in case of a conflict or Occupying Power of which they are not nationals" (Art. 4, al. 1, GC IV).

The Convention is not applicable to the following persons:

> "Nationals of a State which is not bound by the Convention are not protected by it. Nationals of a neutral State who find themselves in the territory of a belligerent State, and nationals of a co-belligerent State, shall not be regarded as protected persons while the State of which they are nationals has normal diplomatic representation in the State in whose hands they are" (Art. 4, al. 2, GC IV).

After four annual sessions, a "Diplomatic Conference on the Reaffirmation and Development of International Humanitarian Law Applicable in Armed Conflicts" adopted on 8 June 1977 in Geneva two Protocols Additional to the Geneva Conventions of 12 August 1949: Protocol I relating to the protection of victims of *international* armed conflicts" (P I) and Protocol II relating to the protection of victims of *non-international* armed conflicts" (P II). Those Protocols pursue three objectives: to unify the law of The Hague and the law of Geneva, to fill in lacunae in the Geneva Conventions of 1949 and to make international humanitarian law to some extent applicable to non-international armed conflicts.

The Protocols of 1977 do not replace the Geneva Conventions of 1949, but they reaffirm and complement those Conventions. Some important innovations of Protocol I are: a recognition under certain conditions of national liberation wars as international armed conflicts, a clarified definition of a military objective, a better protection of the civilian populations and civilian property and some changes in the definition of the combatant in order to adapt it to the reality of guerrilla wars.

According to Article 44 P I,

"combatants are obliged to distinguish themselves from the civilian population while they are engaged in an attack or in a military operation preparatory to an attack". In situations "where, owing to the nature of the hostilities an armed combatant cannot so distinguish himself, he shall retain his status as combatant, provided that, in such situations, he carries his arms openly:

(a) During each military engagement, and

(b) During such time as he is visible to the adversary while he is engaged in a military deployment preceding the launching of an attack in which he is to participate".

According to Article 96 P I,

"That authority representing a people engaged against a High Contracting Party in an armed conflict [...] may undertake to apply the Conventions and the Protocol in relation to that conflict by means of a unilateral declaration addressed to the depository".

By doing so, the said authority assumes the same rights and obligations as those which have been assumed by a High Contraction Party to the Convention and this Protocol.

The most important innovation of Protocol II is that it makes a greater number of international humanitarian rules applicable to non-international conflicts. The field of application of Protocol II is, however, very limited as several conditions enumerated exhaustively in its Article 1.1 must be fulfilled:

"conflicts which take place in the territory of a High Contracting Party between its armed forces and dissident armed forces of other organized armed groups which, under responsible command, exercise such control over a part of its territory as to enable them to carry out sustained and concerted military operations and to implement this Protocol".

Only States already parties to the Geneva Convention of 1949 can become parties to the Protocols. It is, however, possible to become party to only one of the two Protocols.

b. The Normative Provisions

Each of the four Geneva Conventions of 1949, which have a common structure, protects a specific group. Those persons either *do not* (the sick and the civilians) or *no longer* (the wounded, the shipwrecked members and the prisoners of war) participate in the combat. Some important provisions (Articles 1–3) are common to the four Conventions. Common Article 1 reads as follows:

> "The High Contracting Parties undertake *to respect* and *to ensure respect* for the present Convention in all circumstances" (emphasis added).

This provision is the contrary of the *si omnes* clause of The Hague Conventions.

The most important normative provisions of international humanitarian law may be summarised in seven points:

(1) The Parties to a conflict must at all times distinguish between the civilian population and combatants and between civilian objects and military objectives:

- "In order to ensure respect for and protection of the civilian population and civilian objects, the Parties to the conflict shall at all times distinguish between the civilian population and combatants and between civilian objects and military objectives and accordingly shall direct their operations only against military objectives" (Art. 48 P I).
- "The civilian population and individual civilians shall enjoy general protection against dangers arising from military operations" (Art. 51.1, 1st sentence, P I).
- "Indiscriminate attacks are prohibited. Indiscriminate attacks are [...] of a nature to strike military objectives and civilians or civilian objects without distinction" (Art. 51.4 P I).

However, international humanitarian law also takes into account the "necessities of war": "collateral damage" (civilian casualties caused by the attack of a military objective) is not prohibited when it is not excessive in relation to the expected military advantage:

"An attack [is indiscriminate when] it may be expected to cause incidental loss of civilian life, injury to civilians, damage to civilian objects, or a combination thereof, which would be *excessive* in relation to the concrete and direct military advantage anticipated" (Art. 51.5 (b) P I) (emphasis added).

Moreover, all feasible precautions should be taken, as is set out in detail in Art. 57.2 of Additional Protocol I.

(2) The principle of limited warfare: the right of the Parties to a conflict to choose methods or means of warfare is not unlimited (Art. 35.1 P I). "Superfluous injury" of "unnecessary suffering" should be avoided:

"It is prohibited to employ weapons, projectiles and material and methods of warfare of a nature to cause superfluous injury or unnecessary suffering" (Art. 35.2 P I).

Moreover,

"It is prohibited to employ methods or means of warfare which are intended, or may be expected, to cause widespread, long-term and severe damage to the natural environment" (Art. 35.3 P I).
"Care shall be taken in warfare to protect the natural environment against widespread, long-term and severe damage; [...]" (Art. 55 P I).

In its above-mentioned Advisory Opinion, the International Court of Justice notes further that:

"Articles 35, paragraph 3, and 55 of Additional Protocol I provide additional protection for the environment. Taken together, these provisions embody a general obligation to protect the natural environment against widespread, long-term and severe environmental damage; the prohibition of methods and means of warfare which are intended, or may be expected, to cause such damage; and the prohibition of attacks against the natural environment by way of reprisals. These are powerful constraints for all the States having subscribed to these provisions" (§31).

The Court, referring to Article 22 of the 1907 Hague Regulations, also recalled that:

"the right of belligerents to adopts means of injuring the enemy is not unlimited" (§77).

(3) Persons in the power of a party to the conflict shall be treated humanely in all circumstances (Art. 75.1 P I). Murder, torture of all kinds, corporal punishment and mutilation are and shall remain prohibited at any time and in any place (Art. 75.2 (a) P I).

"No one shall be convicted of an offence except on the basis of individual penal responsibility" (Art. 75.4 (b) P I).

(4) Prisoners of war and civilians in the hands of enemy power are entitled in all circumstances to respect for their person and their honour. They are allowed to send and to receive letters and cards.

- "Prisoners of war must at all times be humanely treated. [...] In particular, no prisoner of war may be subjected to physical mutilation or to medical or scientific experiments of any kind [...]. Likewise, prisoners of war must at all times be protected, particularly against acts of violence or intimidation and against insults and public curiosity. Measures of reprisals against prisoners of war are prohibited" (Art. 13 GC III).
- Every prisoner of war is bound to give only his surname, first names and rank, date of birth, and army, regimental, personal or serial number (Art. 17 GC III).
- A prisoner of war who attempts to escape shall be liable only to a disciplinary punishment (Art. 92 GC III).
- Representatives of the Protecting Powers shall be able to interview the prisoners without witnesses (Art. 126 GC III).
- Collective punishments, measures of intimidation or of terrorism, pillage and reprisals against protected persons are prohibited (Art. 33 GC IV).
- The Occupying Power has the duty of ensuring the food and medical supplies of the population (Art. 55 GC IV).

(5) A person who is *hors de combat* shall not be made the object of attack:

"A person is *hors de combat* if (a) He is in the power of an adverse Party; (b) He clearly expresses an intention to surrender; or (c) He has been rendered unconscious or is otherwise incapacitated by wounds or sickness, and therefore is incapable of defending himself" (Art. 41 P I).

(6) "All persons who do not take a direct part or who have ceased to take part in hostilities, [...] are entitled to respect for their person, honour and convictions and religious practices. They shall in all circumstances be treated humanely, without any adverse distinction" (Art. 4.1 P II).

"The following acts are and hall remain prohibited at any time and in any place whatsoever: (a) Violence to the life, in particular murder as well as cruel treatment; (b) Collective punishments; (c) Taking of hostages; (d) Acts of terrorism; (e) Outrage upon personal dignity; (f) Slavery; (g) Pillage; (h) Threats to commit any of the foregoing acts" (Art. 4.2 P II).

(7) "The wounded and sick shall be collected and cared for" (Art. 3.2 GC I).

"They shall be treated humanely and cared for by the Party to the conflict in whose power they may be, without any adverse distinction founded on sex, race, nationality, religion, political opinions, or any other similar criteria" (Art. 12 GC I).

The protection of the Geneva Conventions I and II extends to the medical units and establishments, the medical personnel, the buildings, material and stores of fixed medical establishments and the medical transports bearing the emblem of the Red Cross or the Red Crescent. Wounded and sick, as well as members of the medical personnel and chaplains, may in no circumstances renounce in part or in entirety the rights secured to them by the Convention (Art. 7 GC I).

ANNEX: AT THE CROSSROADS
OF LAW AND POLITICS

*"Les hommes naissent et demeurent
libres et égaux en droits"*[376]

This farewell lecture[377] at the University of Antwerp gives me the opportunity to give some messages dear to my heart. They are based on my experiences in the field of the protection of human rights and they will be linked to a review of those experiences in the form of a personal testimony. The point of departure is the famous year of 1968.

1.   THE PROHIBITION OF DISCRIMINATION

Indeed, on 23 July 1968, two weeks after my graduation as Doctor of Laws at the State University of Ghent, the European Court of Human Rights delivered its judgment in the *Belgian linguistic* case.[378] After a very busy academic year,[379] during which events dominated by linguistic issues had taken a prominent role, it was for me a particularly intriguing case. The question raised before the Court was: "Do the Belgian linguistic laws violate the prohibition of discrimination guaranteed by the European Convention on Human Rights?" And the question I asked myself was: "Is this a legal question or depends the reply on it from the political persuasion of those having to answer it?"

---

[376]   Article 1 of the French Declaration on Human Rights and the Rights of the Citizen of 26 August 1789.

[377]   [Delivered on 28 September 2007 (published in Dutch: *Op het kruispunt van recht en politiek: een persoonlijke terugblik op 35 jaar mensenrechtenbescherming*, Antwerp, Intersentia, 2007, 42 p.; major excerpts have been published in French: Bossuyt, Marc, "Témoignage d'une présence belge au sein des organes des Nations Unies en matière de droits de l'homme", *Revue trimestrielle des droits de l'homme*, 2008, pp. 329–346. Most publications in Dutch are omitted in the present English version; additional references are reproduced between square brackets)].

[378]   ECtHR, judgment of 23 July 1968 in the case *"relating to certain aspects of the laws on the use of languages in education in Belgium (merits)"*.

[379]   In November 1967, I participated in Washington DC, as leader of the Ghent Student body (*Gents Studentenkorps*), in the "Conference on the Atlantic Community" organised at Georgetown University by (the then 21-year-old) Bill Clinton (*My Life*, London, Hutchinson, 2004, p. 112).

It took me several years (the time to write my PhD thesis)[380] to answer that question. In doing so, I entered the field of the international protection of human rights. Important in that context was my participation in the first two sessions (1971 and 1972) of the International Institute of Human Rights (founded in Strasbourg by Nobel Prize winner René Cassin). In my PhD thesis, defended in Geneva in 1975, I concluded that it is possible to depoliticise that question to a great extent by identifying one by one (*in concreto*) the constitutive elements of the prohibition of discrimination.[381] The constitutive elements of a legally unjustified difference in treatment are: the ground on which that difference is made;[382] the right in which that difference is made;[383] and the relation or the connexion (the relevance)[384] between that ground and that right.[385] At that time, there was not the slightest suspicion that I would ever end up in the Belgian Constitutional Court. That court did not yet exist and it was only in 1989 that it became competent to judge whether Belgian legislative norms violate the prohibition of discrimination.

---

[380] Being a student at the Bologna Centre of the School of Advanced International Studies (SAIS) of the Johns Hopkins University, I was encouraged in the choice of my PhD subject by Paolo Mengozzi, then *Rettore del Collegio dei Fiamminghi* (where I stayed in Bologna) and later Advocate General at the Court of Justice of the European Union in Luxembourg. He put me in contact with Georges Abi-Saab (*Les exceptions préliminaires dans la procédure de la Cour internationale*, Paris, Pedone, 1967, 279 p.), who under the guidance of Paul Guggenheim (both professors at the Graduate School of International Studies of the University of Geneva) collaborated in the defence of Belgium in the *Belgian linguistic* case and became the director of my PhD.

[381] BOSSUYT, Marc, *L'interdiction de la discrimination dans le droit international des droits de l'homme*, Brussels, Bruylant, 1976, p. 128.

[382] *Ibid.*, pp. 41–66.

[383] *Ibid.*, pp. 67–92.

[384] *Ibid.*, pp. 97–126 and in particular pp. 126–127; in the same sense, VIERDAG, Egbert, *The Concept of Discrimination in International Law*, The Hague, M. Nijhoff, 1973, p. 61, speaks about a "sufficient connection".

[385] Non-constitutive elements are: the prejudice (BOSSUYT, *supra* note 1, pp. 124–126) and the goal pursued by the difference in treatment. The latter is considered to be a subjective element weakening the judicial settlement of disputes in the matter (*ibid.*, pp. 36–37; see also KEWENIG, Wilhelm, *Der Grundsatz der Nichtdiskriminierung im Völkerrecht der internationalen Handelsbeziehungen, vol. I (Der Begriff der Diskriminierung)*, Frankfurt am Main, Athenäum, 1972, p. 197). The dissenting opinion in the *Belgian linguistic* case (p. 106) of the Norwegian Judge Wold, who was concerned that it would inevitably bring the Court "into the very middle of the internal political questions of each member State, which it has never been the intention that the Court should deal with" was quoted with approval (BOSSUYT, *supra* note 1, p. 119). This is even more the case with the proportionality principle which plays an ever-increasing role in the case law of the European Court of Human Rights in Strasbourg, of the Court of Justice of the European Union in Luxembourg and of the Belgian Constitutional Court; see MARTENS, Paul, "L'irrésistible ascension du principe de proportionnalité", in *Présence du droit public et des droits de l'homme (Mélanges offerts à Jacques Velu)*, Brussels, Bruylant, 1992, vol. 1, pp. 49–68.

2. THE UNITED NATIONS SECRETARIAT

When defending my PhD thesis at the University of Geneva, I was employed at the Division of Human Rights of the United Nations Office in Geneva. Recruited for the updating of a study on racial discrimination,[386] I collaborated in a study on minorities,[387] and serviced the Working Group on the human rights situation in Chile[388] (the first country-oriented procedure initiated by the Commission on Human Rights)[389] and two sessions of the UN Sub-Commission on Human Rights. In addition, I drafted the draft Rules of Procedure[390] of the new Human Rights Committee.[391] I also felt then the need to make the *travaux préparatoires* of the International Covenant on Civil and Political Rights more accessible.[16] This led to the publication in 1987 of a Guide to those *travaux préparatoires*.[392] Servicing the Working Group on Chile was confrontational because the testimonies of the torture practices[393] of the Pinochet regime did not leave anything to imagination. With particular attention, I followed years later the procedures against Pinochet and the debate in Belgium about the so-called Genocide law.[394] Also in Geneva, I cherished the wish to ever become a member of the UN Sub-Commission or even of the UN Commission on Human Rights, not knowing the important place those organs would take in my future career.

---

[386] See the updated report of the Special Rapporteur Hernán SANTA CRUZ (Chile), *Racial Discrimination*, E.76.XIV.2 (1976).

[387] See the report of the Special Rapporteur Francesco CAPOTORTI (Italy), *Study of the Rights of Persons Belonging to Ethnic, Religious and Linguistic Minorities*, E/CN.4/Sub.2/384/Rev.1 and Add. 1–6, E.78.XIV.1 (1979).

[388] *Cf.* BOSSUYT, Marc, "The United Nations and Civil and Political Rights in Chile", *International and Comparative Law Quarterly*, 1978, pp. 462–471 (also reproduced in LILLICH, Richard & NEWMAN, Frank, *International Human Rights: Problems of Law and Policy*, Boston, 1977, pp. 303–311).

[389] *Cf. supra* note 124, pp. 179–210 (excerpts reproduced in NEWMAN, Frank & WEISSBRODT, David, *International Human Rights: Law, Policy and Process*, Cincinnati, Anderson, 1990, pp. 123–129).

[390] BOSSUYT, Marc, "Le règlement intérieur du Comité des droits de l'homme", *Belgian Review of International Law*, 1978–1979/1, pp. 104–156.

[391] BOSSUYT, Marc, "Notes relating to the International Covenants on Human Rights", *Human Rights Journal*, 1977, pp. 297–309.

[392] BOSSUYT, Marc, *Guide to the 'travaux préparatoires' of the International Covenant on Civil and Political Rights*, Dordrecht, M. Nijhoff, 1987, 851 p.[; see also *id.*, "Les travaux préparatoires du Pacte", in Emmanuel DECAUX (Dir.), *Commentaire du Pacte international sur les droits civils et politiques*, Paris, Economica, 2011, pp. 1–9].

[393] See on torture: BOSSUYT, Marc, "Two new regional conventions with respect to the prohibition of torture", in Franz MATSCHER (Ed.), *The Prohibition of Torture and Freedom of Religion and of Conscience: Comparative Aspects*, Strasbourg, Engel Verlag, 1990, pp. 81–92.

[394] The law of 16 June 1993, amended by the laws of 10 February 1999, 10 April and 23 April 2003 and replaced by the law of 5 August 2003. See also BOSSUYT, Marc, "Immunities" (with Stefan SOTTIAUX), in Dinah SHELTON (Ed.), *The Encyclopedia of genocide and crimes against humanity*, New York, Thomson Gale, 2005, vol. II, pp. 485–488.

3. THE DIRECT APPLICABILITY OF HUMAN RIGHTS TREATY PROVISIONS

Back at the University of Antwerp (then the UIA), I concentrated – as far as my publications were concerned – on the so-called "direct applicability" of provisions of the International Covenant on Civil and Political Rights and of the European Convention on Human Rights,[395] as interpreted by the European Court of Human Rights in its *Marckx* judgment.

A. THE INTERNATIONAL COVENANT ON CIVIL AND POLITICAL RIGHTS

As far as the International Covenants on Human Rights are concerned, the legislative section of the *Conseil d'Etat* had stated in its opinion of 1 December 1976 that:

> "Neither the one nor the other treaty[396] contain a provision directly applicable in Belgium without any domestic law intervention other than the approval by the Legislative Chambers and the publication".[397]

Following an extensive argumentation in favour of the "direct applicability" of the suitable provisions of the International Covenant on Civil and Political Rights, I stated that it was the mission and the responsibility of the *Cour de cassation* to pronounce itself on those issues.[398] After a discussion of that matter at the Board of the Belgian Society of International Law, I was entrusted, in my capacity of Secretary General of that Society, to organise on 8 November 1980 a colloquium at the UIA campus of the University of Antwerp. To the surprise of many, Jacques Velu,[399] then Advocate General at the *Cour de cassation*, also concluded in his report[400] that:

---

[395] See also Bossuyt, Marc, "Judges an Judgements: 25 years of judicial activity of the Court of Strasbourg" (with Yolanda Vanden Bosch), *Belgian Review of International Law*, 1984–1985, pp. 695–712.

[396] Neither the International Covenant on Civil and Political Rights, nor the International Covenant on Economic, Social and Cultural Rights, adopted on 16 December 1966.

[397] *Doc. Parl.*, Chambre, 1977–1979, no. 188, p. 29.

[398] Bossuyt, Marc, "De directe werking van het Internationaal Verdrag inzake burgerrechten en politieke rechten" (The direct applicability of the International Covenant on Civil and Political Rights), *Rechtskundig Weekblad*, 1978–1979, col. 235–248, at col. 242.

[399] Velu, Jacques, *Les effets directs des instruments internationaux en matière de droits de l'homme*, Brussels, Swinnen (Prolegomena 2), 1981, 190 p. (see in particular pp. 33–53).

[400] See Bossuyt, *supra* note 173, pp. 317–343, and in S.B.D.I, *L'effet direct en droit belge des traités internationaux en général et des instruments internationaux relatifs aux droits de l'homme en particulier*, Brussels, Bruylant, 1981, pp. 79–105; *id.*, "The Domestic Judge and the International Covenant on Civil and Political Rights", *Topical Law* (North London), October

"The International Covenant on Civil and Political Rights, once approved, ratified and published, will be an integral part of the legal order applicable in Belgium and will have binding force and, moreover, the majority of its norms will have direct effects enabling their application by the judge, without the need of any legislative intervention, and, in case of a conflict with norms of domestic law, the judge will have to give them priority".[401]

The question was settled on 17 January 1984 – hardly six months after Belgium had become a party to the International Covenants on Human Rights – when the *Cour de cassation* added in its judgment in *Kamer*[402] to a reference to Article 9.2 of the International Covenant on Civil and Political Rights the words "provision having direct effect in Belgium".

B. THE MARCKX JUDGMENT OF THE EUROPEAN COURT OF HUMAN RIGHTS

As far as the European Convention on Human Rights was concerned, the direct applicability of most of its provisions was generally accepted. However, on 16 October 1973, Paula Marckx[403] gave birth to her daughter Alexandra in Wilrijk (not far from the UIA campus, now Campus Drie Eiken). This led on 13 June 1979 to an important judgment of the European Court of Human Rights. Not many were surprised that the Court was of the opinion that discrimination against the (then so-called) "natural children" was prohibited. It was the interpretation of Article 8 (the right to respect of family life) of the European Convention that was criticised. In his dissenting opinion (§15), the British Judge Sir Gerald Fitzmaurice reproached the Court to inflate Article 8 by reading "a whole code of family law" in it. There was great controversy in Belgium about the legal consequences of that judgment.[404]

François Rigaux of the *Université Catholique de Louvain* complained about the "adventurous" character of that judgment.[405] He referred to its "frightening

---

       1981, pp. 1–22; also reproduced in *Summary of the Lectures of the 12th study session of the International Institute of Human Rights*, Strasbourg, July 1981.

401   VELU, *supra* note 399, p. 53 (own translation).

402   *Cf.* WOUTERS, Jan (with the collaboration of Maarten VIDAL), *Cases van internationaal recht* (Cases of International Law), Antwerp, Intersentia, 2005, pp. 457–458. The *Kamer* case concerned the request for extradition of a Dutch national, Rienk Kamer (editor, journalist, art collector and expert in investments), by the United States of America where he was later acquitted.

403   Paula Marckx (1925) is a former model, pilot, journalist and business woman.

404   See LEMMENS, Paul, "De moeizame tenuitvoerlegging van het arrest *Marckx* in de Belgische rechtsorde", *N.J.C.M.-Bulletin,* 1992, pp. 673–683.

405   RIGAUX, François ("La loi condamnée. A propos de l'arrêt du 13 juin 1979 de la Cour européenne des droits de l'homme", *Journal des Tribunaux,* 1979, p. 523, no. 76) stated: "*La jurisprudence de la Cour fait parfois penser aux homélies de certains curés qui, en s'adressant en termes très sévères au petit nombre de fidèles qui leur reste, entendent fustiger tous ceux qui ont cessé de fréquenter l'église*".

---

consequences"[406] that would cause an "imbroglio"[407] and "chaos".[408] In his opinion, provisions of the European Convention on Human Rights could create individual rights, as far their scope is negative, but not when a positive interpretation is given to them.[409] In comments on that judgment, I observed in a footnote that "[b] y neglecting the distinction between classic freedom rights and social rights, the Court runs the risk of overstepping the bounds of its jurisdiction".[410]

Contrary to François Rigaux's opinion that Article 8, as interpreted by the Court in the *Marckx* case, could not have "direct effects", I expressed the opinion that this positive interpretation should also be applied by the domestic judges.[411] As long as a modification of the law of filiation was pending,[412] the case law of the French-speaking courts and tribunals[413] and of the *Cour de cassation*·[414] – contrary to the Dutch speaking courts and tribunals[415] – was not willing to recognise any direct effect to that interpretation. The *Cour de cassation* accepted the direct effects of the *Marckx* judgment only after the *Cour d'arbitrage*[416] (renamed the Constitutional Court in 2007), in its judgment of 4 July 1991, and the Court of Strasbourg, in its judgment in *Vermeire* of 29 November 1991, had stated that the unequal treatment found discriminatory by the Strasbourg Court could not be applied anymore.[417]

4. RUANDA-URUNDI[418]

My teaching assignments at the University of Antwerp (UIA) being at that time still limited, I seized in 1980 the opportunity to teach in Bujumbura at the Law

---

[406]   *Ibid.*, p. 522, no. 70.

[407]   *Ibid.*, no. 69.

[408]   *Ibid.*, p. 523, no. 71.

[409]   *Ibid.*, no. 74 *in fine.*

[410]   Bossuyt, Marc, "L'arrêt Marckx devant la Cour européenne des droits de l'homme", *Belgian Review of International Law*, 1980/1, p. 70, note 78. In addition, it was predicted that the method of interpretation of the Court would allow the counsels of individual applicants to expect pleasant surprises (*ibid.*, p. 79).

[411]   *Ibid.*, pp. 76–78.

[412]   Such a law, adopted on 31 March 1987, entered into force on 6 June 1987.

[413]   See Van Leuven, Nathalie, "Art. 8 en 14 EVRM in de Belgische rechtspraak inzake personen- en familierecht", in Patrick Senaeve & Paul Lemmens (Eds.), *De betekenis van de mensenrechten voor het personen- en familierecht*, Antwerp, Intersentia, 2003, p. 53, note 16.

[414]   Cass. B., 3 October 1983, *Rechtskundig Weekblad*, 1983–84, col. 1972.

[415]   See Puelinckx-Coene, Mieken, *Erfrecht*, Antwerp, Kluwer, 1996, p. 168, note 18. This was particularly the case for notaries (*ibid.*, p. 169, note 20), as recommended in "L'arrêt Marckx …", *supra* note 410, p. 72, note 85.

[416]   In its judgment no. 18/91, the *Cour d'arbitrage* decided that (old) article 756 of the Civil Code, still applicable under article 107 of the law of 31 March 1987, violated the constitutional principle of equality and non-discrimination in as far as it was applicable to legacies from 13 June 1979 on (date of the *Marckx* judgment).

[417]   See Cass. B., 15 May 1992, *Arr. Cass.* 1991–92, p. 862, and Cass. B., 21 October 1993, *Rechtskundig Weekblad*, 1993–94, col. 984.

[418]   [Ruanda-Urundi, since 1885 with Tanganyika a part of German East-Africa, was conquered by Belgium in 1916. Ruanda-Urundi became a mandate under the League of Nations in 1923,

Faculty of the *Université du Burundi*. Many times I returned enthusiastically,[419] last in 2003, when *katchuska* missiles were whistling over our heads. Three times, I also went to teach at the Law Faculty of the *Université Nationale du Rwanda* at Butare (now Huye). The latter Faculty was a project of our own Law Faculty in Antwerp. Some felt so closely connected with that project that an objective evaluation of the political situation in Rwanda and Burundi was lacking. The Board of the Law Faculty decided to distance itself from my missions to Burundi, because teaching there would only reinforce the repression in that country, while in Rwanda – "the paradise on earth" as was generally known – democratisation was progressing steadily. In any case, it has always been my conviction that teaching in a developing country is one of the most useful forms of development cooperation. Doing so contributes to better training of the future leaders of the country that will be rapidly entrusted with great responsibilities. Moreover, trained lawyers are one of the necessary – but not sufficient – conditions to build the rule of law and respect for human rights.[420] In addition, I am convinced that we in Belgium have an historic responsibility to our former overseas territories. That is why I continue to support institutional university cooperation with the University of Burundi, with the National University of Rwanda and with universities in the Democratic Republic of Congo.

Great was my frustration when in 1994 Rwanda became the scene of a gruesome genocide while neither the United Nations – nor any country – tried to intervene.[421] After the killing in a most atrocious manner of ten Belgian paratroopers wearing a blue beret, the Belgian troops only cared for the evacuation of their own compatriots and other foreigners.[422] The Rwandese were left to their tragic fate. During 100 days an average of 10,000 Rwandese each day were killed, mostly with machetes. In his first report to the UN Commission on Human Rights, the Special Rapporteur René Degni

---

a trusteeship territory under the United Nations in 1946 and independent on 1 July 1962 as two separate countries: Rwanda and Burundi].

[419]   [See SAGAERT, Vincent, "De betekenis van Marc Bossuyt voor de Burundese rechtstaat: 'Munshingantahe' als eretitel" (and *post-scriptum* by Stanislas MAKOROKA), in André ALEN, Véronique JOOSTEN, Riet LEYSEN & Willem VERRIJDT (Eds.), *supra* note 348, pp. 543–557; BOSSUYT, Marc, "Perspectives extérieures sur le développement des libertés publiques et des droits de l'homme au Burundi", in Jean-Marie BARAMBONA, Stanislas MAKOROKA, Vincent SAGAERT & Raf VAN RANSBEECK (Dir.), *L'Etat du Burundi après 50 ans d'indépendance*, Brussels, Bruylant, 2015, pp. 327–333].

[420]   See BOSSUYT, Marc, "Human Rights as an element of foreign policy", *Bulletin of Human Rights*, Geneva, United Nations, 1989, pp. 27–33.

[421]   See BOSSUYT, Marc, "Human Rights and Non-Intervention in Domestic Matters", *I.C.J. The Review*, December 1985, pp. 45–52.

[422]   BOSSUYT, Marc, "La Belgique et le génocide rwandais: Responsabilités en droit international", *Journal des Procès*, 20 February 1998, pp. 12–16; see in particular the Chapter on "Disfonctionnements, fautes et responsabilités" (pp. 702–722) in the "Rapport au nom de la Commission d'enquête parlementaire concernant les événements du Rwanda", by Philippe MAHOUX & Guy VERHOFSTADT (6 December 1997), *Doc. Parl.*, Sénat, 1997–98, no. 1–611, 736 p. and 13 annexes.

Segui (Côte d'Ivoire) already unequivocally referred to "genocide" as regards the Tutsi.[423] The Commission of Experts established by the Security Council stressed the "concerted, planned, systematic and methodical way" of the mass exterminations.[424] Out of respect for the hundreds of thousands of victims of such massacres, the term "genocide" may not be used lightly, risking otherwise to trivialise the exceptional gravity of that "crime against mankind"[425] (rather than against "humanity").[426] This is also the tendency of the report of the International Commission of Inquiry on Darfur[427] of 25 January 2005 and of the judgment of 26 February 2007 of the International Court of Justice in the case *concerning the Application of the Convention on the Prevention and Punishment of the Crime of Genocide*.[428]

5. THE UN SUB-COMMISSION ON HUMAN RIGHTS

Being associated since 1981 without interruption with the United Nations human rights activities, I was even more shocked by the failure of the

---

[423] E/CN.4/1995/7 (28 June 1994): "a human tragedy that appears to be well-orchestrated" (§24); "The massacres [...] give the impression of being planned, systematic and atrocious" (§25) and "the term 'genocide' should henceforth be used as regards the Tutsi" (§48). In its resolution of 25 May 1994, the UN Commission on Human Rights had expressed its belief that "genocidal acts may have occurred in Rwanda". In its resolution 925 (1994) of 8 June 1994, the Security Council noted that "acts of genocide have occurred in Rwanda which constitute a crime punishable under international law"; see also BOSSUYT, Marc, *Out of the Ashes: Reparation for Victims of Gross and Systematic Human Rights Violations* (with Koen DE FEYTER, Stefan PARMENTIER & Paul LEMMENS, Eds.), Antwerp, Intersentia, 2005, 522 p.

[424] See the Preliminary Report of the Commission of Independent Experts established in implementation of Security Council resolution 935 (1994), annex to document S/1994/1125 of 29 September 1994, §44: "Overwhelming evidence indicates that the extermination of Tutsi by Hutu had been planned months in advance of its actual execution. The mass exterminations of Tutsis were carried out primarily by Hutu elements in a *concerted, planned, systematic and methodical way* and were motivated out of ethnic hatred. These mass exterminations were clearly 'committed with intent to destroy, in whole or in part, a national, ethnic, racial, or religious group, as such' within the meaning of article II of the Convention on the Prevention and Punishment of the Crime of Genocide of 1948".

[425] ICTY, Appeals Chamber, judgment of 19 April 2004 in the case of *Krstic*, §36: "The crime is horrific in its scope; its perpetrators identify entire human groups for extinction. Those who devise and implement genocide seek to deprive humanity of the manifold richness its nationalities, races, ethnicities and religions provide. This is a crime against *all humankind*, its harm being felt not only by the group targeted for destruction, but by all of humanity".

[426] BOSSUYT & WOUTERS, *supra* note 139, p. 244, note 784.

[427] UN Doc., "Report of the International Commission of Inquiry on Darfur to the United Nations Secretary-General", S/2005/60, 25 January 2005, in particular §§489–522.

[428] ICJ, *Case concerning the Application of the Convention on the Prevention and Punishment of the Crime of Genocide* (Bosnia and Herzegovina v. Serbia and Montenegro), judgment of 26 February 2007, at §§161–179 and 186–189.

international community in Central Africa.[429] Indeed, in 1981, while teaching in Burundi, I was elected a member of the UN Sub-Commission on the Prevention of Discrimination and the Protection of Minorities. That Sub-Commission – the only sub-commission of the United Nations system – has always been the think-tank of the UN Commission on Human Rights. Among the 26 independent experts[430] of the Sub-Commission, there was a great variety in independence and in expertise. Because the Sub-Commission members did not act on behalf of their governments, the Sub-Commission could take many initiatives that have guided the Commission in its activities. The Sub-Commission undertook several studies and collaborated in the drafting of several human rights instruments. The Sub-Commission was also at the origin of the development of the confidential complaint procedure 1503 and the public country-oriented procedures. Personally, I was sent on a mission to Mauritania to examine the situation with respect to slavery.[431] Quite early on, I became the Western member of the Working Group on communications examining human rights complaints, and, at the end of my first membership of the Sub-Commission (1981–1985), I was entrusted with a study on the drafting of a second optional protocol to the International Covenant on Civil and Political Rights, aiming at the abolition of the death penalty.[432]

During that period, the Cold War was raging heavily and that was keenly felt in the Sub-Commission. The image we had of the world was rather simple. The Western experts stood diametrically opposed to the Soviet expert. The Third World experts stood in the middle and we tried to persuade them – with varying success – to support – or at least not to oppose – our endeavours to reinforce the UN human rights mechanisms. Apartheid in South Africa and the situation in the Israeli-occupied territories were easy targets and the human rights violations

---

[429] BOSSUYT, Marc, "La Commission des Nations Unies des droits de l'homme et la crise en Afrique centrale", *Revue de droit international et de droit comparé*, 1998, pp. 103–118; *id.*, "United Nations Human Rights Procedures Regarding Burundi, Rwanda and Zaire (1994–1997)", in Karel WELLENS (Ed.), *International Law: Theory and Practice (Essays in Honour of Eric Suy)*, The Hague, M. Nijhoff, 1998, pp. 493–504.

[430] BOSSUYT, Marc, "Le mandat et le statut des experts indépendants" in Emmanuel DECAUX (Ed.), *Les Nations Unies et les Droits de l'Homme*, Paris, Pedone, 2006, pp. 209–216.

[431] BOSSUYT, Marc, "Report of a United Nations Mission to Mauritania" (13–22 January 1984), E/CN.4/Sub.2/1984/23, 18 p. & 7 annexes; *id.*, "Follow-up Report on the Mission to Mauritania", E/CN.4/Sub.2/1987/27, 18 p. (UN documents can be found on unbisnet.un.org/, also in French, Spanish, Russian, Chinese and Arabic). One year earlier (25 February–4 March 1983) I was sent on a mission to Suriname by the International Commission of Jurists after the killings that had taken place on 8–9 December 1982 (*cf. id.*, "Human Rights in Suriname" (with John GRIFFITHS), *I.C.J.-Review*, July 1983, pp. 52–62).

[432] BOSSUYT, Marc, "Analysis concerning the proposition to elaborate a second optional protocol to the International Covenant on Civil and Political Rights aiming at the abolition of capital punishment", E/CN.4/Sub.2/1987/20, 69 p. The Minister of Foreign Affairs of the Federal Republic of Germany, Hans-Dietrich Genscher, had proposed in 1980 in the UN General Assembly to examine the idea of elaborating such a protocol (*cf.* GA decision 35/437 of 15 December 1980).

by Latin American[433] dictatorships were at the centre of attention. We played a pioneering role with respect to Afghanistan and Iran, and also with respect to East-Timor, but without much effect as far as the latter was concerned. In the confidential complaint procedure, special attention was given to the human rights situation in countries such as Albania, the German Democratic Republic and Turkey.

6. THE UN COMMISSION ON HUMAN RIGHTS

When, after 25 years of absence, Belgium was elected in 1986 a member of the UN Commission on Human Rights,[434] the Minister of Foreign Affairs, Leo Tindemans,[435] asked me to resign from the Sub-Commission and to become the leader of the Belgian delegation to the Commission.[436] It provided me with an extremely interesting experience.[437] There are many misunderstandings about that Commission. It is not a tribunal of independent judges, nor an academy of human rights experts or a club of human rights activists. It is a political organ that consists of States represented by government delegates. It is precisely because the Commission (now the Human Rights Council) is a political organ that it occupies such a unique place in the world. Criticising a political organ for being politicised is completely missing the point. As is the case with the Organisation of the United Nations as a whole, the composition of its main human rights organ reflects the world as it is (and not as we would like it to be). Conscious of the very nature of the Commission, one can better appreciate at its true value the enormous merits that Commission has in having – despite its composition – elaborated a great variety of human rights treaties and established a broad spectrum of special procedures in the field of human rights.

---

[433]   The main countries concerned were Chile, El Salvador, Guatemala, Paraguay and Uruguay and, in the confidential procedure 1503, Argentina. On the latter, see GUEST, Iain, *Behind the Disappearances. Argentina's Dirty War against Human Rights and the United Nations*, Philadelphia, University of Pennsylvania Press, 1990, 624 p.

[434]   BOSSUYT, Marc, "The U.N. Human Rights Commission", in Karel WELLENS (Ed.), *Peace and Security: Justice and Development*, The Hague, Asser Institute, 1986, pp. 77–80; id., "La diversité culturelle au sein de la Commission des droits de l'homme des Nations Unies", in Claudio ZANGHI (Ed.), *I diritti dell'uomo alle soglie del terzo milennio: universalità et dialogo interculturale*, Messina, 2000, pp. 389–402.

[435]   As Prime Minister of Belgium, he had signed on 1 August 1975 the Final Act of Helsinki which became the basis for the Conference (since 1 January 1995 the "Organisation") for Security and Cooperation in Europa. After the changes in Eastern Europe that Organisation has delivered invaluable services in accompanying the dissolution of the Soviet Union and Yugoslavia.

[436]   The delegation in Geneva consisted of Paul Rietjens (from Brussels) and, consecutively, Guy Trouveroy and Machteld Fostier (from New York) and Luc Willemarck, Dominique Struye de Swielande and Marc Van Craen (in Geneva) and, in Brussels, Guy Genot.

[437]   BOSSUYT, Marc, "La Belgique et la Commission des Droits de l'Homme de l'ONU (1986–1991)", in *La Belgique et 50 Ans de Nations Unies*, Brussels, Vif éd., 1995, pp. 47–56.

There was nowhere better than in the Commission on Human Rights to observe the sensational changes[438] happening in international relations. In 1986, the Soviet delegation was still acting in a pure Cold War style. From 1987 on, however, the Soviets undertook frantic efforts to make it clear that the reforms by Mikhail Gorbachev (*perestroika*)[439] were drastic and that the new transparency (*glasnost*) was aimed at making them irreversible. It took quite some time before – in particular the Western – political leaders understood the importance and the seriousness of those reforms. An active delegation of a small country could play an important role. The human rights debate was essentially a confrontation of ideas. Representing a small country was not disadvantageous – quite the contrary. Not being suspected of defending major interests, Belgium could without any inhibition put forward its conception of human rights. Some expertise, familiarity with precedents, advanced knowledge of the Rules of Procedure (very important in a period of confrontation) and most of all the courage to express its convictions were sufficient to exercise real influence. This was foremost the case in the framework of the Group of Western European States and Others (WEOG),[440] which met for six weeks every morning before the plenary meetings of the Commission. The members (12 since 1986) of the European Economic Community met only sporadically and there was no question of a common foreign policy. It was not evident at that time that to be or not be a member of the European Economic Community should influence the human rights positions of those countries to great extent.

7. THE YEAR 1989

The pinnacle was undoubtedly the year of 1989, the year of the bloody crash down of the student revolt on the Celestial Peace place in Beijing (the beginning of June) and the year of the fall of the Berlin Wall (on 9 November), and for me, the year that I chaired[441] the Commission on Human Rights. It was an unforgettable experience. During the session of the Commission, a practice started of visits by high dignitaries (in French "*des visiteurs de marque*") coming to deliver speeches at the Commission. Among them were the Prime Minister of France, Michel Rocard, and the *Segretario di Stato* of the Holy See, Agostino Cardinal Casaroli. A particularly impressive moment was

---

438   On the changes in the World Order (which became progressively a World Disorder), see Bossuyt, Marc, "Nouvel ordre ou nouveau désordre international", *Libéralisme*, 1995, pp. 87–95.

439   Gorbachev, Mikhail, *Perestroika: New Thinking for Our Country and the World*, November 1987, HarperCollins, 255 p.

440   Western European and Others Group.

441   *Cf.* E/CN.4/1989/SR.1, §§53–66.

the speech[442] of the Hungarian Secretary of State (and later Prime Minister) Gyula Horn, who came to complain (in Russian) about the human rights violations in Rumania. He was the man who a few months later[443] – by cutting the Iron Curtain between Hungary and Austria – showed the East Germans with their small Trabant cars the road to the West, which led to the crumbling of the Berlin Wall. At the end of the session, I was asked to appoint a Special Rapporteur for Romania.[444] That this could happen without opposition of the Eastern European countries (including the Soviet Union and the German Democratic Republic) showed the isolation of Nicolae Ceausescu.[445] The session was dominated by the confrontation between the United States of America[446] and Cuba,[447] but we got out of it intact. During that session, it was possible to adopt two new human rights treaties: the Second Optional Protocol to the International Covenant on Civil and Political Rights, aiming at the abolition of the death penalty,[448] which I had drafted as a Special Rapporteur of the Sub-Commission,[449] and the Convention on the Rights of the Child,[450] which would become the human rights treaty with the highest number of States parties.[451]

1991 was my last year in the Commission. Having several times tried unsuccessfully to have Iraq blamed for its human rights violations, I was proud to be able as Representative of Belgium – even if it was only after the invasion of Kuwait – to act as the main sponsor of a resolution requesting the appointment

---

[442] On 27 February 1989.

[443] On 2 May 1989.

[444] The Swiss national Joseph Voyame was appointed Special Rapporteur. Commission resolution 1989/75 was adopted on 9 March 1989 by 21 votes to 7, with 10 abstentions. Five States did not participate in the vote, among them Bulgaria, the German Democratic Republic, the USSR and the Ukraine SSR.

[445] He was killed on 25 December 1989.

[446] The leader of the US Delegation was Armando Valladares, who had been a political prisoner in Cuba from 1960 till 1982. He expressed himself in Spanish only.

[447] NEWMAN & WEISSBRODT, *supra* note 389, pp. 133–135.

[448] This Protocol was adopted by 59 votes to 26, with 48 abstentions, on 15 December 1989 by the UN General Assembly in its resolution 44/128.

[449] BOSSUYT, Marc, "International Protocols aiming at the Abolition of the Death Penalty", *Revue internationale de droit pénal* 1987, pp. 371–385; *id.*, "The Death Penalty in the 'travaux préparatoires' of the International Covenant on civil and political rights", in *Essays on the Concept of a "Right to Live"* (*In memory of Yougindra Khushalani*), Brussels, Bruylant, 1988, pp. 251–265.

[450] BOSSUYT, Marc, "La Convention des Nations Unies sur les droits de l'enfant", *Revue universelle des droits de l'homme*, 1990, pp. 141–144.

[451] [There are 196 States party to the Convention on the Rights of the Child, adopted on 20 November 1989. The most recent States party to that Convention are the State of Palestine (accession on 2 April 2014), South Sudan (accession on 23 January 2015) and Somalia (ratification on 1 October 2015). The only Member State of the United Nations not party to that Convention is the USA.]

of a Special Rapporteur on Iraq.[452] The only country voting against that resolution[453] was Iraq itself.[454] After leaving the Commission, the composition of which was enlarged (with ten Third World countries) from 43 to 53 members, I was again elected a member of the Sub-Commission where I fulfilled two new mandates of four years.

8. THE UN SUB-COMMISSION ON HUMAN RIGHTS (*BIS*)

The adoption of country resolutions by the Sub-Commission was at that time very important.[455] In view of the rather hypocritical criticism that the Sub-Commission was too occupied with countries already dealt with by the Commission ("duplication"), I took in 1996 the initiative[456] to have the Sub-Commission decide that it would no longer take any action "in respect of human rights situations which the Commission was considering under the public procedure for dealing with human rights violations". From then on, only resolutions were adopted concerning such countries as the Democratic People's Republic of Korea, Mexico, the Republic of the Congo (Brazzaville) and Belarus.[457] Convinced of the adverse consequences for human rights of economic sanctions imposed on countries such as Burundi, Cuba and Iraq, I took the initiative in 1997 to submit a resolution requesting attention for this problem.[458] In 1999, The Sub-Commission asked[459] me to draft a working paper on this question. That working paper,[460] presented to the Sub-Commission (since 1999

---

452   Max van der Stoel, former Minister of Foreign Affairs of the Netherlands, became Special Rapporteur.

453   Resolution 1991/74 adopted on 6 March 1991 by 30 votes to 1, with 10 abstentions.

454   The leader of the Delegation of Iraq in 1989 and 1990, Barzan Al-Tikriti (half-brother of President Sadam Hussein), was hanged on 15 January 2007.

455   In 1991–1996, the Sub-Commission adopted country resolutions concerning Albania, Bougainville, Colombia, Haiti, East-Timor, Peru, Somalia, Togo and Chad, besides countries also dealt with by the Commission such as Burundi, El Salvador, Iraq, Iran, the former Yugoslavia (Kosovo) and Rwanda. I took a special interest in the situation in Burundi and in Rwanda. The Sub-Commission adopted resolutions concerning those two countries in 1994, 1995 and 1996.

456   Together with José Augusto Lindgren Alves (Brazil) and Stanislav Chernichenko (Russian Federation): Sub-Commission decision 1996/115 adopted on 29 August 1996 by 19 votes to 3, with 2 abstentions.

457   In 1999 (the year before the Sub-Commission was forbidden to adopt country resolutions), such a resolution was only adopted with respect of the Republic of Congo and declarations of the Chairperson were adopted with respect of Indonesia, Togo, Mexico, Belarus and concerning persons in Nepal alleging to be refugees from Bhutan.

458   Sub-Commission resolution 1997/35 adopted on 28 August 1997 without a vote.

459   Sub-Commission resolution 1999/111 adopted on 26 August 1999 without a vote.

460   BOSSUYT, Marc, "The adverse consequences of economic sanctions on the enjoyment of human rights", E/CN.4/Sub.2/2000/33, Geneva, 2000, 43 p.

finally renamed Sub-Commission on the Promotion and Protection of Human Rights) on 16 August 2000[461] was sharply criticised by the US Government,[462] but it received a wide response.

In 1997 the Sub-Commission asked[463] me to draft a Working Paper on the concept of "affirmative action",[464] bringing me back into the familiar field of discrimination. To speak about "positive discrimination" would be a *contradictio in terminis* because either the difference in treatment is positive and, consequently, not discriminatory, or it is discriminatory and, consequently, not positive. The Working Paper led to a final report[465] presented to the Sub-Commission on 8 August 2002.[466] The most important conclusion of that report is that affirmative action is no exception to the principle of non-discrimination, rather, "it is the principle of non-discrimination that establishes limits to each affirmative action".[467] It would for example not be justifiable

> "to provide special social benefits to persons who do not need them but who belong to a category which formerly was in a disadvantaged position, and to deny the same benefits to persons who do need them but belong to a category which previously enjoyed better conditions in society".[468]

9. THE ELIMINATION OF RACIAL DISCRIMINATION

In the meantime, I had left the Sub-Commission – in application of alternation agreements with the Netherlands[469] – to be elected for four years, from 2000 on,

---

461   E/CN.4/Sub.2/2000/SR.24, §§12–69, and *ibid.*, SR.25, §§37–40, 47–52, 59–60.

462   "That part of the paper relating to sanctions applied to Iraq was incorrect, biased and inflammatory, and risked the Sub-Commission's credibility" (*ibid.*, §37).

463   On a proposal of the UN Committee on the Elimination of Racial Discrimination (Sub-Commission decision 1997/118 adopted on 28 August 1997 without a vote).

464   BOSSUYT, Marc, "L'interdiction de la discrimination et l'action positive", in Kalliopi KOUFA (Ed.), *Might and Right in International Relations,* Thesaurus Acroasium, vol. XXVIII, Athens-Thessaloniki, Sakkoulas Publ., 1999, pp. 325–344; *id.*, "Prohibition of Discrimination and the Concept of Affirmative Action", in *Bringing International Human Rights Law Home*, New York, United Nations, 2000, pp. 93–106; *id.*, "The concept and practice of affirmative action", in Ineke BOEREFIJN ET AL. (Eds.), *Temporary Special Measures. Accelerating* de facto *equality of women under article 4(1) UN Convention on the Elimination of all forms of Discrimination against Women*, Antwerp, Intersentia, 2003, pp. 65–74[; *id.*, "La notion d'action positive", in *La pauvreté: un défi pour les droits de l'homme,* Paris, Pedone, 2009, pp. 97–102].

465   BOSSUYT, Marc, "Working Paper on the concept of affirmative action", E/CN.4/Sub.2/1998/5, Geneva, 1998, 10 p.; *id.*, "The concept and practice of affirmative action", preliminary report, E/CN.4/Sub.2/2000/11, Geneva, 2000, 22 p. & progress report, E/CN.4/Sub.2/2001/15, 2001, Geneva, 2001, 32 p. & final report, E/CN.4/Sub.2/2002/21, Geneva, 2002, 40 p.

466   *Cf.* E/CN.4/Sub.2/2002/SR.13, §§19–41.

467   E/CN.4/Sub.2/2002/21, §113.

468   *Ibid.*, §111.

469   It is appropriate to stress the excellent understanding in this context with Professor Theo van Boven (Maastricht), former Director of the Human Rights Division of the UN Secretariat,

as one of the 18 members of the UN Committee on the Elimination of Racial Discrimination (CERD),[470] the oldest of the UN human rights treaty bodies. The CERD does not cover the very large field of attention of the Sub-Commission and the calendar of its meeting was difficult to reconcile with my other professional obligations. In the framework of the division of labour applicable in the Committee, I was rapporteur for countries such as the Czech Republic, Germany, Italy, Saudi Arabia and Iran. I was concerned by the position taken by some colleagues in the Committee according to whom all minorities,[471] regardless of their origin, might claim to be entitled to allowances of States where they reside. If every person considering himself to belong to a minority were to be treated like the German-speaking minority in Belgium, exciting times would be ahead. The protection of human rights and the protection of minorities cannot be put on the same footing.

Also because of my membership of CERD, I was included at the end of August 2001 in the Belgian delegation to the World Conference against Racism in Durban.[472] In the absence of other Western volunteers, I became *in extremis*, on the proposal of the Belgian Minister of Foreign Affairs, Louis Michel, who chaired the European Union at the World Conference, chairperson of one of the

---

former Member of the Sub-Commission and of the CERD and former Special Rapporteur on Torture.

[470] Bossuyt, Marc, "Les lois belges relatives à la répression du racisme", in Emmanuel Decaux (Ed.), *Le droit face au racisme*, Paris, Pedone (Publ. Fond. Marangopoulos, Série no. 4), 1999, pp. 118–125; Bossuyt, Marc, "Hate Speech" (with Stefan Sottiaux), in Dinah Shelton (Ed.), *supra* note 394, vol. I, pp. 433–436.

[471] Bossuyt, Marc, "La définition du concept de 'minorités' en droit international", in Francis Delpérée & Laslo Trocsanyi (Dir.), *L'unité et la diversité de l'Europe: les droits des minorités (Les exemples belge et hongrois)*, Brussels, Bruylant, 2003, pp. 21–35. See also: *id.*, "Protection internationale des minorités: le cas particulier de la Belgique", in *Droit constitutionnel & minorités*, Académie Internationale de Droit Constitutionnel, Recueil des cours, vol. XII, Tunis, 2003, pp. 15–39; *id.*, "Droits linguistiques: une perspective européenne", *Manitoba Law Journal*, 1983, pp. 663–667; *id.*, "Coexistence in some plural European societies: Belgium, Part I", *The Minority Rights Group Report*, No. 72, 1986, pp. 11–12; *id.*, "Belgium" (with Dick Leonard), in *Minorities and Autonomy in Western Europe* (A Minority Rights Report), London, MRG, 1991, pp. 19–23[; *id.*, "Nationalité et minorités en droit international", in S.F.D.I., *Droit international et nationalité* (Colloque de Poitiers), Paris, Pedone, 2012, pp. 145–163]. On 19–28 September 1993, I was sent on a mission with Frank Horn (Lapland) and Karen Knop (Toronto) by Max van der Stoel, High Commissioner for National Minorities of the Conference for Security and Cooperation in Europe (now the OSCE), to Slovakia and Hungary to report on the situation of their respective minorities.

[472] On the World Conference against Racism, Racial Discrimination, Xenophobia and Related Intolerance, (A.CONF.189/12, Part I–III), see Pits III, Joe W. (Chip), "Anatomy of a World Conference: was Durban worthwhile?", *Human Rights Monitor*, 2001/56, pp. 15–23; Lindgren Alves, José Augusto, "The Durban Conference against Racism and everyone's responsibilities", *Netherlands Quarterly of Human Rights*, 2003, pp. 361–384; see also Bossuyt, Marc, "The Issue of Reparation for Slavery and Colonialism and the Durban World Conference against racism" (with Stef Vandeginste), *Human Rights Law Journal*, 2001, pp. 341–350.

two plenary working groups of that Conference in which 171 States participated. Those were the most hectic eight days of my professional life. Applying endless patience, strict neutrality, all the procedural tricks proper to UN meetings and some occasional humour, several dozens of paragraphs of the final declaration could be adopted by consensus.[473] During the very last hours of the Conference, on Saturday 8 September 2001, it was possible, after a heated procedural debate,[474] to reject the Syrian attempts to have it their way. Contrary to all expectations, a no action motion,[475] originally raised by Brazil and reintroduced by Belgium, could be adopted.[476] Three days later (on 11 September, called 9/11 by the Americans), two planes flew into the Twin Towers in New York. For those who had experienced the animosity at the World Conference between the Organisation of Islamic States and the Western States in general, and the United States and Israel in particular, this action – even if it may seem peculiar – appeared less surprising than to many others. It was the beginning of a period of heavy and grey shadows for the international protection of human rights in particular[477] and for international law in general.

10. THE UN SUB-COMMISSION ON HUMAN RIGHTS (*TER*)

It was a pleasure to return in 2004 to the Sub-Commission. At the end of the session of that year, I was appointed Special Rapporteur for a study[478] on the prohibition of discrimination in the International Covenant on Economic, Social and Cultural Rights. I took advantage of the presentation to the Sub-Commission, on 3 August 2005,[479] of the preliminary report[480] on that issue to clarify some elements of the controversy[481] that was arisen concerning

---

[473] During the three preparatory conferences held in Geneva, only 40% of the paragraphs of the Declaration could be adopted.

[474] "Procedural Confusion at the Main Committee of the Durban Conference against Racism", *Human Rights Monitor*, 2001/56, pp. 12–15.

[475] "A motion requiring that no decision be taken on a proposal shall be put to the vote before a vote is taken on the proposal in question".

[476] The motion was adopted by 51 votes to 37, with 11 abstentions; not less than 70 States – mainly African and Asian States did not participate in the vote.

[477] See SOTTIAUX, Stefan, *Terrorism and the Limitation of Rights. The ECHR and the US Constitution*, Oxford, Hart Publ., 2008, 443 p.

[478] On a proposal of the Committee on Economic, Social and Cultural Rights (Sub-Commission resolution 2004/5 adopted on 9 August 2004 without a vote).

[479] E/CN.4/Sub.2/2005/SR.9, §§60–96.

[480] BOSSUYT, Marc, "Non-discrimination as enshrined in article 2, paragraph 2, of the International Covenant on Economic, Social and Cultural Rights", E/CN.4/Sub.2/2005/19, Geneva, 2005, 18 p.

[481] See VAN HOOF, G.J.H., "The Legal Nature of Economic, Social and Cultural Rights: a Rebuttal of Some Traditional Views", in Philip ALSTON & Katharina TOMASEVSKI, *The Right to Food*, The Hague, M. Nijhoff, 1990, pp. 97–110; MEYER-BISCH, Patrice, *Le corps des*

the legal distinction stressed in my PhD thesis[482] between classic freedom rights and socio-economic rights. That controversy had given rise to some misunderstandings and some incorrect interpretations. I stressed again that both categories of rights are interdependent and equally important and urgent,[483] but that the disputed distinction, which had never been presented as a black/white opposition,[484] is nevertheless an appropriate means to provide a better insight into the legal characteristics of those different categories.[485] Indeed, it makes it possible to better understand which measures are necessary to ensure respectively the respect or the implementation of those categories of rights.[486] The implementation of social rights, indisputably a legal obligation for States parties to social rights treaties, requires further regulation before they can be sanctioned as individual rights by a judge.

The prohibition of discrimination is, without any doubt, as much applicable to social rights as to classic freedom rights, but it has further reaching effects (and possibly important financial implications), because they can provide the legal subjects with new rights not attributed to them neither by a treaty nor by domestic regulations.[487] The question is not whether discrimination is allowed, and even less whether human rights may be violated. The question is whether it is up to national authorities to pronounce themselves on those questions or rather whether – and to what extent – States have accepted to entrust the supervision on this questions to international judicial instances – and in particular to 27 [now 28] European judges in Luxembourg or to 46 [now 47] in Strasbourg.

---

droits de l'homme. L'indivisibilité comme principe d'interprétation et de mise en œuvre des droits de l'homme, Freiburg, Editions universitaires, 1992, 401 p. (in particular pp. 135–155); ARAMBULO, Kitty, Strengthening the Supervision of the International Covenant on Economic, Social and Cultural Rights. Theoretical and Procedural Aspects, Antwerp, Intersentia, 1999, 449 p. (in particular pp. 71–81); MAES, Gunter, De afdwingbaarheid van sociale rechten, Antwerp, Intersentia, 2003, 523 p. (in particular pp. 28–30 and 488–491).

[482]   BOSSUYT, supra note 1, pp. 169–217; see also supra note 51, pp. 783–820; VIERDAG, Egbert, "The Legal Nature of the Rights granted by International Covenant on Economic, Social and Cultural Rights", Netherlands Yearbook of International Law, 1978, pp. 69–105; BOSSUYT, Marc, "International Human Rights Systems: Strengths and Weaknesses", in Kathleen MAHONEY & Paul MAHONEY, Human Rights in the Twenty-first Century, Kluwer, 1990, pp. 52–55.

[483]   Cf. BOSSUYT, supra note 1, pp. 195 en 210.

[484]   Ibid., p. 195, note 10: "Ici, comme d'habitude dans les sciences humaines, il n'y a pas que du noir et du blanc. Il y a du gris, surtout du gris, du gris foncé et du gris clair".

[485]   It is trendy to minimise that distinction or even to ignore it, overlooking the necessity (which is greater for the one category of rights than for the other) of national regulations determining with precision the content, the modalities and the beneficiaries of those (social) rights.

[486]   In particular, entrusting the supervision of the respect of the prohibition of discrimination to international jurisdictions amounts to an abandonment of sovereignty (from the national legislator to the international judge) which is significantly greater than when classic civil rights are concerned.

[487]   This is also the effect of a generalised prohibition of discrimination as contained in the 12th Additional Protocol to the European Convention on Human Rights.

On my return to the Sub-Commission, I found out that, as a consequence of the pernicious reforms of 1999–2000, the Sub-Commission had lost much of its importance and its prestige. The length of the annual session was reduced from four to three weeks but, more importantly, the reform of the confidential complaints procedure[488] and the prohibition on adopting country resolutions[489] had considerably impaired its strength. States were less concerned about initiatives from the Sub-Commission and several non-governmental organisations stayed aloof because there was no longer any chance to obtain one of the country resolutions they were so much looking for. Under pressure from the United States, which were in matters of human rights less and less irreproachable (with their attitude towards the death penalty, their policy in Iraq and the treatment of prisoners in Guantanamo and Abu Ghraib as major downfalls), the Western Group took a more defensive approach, also with respect of the Sub-Commission. Ill-considered proposals to reform the Commission on Human Rights – naively accused of being politicised – led to its transformation into a Human Rights Council.[490]

11. THE UN HUMAN RIGHTS COUNCIL

In that new Human Rights Council, the Western influence has been further reduced.[491] Achievements of the Commission risked falling into decline. Warnings expressed at the Sub-Commission fell on deaf ears.[492] A lack of vision of the Western Group, a lack of familiarity with the historic development of the UN human rights programme, and the lack of readiness for battle of an

---

[488] See resolution 2000/3, adopted on 16 June 2000 by the Economic and Social Council, eliminating the intervention of the Sub-Commission in the confidential complaints procedure, except for the appointment of the five members of the Working Group.

[489] See the annex to decision 2000/109 adopted by the Commission on Human Rights on 26 April 2000, §52: "The Sub-Commission should not adopt country specific resolutions;".

[490] Bossuyt, Marc, "De la 'Commission' au 'Conseil' des droits de l'homme: Un nom pour un autre?" (with Emmanuel Decaux), www.droits-fondamentaux.org, January/December 2005, no. 5; id., "Commission des droits de l'homme: fallait-il réformer?", Le Mensuel de l'Université, June 2006, 3 p.; id., "The New Human Rights Council: A first appraisal", Netherlands Human Rights Quarterly, 2006, pp. 551–555; id., "Le Conseil des droits de l'homme: une réforme douteuse?", in Droit du pouvoir, pouvoir du droit (Mélanges offerts à Jean Salmon), Brussels, Bruylant, 2007, pp. 1184–1192; see also Obembo, Jean-Pascal, "Recreating the Human Rights Commission with only a name change while replicating its main flaw", Journal of International Law of Peace and Armed Conflict, 2007, pp. 91–104.

[491] The States belonging to the Group of Western European States and Others disposed in the Commission of 10 out 53 seats (43 until 1991). They have in the new Human Rights Council only 7 out of 47 seats. The States belonging to the African Group and the Asian Group had 27 of the 53 seats in the Commission and they have 26 of the 46 seats in the Human Rights Council. Where the ratio between the Western Group, on the one hand, and the African and Asian Groups, on the other hand, was 10 versus 20, it is now 7 versus 26.

[492] E/CN.4/Sub.2/2005/SR.5, §§47–53 (28 July 2005).

enlarged European Union, including some Member States blindly following the United States, brought the Sub-Commission itself into the line of fire. The Sub-Commission was criticised for the lack of independence of its members but, as a matter of fact, it was rather the independence of the Sub-Commission with respect to its "parent body" that for many States, including Western States, was considered embarrassing. It was fine to end my UN activities by chairing the Sub-Commission in 2006.[493] It was sad, however, that it was the last session of the Sub-Commission. It was nevertheless a source of pride to be able to address by consensus recommendations to the Human Rights Council on a future advisory mechanism.[494] The Sub-Commission had no any doubt that the assistance of a permanent, collegial and independent advisory mechanism with general competences in the field of human rights would reinforce the credibility of the Human Rights Council.

12. THE PROTECTION OF REFUGEES

Hardly two years after I became the Representative of Belgium in the UN Commission on Human Rights, I was appointed, starting on 4 November 1987, Commissioner General for Refugees and Stateless Persons, on the proposal of the Minister of Justice, Jean Gol. In Belgium, it was the Representative of the UN High Commissioner for Refugees that had been made competent to decide on refugee applications. The High Commissioner having requested to be discharged of this burden, that competence was transferred to a new Belgian independent administrative authority. For nine years, I exercised that role with my heart and soul. Since refugees in the sense of the Geneva Convention relating to the Status of Refugees have left their country owing to a well-founded fear of being persecuted for reasons[495] mentioned in that Convention, the link between the protection of human rights and the protection of refugees is particularly strong.[496]

---

493   *Cf.* A/HRC/Sub.1/58/SR.1, §§27–41.

494   See the annex (A/HRC/2/2, pp. 79–119) to decision 2006/11, adopted without a vote on 25 August 2006 by the UN Sub-Commission on the Promotion and the Protection of Human Rights.

495   "[F]or reasons of race, religion, nationality, membership of a particular social group or political opinion".

496   Bossuyt, Marc, "For an Integrated Refugee Policy Better Adapted to Present Circumstances", in *Refugees in the World: The European Community's Response*, Utrecht, SIM (Special No. 10), 1989, pp. 37–44; *id.*, "Pour une politique intégrée en matière de réfugiés mieux adaptée aux circonstances actuelles", *Revue trimestrielle des droits de l'homme*, 1990, pp. 257–265; *id.*, "La mise en œuvre de la nouvelle loi belge sur les réfugiés", *Belgian Review of International Law*, 1989, pp. 171–187 and in *La Reconnaissance de la qualité de réfugié et l'octroi de l'asile*, Brussels, Bruylant (Collection de droit international, no. 25), 1990, pp. 171–187; *id.*, "Des malentendus au sujet de certains motifs d'irrecevabilité dans la procédure belge de reconnaissance du statut de réfugié", *Documentation-Réfugiés*, 1993, Suppl. no. 208, Corresp.

I was astonished to discover that only a few asylum seekers were refugees in the sense of the Geneva Convention.[497] Despite a large interpretation of the Geneva Convention and a great benefit of the doubt, more than 90% of

pp. 1–4; *id.,* "La conformité à la Convention européenne des droits de l'homme des mesures d'éloignement du territoire de demandeurs d'asile déboutés" (with Isabelle LAMMERANT), *Revue trimestrielle des droits de l'homme,* 1993, pp. 417–430; *id.,* "Les demandeurs d'asile: Protéger les réfugiés tout en réduisant le nombre des étrangers illégaux", *Libéralisme,* 1993, pp. 33–45; *id.,* "L'incompétence du juge civil des référés en matière d'asile", *Journal des procès,* 18 March 1994, pp. 18–24, and 1 April 1994, pp. 12–14; *id.,* "La Cour d'arbitrage: Contrôle d'égalité ou contrôle d'opportunité? A propos de la faculté de suspension par le Conseil d'Etat des décisions confirmatives du Commissaire général aux réfugiés et aux apatrides", *Revue trimestrielle des droits de l'homme,* 1996, pp. 551–571; *id.,* "Le C.G.R.A. et les personnes déplacées de l'ex-Yougoslavie", *Revue du droit des étrangers,* 1995, pp. 467–477; *id.,* "Overview of Council of Europe standards on the status and rights of aliens, including refugees and asylum-seekers", in *Council of Europe, Seminar on the 'Legal Status of Aliens. European Standards and Unification Trends and their possible impact on Central and Eastern European Countries'* (Warsaw, 7–9 November 1995) (DEMO-DROIT CR (96) 1), 17 p. & *Polish Yearbook of International Law,* 1995/1996, pp. 37–48; *id.,* "La procédure d'asile en Belgique: Evolution récente", *Revue du droit des étrangers,* 1996, pp. 563–571, and in Société Française de Droit International, *Droit d'asile et des réfugiés* (Colloque de Caen), 1997, pp. 325–338; *id.,* "La protection internationale des réfugiés à la lumière de la Convention de Genève relative au statut des réfugiés et de la Convention européenne des droits de l'homme", in Vincent CHETAIL (Ed.), *La Convention de Genève du 28 juillet 1951 relative au statut des réfugiés 50 ans après: Bilan et perspectives,* Brussels, Bruylant, 2001, pp. 239–256; *id.,* "Les incidences de la Convention européenne des droits de l'homme sur l'application de la Convention relative au statut des réfugiés", in *Avancées et confins actuels des droits de l'homme aux niveaux international, européen et national* (*Mélanges offerts à Silvio* MARCUS HELMONS), Brussels, Bruylant, 2003, pp. 11–28[; *id., Strasbourg et les demandeurs d'asile: des juges sur un terrain glissant,* Brussels, Bruylant, 2010, 189 p.; *id.,* "Le rôle de la Cour de Strasbourg à l'égard des demandeurs d'asile / Sur les arrêts Čonka et Mubilanzila Mayeka et Kaninki Mutanga c. Belgique, Mamatkoulov et Askarov c. Turquie, N. c. Finlande, Saadi, N. et NA. c. Royaume Uni", *Revue universelle des droits de l'homme,* 2007–2010, pp. 16–34; *id.,* "Judges on thin ice: the European Court on Human Rights and the Treatment of Asylum Seekers", *Inter-American and European Human Rights Journal,* 2010, pp. 3–48; *id.,* "Belgium condemned for inhuman or degrading treatment due to violations by Greece of EU Asylum Law, M.S.S. v. Belgium and Greece,* Grand Chamber, European Court of Human Rights, January 21, 2011", *European Human Rights Law Review,* 2011, pp. 581–596; *id.,* "Strasbourg et les demandeurs d'asile (*M.S.S. c. Belgique et Grèce et Sufi et Elmi c. Royaume-Uni*)", *Annuaire international des droits de l'homme 2011,* Athens, Ant. N. Sakkoulas, 2012, pp. 663–667; *id., "You cannot try them, you cannot detain them and you cannot deport them* (Observations sous *C.E.D.H., M.S. c. Belgique,* 31 janvier 2012)", *Journal des tribunaux,* 2012, pp. 351–355; *id.,* "The Court of Strasbourg acting as an Asylum Court", *European Constitutional Law Review,* 2012, pp. 203–245; *id.,* "The European Court of Human Rights and irreducible life sentences. The *Trabelsi v. Belgium* judgment of 4 September 2014", *Human Rights Law Journal,* 2014, pp. 269–276; *id.,* "*Tarakhel c. Suisse:* La Cour de Strasbourg rend encore plus difficile une Politique commune européenne en matière d'asile", *Revue suisse de droit international et européen,* 2015, pp. 1–6; *id.,* "The European Union Confronted with an Asylum Crisis in the Mediterranean: Reflections on Refugees and Human Rights Issues", *European Journal of Human Rights,* 2015/5, pp. 581–605].

[497]   Premier (118 p.), Deuxième (128 p.), Troisième (93 p.), Quatrième (93 p.), Cinquième (118 p.), Sixième (80 p.), Septième (133 p.), Huitième (p. 174) et Neuvième (p. 217) *Rapport(s) annuel(s) du Commissaire général aux réfugiés et aux apatrides* (années d'activité 1988, 1989, 1990, 1991, 1992, 1993, 1994, 1995, 1996).

the asylum seekers at that time could not – even after the exhaustion of all possibilities of appeal at the Permanent Appeals Commission and at the *Conseil d'Etat* – be recognised as refugees. Moreover, it was often assumed that 90% of them were refugees. This major misunderstanding, entertained by certain lobby groups, makes it very difficult to deal calmly with this issue. I was staggered by the means employed to raise doubts about the integrity of the asylum procedure and to prolong it endlessly or to start new or other procedures over and over again.

Some felt that as a human rights specialist I should have shut my eyes to this or at least that I should have remained silent. Being Commissioner General for Refugees, I did not do so, convinced as I was that the improper use of the asylum procedure was detrimental to the refugees in the sense of the Geneva Convention and causes a lot of problems in our society. To frame it in the words of the Final Report of the Flemish Commission on "Norms and Values":[498]

> "Those forms of illegality and those abuses expose those concerned to practices of exploitation which are not compatible with the exigencies of human dignity, and they cause among the population sentiments of social uneasiness impairing the harmonious living together of persons of different national origin".

Over a period of nine years, nearly 100,000 individual decisions (two thirds of them in the so-called admissibility phase and one third on the merits) were taken by me or by one of my two deputies. During that period, more than 8,000 refugees were recognised.[499] Having faced an ever-increasing backlog for six years, due to a lack of means, it was possible to catch up on that backlog from 1994 on,[500] thanks to measures taken by the newly competent Minister of the Interior, Louis Tobback.[501] At the start of my mandate five staff members with a university degree were put at the disposal of the Commissioner General. When I left that role (at the beginning of 1997), there were already 118 of them.[502] At that time, the number of asylum applications had been stable for nearly three years at an average of about 1,000 a month. The Government being then unwilling to

---

[498] The Final Report of the *"Commissie ter invulling van de cursus maatschappelijke oriëntatie"*, established by the Flemish Minister for Integration Marino Keulen. That Commission, which I chaired, consisted of Ludo Abicht, Abied Alsulaiman, Naima Charkaoui, Marie-Claire Foblets, Rik Torfs and Etienne Vermeersch. Its report was presented to the Flemish Parliament on 4 May 2006 (*Parl. St.*, Vl. Parl., 2005–2006, no. 860–1, 17 p.).

[499] Later, the stay of more foreigners was legalised in one year than refugees were recognised in nine years.

[500] During that year, the Commissioner General for Refugees and Stateless Persons took 20,214 decisions.

[501] And also thanks to a strict application by the Commissioner General of the LIFO principle ("last in, first out").

[502] By comparison, in 2005 the Commissioner General for Refugees and Stateless Persons took, assisted by 329 staff members with a university degree, 20,785 decisions.

settle the status of the Commissioner general in a satisfactory manner, I took advantage of a unique opportunity to join the constitutional court.

13. THE CONSTITUTIONAL COURT

By Royal Decree of 28 January 1997, I was appointed judge in the Belgian *Cour d'arbitrage*.[503] The link with the beginning of this story (the prohibition of discrimination) was back again. Since the enlargement of the competence of that Court,[504] by special law of 6 January 1989, to the principle of equality and non-discrimination, it had fully exploited the possibilities to exercise its supervision trough that principle with reference to all human rights provisions of the Constitution. The enlargement of the competence of the Court, by special law of 9 March 2003, enabling it to exercise its supervision with reference to all rights and freedoms guaranteed in the Constitution, did not change very much. By participating in meetings of the Conference of European Constitutional Courts and of the *Association des Cours constitutionnelles ayant en partage l'usage du français* (ACCPUF), it became clear that the Belgian Constitutional Court (not yet named as such) had more competences than most constitutional courts bearing that name.[505] Since on 7 May 2007 the Constitution renamed the Constitutional Court as such, it may be hoped that it will be possible to have in Belgium and abroad a more precise idea of the role of that Court[506] in our

---

[503] [See ALEN, André, *Treatise of Belgian Constitutional Law*, Deventer, Kluwer, 1992, 288 p.;] VELAERS, Jan, *Van Arbitragehof tot Grondwettelijk Hof*, Antwerp, Maklu, 1990, 578 p.

[504] BOSSUYT, Marc, "The Court of Arbitration" in Kas DEPREZ ET AL. (Eds.), *Multilingualism and Government: Belgium, Luxembourg, Switzerland, former Yugoslavia, South Africa*, Pretoria, Van Schaik, 2000, pp. 62–68.

[505] In cooperation with the University of Liège (with Bob Kabamba and Pierre Verjans), I was associated in 2005 in Kinshasa with the elaboration of the Constitution and in 2007 (together with André Alen, Paul Lemmens and Jean Spreutels) with the preparation of the Constitutional Court of the Democratic Republic of Congo: BOSSUYT, Marc, "République démocratique du Congo: une Constitution pour une Troisième République équilibrée" (with Nicolas BANNEUX, Evariste BOSHAB, Bob KABAMBA and Pierre VERJANS), in *Fédéralisme – Régionalisme 2004-2005, La IIIe République Démocratique du Congo. Un nouveau régionalisme*, pp. 81-101. [I also participated in conferences organised by constitutional courts in Alger (Algeria), Andorra (Principality of Andorra), Bucharest (Romania), Budapest (Hungary), Cape Town (South Africa), Cotonou (Benin), Istanbul (Turkey), Libreville (Gabon), Marrakech (Morocco), Mexico City (Mexico), Moscow and Saint-Petersburg (Russian Federation), Nicosia (Cyprus), Paris (France), Rio de Janeiro (Brazil), Rome (Italy), Sofia (Bulgaria), Vilnius (Lithuania) and Yerevan (Armenia) and visited constitutional courts in Amman (Jordan), Ankara (Turkey), Bujumbura (Burundi), Johannesburg (South Africa), Ljubljana (Slovenia), Maputo (Mozambique), Monaco (Monaco), Rabat (Morocco) and Taipei (Taiwan)].

[506] [On the Belgian Constitutional Court, see POPELIER, Patricia, "The Belgian Constitutional Court: guardian of consensus democracy or venue for deliberation?", in *supra* note 348, pp. 499-514; RIGAUX, Marie-Françoise & RENAULD, Bernadette, *La Cour constitutionnelle*, Brussels, Bruylant, 2008, 330 p.; VERDUSSEN, Marc, *Les douze juges. La légitimité de la Cour*

country. Usually, judges do not discuss the internal functioning of the court to which they belong.[507] This will also not happen now, except by stating that it is an extraordinary privilege to spend the time I have left to be professionally active in presiding[508] over the Court. Thanks to eminent colleagues, it is an intellectual pleasure to look together for answers on the generally highly relevant questions put to the Court.

14. AT THE CROSSROADS OF LAW AND POLITICS

In conclusion, the protection of human rights brings us to the crossroads of law and politics. Both have to play their role and should know their proper place. Human rights policy touches the heart of government policy. In cases of a consistent practice of human rights violations, there are only two ways to put an end to it: either the government concerned should change its policy or the government should be changed. The protection mechanisms of the United Nations exercise pressure to that effect. In the case of flagrant human rights violations, only political pressure works, and the UN human rights organs are such instruments that should not be underestimated.

In order to divorce (so far as is possible) human rights disputes from political considerations, the settlement of such disputes in States functioning under the rule of law is entrusted to judicial organs. In the first instance, this is entrusted to national judicial organs and, in a growing number of countries, to a constitutional court in so far as the supervision of the acts of the legislator is concerned (the most sensitive disputes). States may also enter into treaties by which they undertake the mutual obligation to entrust such supervision to an international court. The competence of such a court is doubly subsidiary:[509] it

---

constitutionnelle, Brussels, Larcier, 2004, 95 p., and Justice constitutionnelle, Brussels, Larcier, 2012, 436 p.]

[507] See nevertheless MARTENS, Paul, "Le métier du juge constitutionnel", in Francis DELPÉRÉE & Pierre FOUCHER (Dir.), La saisine du juge constitutionnel – Aspects de droit comparé, Centre d'études constitutionnelles et administratives, Brussels, Bruylant, 1998, pp. 25–42; ARTS, Alex, "Achter de schermen van het Arbitragehof", in L'Humanisme dans la résolution des conflits. Utopie ou réalité? (Liber amicorum Paul Martens), Brussels, De Boeck & Larcier, 2007, pp. 735–746[; DELRUELLE, Janine, "Il était une fois … une femme à la Cour d'arbitrage", in En hommage à Francis Delpérée: itinéraires d'un constitutionnaliste, Brussels, Bruylant, 2007, pp. 425–435].

[508] [DEBRY, Jean-Thierry, "La désignation et les attributions des présidents de la Cour constitutionnelle", in supra note 62, pp. 49–71; RIGAUX, Marie-Françoise, "Les présidents siègent dans toutes les affaires", ibid., pp. 73–90.]

[509] The European Court of Human Rights was fully aware of its subsidiary role in the Belgian linguistic case. As to the Law, I, B, §10: "the Court […] cannot assume the role of the competent national authorities, for it would thereby lose sight of the subsidiary nature of the international machinery of collective enforcement established by the Convention. The national authorities remain free to choose the measures which they consider appropriate in

has to be exercised after the national legislator (the only body that is politically responsible) and after the national judicial organs have exercised their competence in the matter.

At the international level, it is not unusual for a distinction to be made between, on the one hand, the normative obligations (*in casu* the respect of rights and freedoms) and, on the other hand, the institutional obligations (the recognition of jurisdiction to exercise supervision over the normative obligations).[510] The practice has shown that States are more likely[511] to accept international judicial supervision for civil rights and fundamental freedoms, as is the case in the European Convention on Human Rights,[512] than for social rights.[513] For the latter, each State has to determine, "by all appropriate means, including particularly the adoption of legislative measures" and "to the maximum of its available resources", for which rights (*ratione materiae*) "progressively the full realization" should be achieved for the benefit of which persons (*ratione personae*) and at what moment (*ratione temporis*).[514] Interpreting the rights guaranteed by the European Convention in a manner designed to expand the jurisdiction of the Court of Strasbourg to include social rights[515] is

---

those matters which are governed by the Convention. Review by the Court concerns only the conformity of these measures with the requirements of the Convention".

[510] The International Court of Justice was mindful of that distinction in the case *concerning the Application of the Genocide Convention*, §148: "the Court recalls the fundamental distinction between the existence and binding force of obligations arising under international law and the existence of a court or tribunal with jurisdiction to resolve disputes about compliance with those obligations. The fact that there is not such a court or tribunal does not mean that the obligations do not exist".

[511] Compare the mechanism of supervision of the European Convention on Human Rights 1950) with that of the European Social Charter (1961) and that of the International Covenant on Civil and Political Rights with that of the International Covenant on Economic, Social and Cultural Rights (both of 1966).

[512] See the fifth preambular paragraph of the European Convention on human Rights: "Being resolved [...] to take *the first steps* for the collective enforcement of *certain* rights stated in the Universal Declaration".

[513] [See BOSSUYT, Marc, "Les droits sociaux: une catégorie spécifique de droits de l'homme?", in Leif BERG, Monserrat ENRICH MAS, Peter KEMPEES & Dean SPIELMANN (Eds.), *Cohérence et impact de la jurisprudence de la Cour européenne des droits de l'homme (Liber amicorum Vincent Berger)*, Oisterwijk, Wolf Legal Publ., 2013, pp. 43–58; see also *id.*, "The South African Constitutional Court and socio-economic rights", *supra* note 62, pp. 281–309.]

[514] See Article 2.1 of the International Covenant on Economic, Social and Cultural Rights.

[515] See ECtHR, *Koua Poirrez v. France*, 30 September 2003, in which a claim to allowances for disabled persons was considered to be "property" (see also the admissibility decision of 6 July 2005 in the case of *Stec and Others v. the United Kingdom*, particularly §§5 and 7) and a distinction as to citizens and non-citizens of a State towards whom another State – on the basis of reciprocity – had undertaken to confer to those citizens the same social benefits as to its own citizens (a fundamental principle in the European Union) was considered "discriminatory". The Court now requires that some countries should confer certain social rights to citizens of other countries even if those other countries do not confer those rights neither to their own citizens nor to citizens of other countries residing in their countries. It remains an open question whether the human rights protection is not better served by ensuring that the Court is dealing within a reasonable time with the rights and freedoms

difficult to reconcile with the subsidiary nature of jurisdiction conferred by an international treaty.[516]

Except for those that believe in "divine law", provisions of a treaty are only binding because they result from the common expression of the will of States. Treaties are only binding because – and to the extent that – States have expressed their will to be bound by them. That is the reason why international judicial organs – even more than national judicial organs – should exercise their competence with caution and circumspection, with restraint and reservation.[517] To disregard, willingly and knowingly, the intention of the authors of a treaty amounts to a limitation of State sovereignty[518] without democratic legitimation. Ignoring those intentions is likely to undermine confidence in international law and in its primacy. Arguing that a treaty has a constitutional character[519] should only increase the required vigilance. The legal analysis should not be tributary to political goals, no more so today than 35 years ago, even if they correspond to the spirit of the present time.

15. FAREWELL

Today is my last working day at the University of Antwerp. Teaching there was a real pleasure and the protection of human rights took a prominent place in my classes, in particular in the advanced study of international law and international

---

belonging without any dispute to its jurisdiction rather than by trying continuously to expand that jurisdiction.

[516] [See BOSSUYT, Marc, "Is the European Court of Human Rights on a Slippery Slope?", in Spyridon FLOGAITIS, Tom ZWART & Julie FRASER (Eds.), *The European Court of Human Rights and its Discontents: Turning Criticism into Strength*, Cheltenham, Edward Elgar, 2013, pp. 27–36; *id.*, "Des limites à la juridiction de la Cour de Strasbourg?", *L'homme et le droit: en hommage au Professeur Jean-François Flauss*, Paris, Pedone, 2014, pp. 117–127.]

[517] [See BOSSUYT, *supra* note 54, pp. 321–332; *id.*, "L'extension de la compétence de la Cour de Strasbourg aux prestations sociales: sur l'interprétation de l'article 14 de la Convention combiné avec l'article 1er du Protocole n° 1 dans les affaires *Gaygusuz, Koua Poirrez, Stec et autres, Burden* et *Andrejeva*", *Revue de droit monégasque*, 2009–2010, pp. 91–130.]

[518] The famous dictum of the Permanent Court of International Justice in its judgment of 7 September 1927 in the *Lotus* case ("The rules of law binding upon States [...] emanate from their own free will as expressed in conventions or by usages generally accepted as expressing principles of law [...] Restrictions upon the independence of States cannot therefore be presumed") remains valid for the law of treaties.

[519] See FLAUSS, Jean-François, "La Cour européenne des droits de l'homme est-elle une Cour constitutionnelle?", in Jean-François FLAUSS & Michel DE SALVIA (Eds.), *La Convention européenne des droits de l'homme: Développements récents et nouveaux défis (à la mémoire de Marc-Andre Eissen)* (Droit et Justice no. 19), Brussels, Nemesis, 1997, p. 72: "*la Cour européenne des droits de l'homme a tendance à se comporter comme une juridiction constitutionnelle, à se prendre pour une Cour constitutionnelle et même à affirmer* in corpore *qu'elle est (ou est devenue) une Cour constitutionnelle européenne dans le domaine des droits de l'homme*". He concludes: "*la Cour européenne des droits de l'homme n'est pas [...] vraiment assimilable à une Cour constitutionnelle*" (p. 91).

organisations. Few had expected that over the years so many universities would successfully organise academic programmes on the international protection of human rights. Even in this Faculty, a vacancy in human rights protection could be filled. With the world becoming ever more international, a solid branch of international law can help to compensate for the too often provincial composition of the Antwerp student body. To avoid misunderstanding, it may not be superfluous to add that teaching our own students – even in that field – can and should be in Dutch. I wish success to my successor Koen De Feyter.

And now, some words of thanks. It could be very elaborate, but let's keep it short. Those who are familiar with me know that much of what I have done could not have been possible without the encouragement and the support of my wife Kristien. She accompanied me on my multiple peregrinations. The birthplaces of my children (Kristof in Geneva and Anneleen in Butare) testify to that. There are in our family sometimes divergences of opinion about the "direct applicability" at home of women's rights and children's rights. As far as necessary, I consider it an appropriate moment to offer – in the words of the Durban World Conference[520] – "regrets" or to express "remorse" or to present "apologies".

Special thanks to my assistants (successively Yolanda Vanden Bosch, Koen De Feyter, Fauzaya Talhaoui, Olivier Lins and Veronique Joosten), and to my scientific collaborators[521] and to the staff of the secretariat.[522] Last but not least, because without them there would be no universities, I thank the students of both the Faculty of Law and the Faculty of Political and Social Sciences (International Relations). Their sympathy was heart-warming. It was a pleasure to teach them and also to participate in some of their activities and to meet them after their studies were over. I'll miss them most. That is the end of this farewell lecture. May everything go well with you all.

---

[520] Paragraph 101 of the Durban Declaration: "some have taken the initiative of regretting or expressing remorse or presenting apologies".

[521] Dirk Ceulemans, Filip De Pillecyn, Marleen Maes, Peter Meeus, Nieke Vanavermaete, Stef Vandeginste, Hans Vanhevele and Hilda Wyckers.

[522] In particular Dina Andries, Greet de Ruijter, Ann Janssens, Godelieve Smekens, Peggy Van de Perre, Gaby Van Hecke and Ingrid Van Zele.

BIBLIOGRAPHIES

I. SPECIFIC BIBLIOGRAPHY[523]

A. CASE LAW

1. International Courts: PCIJ – ICJ – ICTY

- PCIJ, *Lotus* case, 7 September 1927
- ICJ, Advisory Opinion on *"the Legality of the Threat or Use of Nuclear Weapons"*, 8 July 1996
- ICJ, *Case concerning Avena and Other Mexican Nationals* (Mexico v. United States of America), 31 March 2003
- ICTY, Appeals Chamber, *Krstic case,* 19 April 2004
- ICJ, *Case concerning the Application of the Convention on the Prevention and Punishment of the Crime of Genocide* (Bosnia and Herzegovina v. Serbia and Montenegro), 26 February 2007

2. European Courts

a. European Court of Human Rights

- Case *"relating to certain aspects of the laws on the use of languages in Belgium"* v. *Belgium* (merits), Pl. Ct., 23 July 1968
- *Golder v. the United Kingdom*, Pl. Ct., 21 February 1975
- *National Union of Belgian Police v. Belgium*, Pl. Ct., 27 October 1975
- *Ireland v. the United Kingdom,* Pl. Ct., 8 January 1978
- *Tyrer v. the United Kingdom*, 25 April 1978
- *Marckx v. Belgium*, Pl. Ct., 13 June 1979
- *Airey v. Ireland*, 9 October 1979
- *Abdulaziz, Cabales and Balkandali v. the United Kingdom*, Pl. Ct., 28 May 1985
- *Shankerath Lukka v. the United Kingdom*, dec. 16 October 1986
- *Soering v. the United Kingdom*, Pl. Ct., 7 July 1989
- *Cruz Varas and Others v. Sweden*, Pl. Ct., 20 March 1991
- *Vilvarajah and Others v. the United Kingdom*, 30 October 1991
- *McCann and Others v. the United Kingdom*, GC, 27 September 1995
- *Gaygusuz v. Austria*, 16 September 1996
- *Chahal v. the United Kingdom*, GC, 15 November 1996

---

[523]   Cases, books and articles referred to in the present book.

- *Ahmed v. Austria*, 17 December 1996
- *D. v. the United Kingdom*, 2 May 1997
- *Denmark v. Turkey*, dec. 8 June 1999; 5 April 2000
- *Selmouni v. France*, GC, 28 July 1999
- *Jabari v. Turkey*, 11 July 2000
- *Maaouia v. France*, GC, 5 October 2000
- *Dougoz v. Greece*, 6 March 2001
- *Čonka and Others v. Belgium*, dec. 13 March 2001; 5 February 2002
- *Cyprus v. Turkey*, GC, 10 May 2001
- *Nivette v. France*, dec. 3 July 2001
- *Einhorn v. France,* dec. 16 October 2001
- *Stanford v. the United Kingdom*, dec. 12 September 2002
- *Wynne v. the United Kingdom*, dec. 22 May 2003
- *Hatton and Others v. the United Kingdom*, 2 October 2001; GC, 8 July 2003
- *Mamatkulov and Askarov v. Turkey*, 6 February 2003; GC, 4 February 2005
- *Koua Poirrez v. France*, 30 September 2003
- *Shamaev and Others v. Georgia and Russia*, 12 April 2005
- *Stec and Others v. the United Kingdom* (merits), GC, 12 April 2006
- *Gebremedhin [Gaberamadhien] v. France*, 26 April 2007
- *Salduz v. Turkey*, 26 April 2007; GC, 27 November 2008
- *Kafkaris v. Cyprus*, GC, 12 February 2008
- *Andrejeva v. Latvia*, GC, 18 February 2009
- *Šilih v. Slovenia*, GC, 9 April 2009
- *Varnava and Others v. Turkey*, GC, 18 September 2009
- *Munoz Diaz v. Spain*, 8 December 2009
- *Oršuš and Others v. Croatia*, GC, 16 March 2010
- *Alajos Kiss v. Hungary*, 20 May 2010
- *Lautsi and Others v. Italy*, 3 November 2009; GC, 18 March 2011
- *Al-Skeini and Others v. the United Kingdom,* GC, 7 July 2011
- *Georgel and Georgeta Stoicescu v. Romania*, 26 July 2011
- *M.S.S. v. Belgium and Greece*, GC, 21 January 2011
- *Di Sarno and Others v. Italy*, 10 January 2012
- *Othman (Abu Qatada) v. the United Kingdom*, 17 January 2012
- *Harkins and Edwards v. the United Kingdom*, 17 January 2012
- *Vinter and Others v. the United Kingdom,* 17 January 2012; GC, 9 July 2013
- *Hirsi Jamaa and Others v. Italy*, GC, 23 February 2012
- *Babar Ahmad and Others v. the United Kingdom*, 10 April 2012
- *I.K. v. Austria*, 28 March 2013
- *I. v. Sweden*, 5 September 2013
- *S.J. v. Belgium*, 27 February 2014; GC, 19 March 2015
- *Öcalan v. Turkey (No. 2)*, 18 March 2014
- *M.G. v. Bulgaria*, 23 March 2014
- *László Magyar v. Hungary*, 20 May 2014
- *Georgia v. Russia*, GC, 3 July 2014
- *M.V. and M.T. v. France*, 4 September 2014
- *Trabelsi v. Belgium*, 4 September 2014

- *Sharifi and Others v. Italy*, 21 October 2014
- *Tarakhel v. Switzerland*, 4 November 2014

b.   Court of Justice of the European Union

- *Kalanke v. Freie Hansestadt Bremen* (C-450/93), 17 October 1995
- *Marschall v. Land NordrheinWestfalen* (C-409/95), 11 November 1997
- *Briheche* (C-319/03), 30 September 2004

3.   *National Courts*

a.   US Supreme Court

- *Foster v. Neilson*, 27 U.S. (2 Pet.) 253, 314–15 (1829)
- *United States v. Percheman*, 32 U.S. (7 Pet.) 51, 88–89 (1833)
- *Plessy v. Ferguson*, 163 U.S. 537 (1896)
- *Korematsu v. United States*, 323 U.S. 214 (1944)
- *Brown v. Board of Education*, 374 U.S. 483 (1954)
- *DeFunis v. Odegaard* case, 416 U.S. 312 (1974)
- *Regents of the University of California v. Bakke*, 438 U.S. 265 (1978)
- *Steelworkers v. Weber*, 443 U.S. 193 (1979)
- *Fullilove v. Klutznick*, 448 U.S. 149 (1980)
- *Firefighters v. Stotts*, 476 U.S. 561 (1984)
- *Sheet Metal Workers v. EEOC (Equal Employment Opportunity Commission)*, 478 U.S. 421 (1986)
- *Wygant v. Jackson Board of Education*, 476 U.S. 267 (1986)
- *United States v. Paradise*, 480 U.S. 149 (1987)
- *Johnson v. Santa Clara County*, 480 U.S. 1442 (1987)
- *City of Richmond v. Croson*, 488 U.S. 469 (1989).
- *Metro Broadcasting Inc. v. FCC (Federal Communications Commission)*, 497 U.S. 547 (1990)
- *Adarand Constructors, Inc. v. Pena*, 515 U.S. 200 (1995)
- *Grutter v. Bollinger*, 539 U.S. 306 (2003)
- *Medellín v. Texas*, 552 U.S. 491 (2008)
- *Fisher v. University of Texas*, 570 U.S. ___ (2016)

b.   Constitutional Court of South Africa

- *Certification of the Republic of South Africa*, CCT 32/96, [1996] *ZACC* 26; 1196 (4) SA 744 (CC); 1196 (10) *BCLR* 1253 (CC) (6 September 1996)
- *Soobramoney v. Minister of Health KwaZulu-Natal*, CCT 32/97, [1997] *ZACC* 17; 1998 (1) SA 765 (CC); 1997 (12) *BCLR* 1696 (27 November 1997)
- *Government of the Republic of South Africa and Others v. Grootboom and Others*, CCT 11/00, [2000] *ZACC* 19; 2001 (1) SA 46 (CC); 2000 (11) *BCLR* 1169 (4 October 2000)

- *Minister of Health and Others v. Treatment Action Campaign and Others (No. 1)*, CCT 9/02, [2002] *ZACC* 16; 2002 (5) SA 703; 2002 (10) *BCLR* 1075 (5 July 2002)
- *Khosa and Others v. Minister of Social Development and Others; Mahlaule and Another v. Minister of Development and Others,* CCT 13/03, CCT 12/03, [2004] *ZACC* 11; 2004 (6) SA 505 (CC); 2004 (3) *BCLR* 569 (CC) (4 March 2004)
- *Occupiers of Olivia Road, Berea Township, and 197 Main Street, Johannesburg v. City of Johannesburg and Others,* CCT 24/07, [2008] *ZACC* 1; 2008 (3) SA 208 (CC); 2008 (5) *BCLR* 475 (CC) (19 February 2008)
- *Lindiwe Mazibuko and Others v. City of Johannesburg and Others,* CCT 39/09, [2009] *ZACC* 28; 2010 (3) *BCLR* 239 (CC); 2010 (4) SA 1 (CC) (8 October 2009)
- *Leon Joseph and Others v. City of Johannesburg and Others,* CCT 43/09, [2009] *ZACC* 30; 2010 (3) *BCLR* 212 (CC); 2010 (4) SA 55 (CC) (9 October 2009)
- *Abahlali Basemjondolo Movement SA and Sibusiso Zikode v. Premier of the Province of KwaZulu-Natal,* CCT 12/09, [2009] *ZACC* 31; 2010 (2) *BCLR* 475 (CC) (14 October 2009)
- *Head of Department: Mpumalanga Department of Education and Another v. Hoërskool Ermelo & Others,* CCT 40/09, [2009] *ZACC* 32; 2010 (2) SA 415 (CC); 2010 (3) *BCLR* 177 (CC) (14 October 2009)
- *City of Johannesburg Metropolitan Municipality v. Blue Moonlight Properties 39 (Pty) Ltd and Another,* (CC) [2011] *ZACC* 33; 2012 (2) *BCLR* 150 (CC); 2012 (2) SA 104 (CC) (1 December 2011)
- *Oppelt v. Head: Health, Department of Health Provincial Administration: Western Cape,* CCT 185/14 [2015] *ZACC* 33; 2016 (1) SA 325 (CC) (14 October 2015)

B.   BOOKS AND ARTICLES

1.   Books

- ABI-SAAB, Georges, *Les exceptions préliminaires dans la procédure de la Cour internationale,* Paris, Pedone, 1967, 279 p.
- ALEN, André, *Treatise of Belgian Constitutional Law,* Deventer, Kluwer, 1992, 288 p.
- ALSTON, Philip & CRAWFORD, James (Eds.), *The Future of UN Human Rights Treaty Monitoring,* Cambridge, Cambridge Univ. Pr., 2000, 563 p.
- ANAGNOSTOU, Dia, & PSYCHOGIOPOULOU, Evangelia, *The European Court of Human Rights and the Rights of Marginalised Individuals and Minorities in National Context,* Leiden, Brill, 2009, 244 p.
- ANDO, Nisuke, *Toward Implementing Universal Human Rights. Festschrift for the Twenty-Fifth Anniversary of the Human Rights Committee,* Leiden, Brill, 2004, 279 p.
- ARAMBULO, Kitty, *Strengthening the Supervision of the International Covenant on Economic, Social and Cultural Rights. Theoretical and Procedural Aspects,* Antwerp, Intersentia, 1999, 449 p.
- AROLD, Nina-Louisa, *The Legal Culture of the European Court of Human Rights,* Leiden, Brill, 2007, 211 p.
- BAIR, Johann, *The International Covenant on Civil and Political Rights and its (first) Optional Protocol: A Short Commentary based on Views, General Comments, and*

Concluding Observations by the Human Rights Committee, New York, P. Lang, 2005, 222 p.

- BAYEFSKY, Anne, *The UN Human Rights Treaty System in the 21st Century*, The Hague, Kluwer Law International, 2000, 1116 p.

- BAYEFSKY, Anne, *How to Complain to the UN Human Rights Treaty System*, The Hague, Kluwer Law International, 2003, 384 p.

- BENELHOCINE, Carole, *The European Social Charter*, Strasbourg, Council of Europe, 2012, 137 p.

- BURGERS, Hermann, *The United Nations Convention Against Torture: A Handbook on the Convention Against Torture and Other Cruel, Inhuman, Or Degrading Treatment or Punishment*, M. Nijhoff, 1988, 271 p.

- CALLEJON, Claire, *La réforme de la Commission des droits de l'homme des Nations Unies: de la Commission au Conseil des droits de l'homme*, Paris, Pedone, 2008, 427 p.

- CHENWI, Lilian, *Towards the Abolition of the Death Penalty in Africa. A Human Rights Perspective*, Pretoria University Law Press, 2007, 239 p.

- CHOLEWINSKI, Ryszard, GUCHTENEIRE, Paul DE & PECOUD, Antoine, *Migration and Human Rights. The United Nations Convention on Migrant Workers' Rights*, Cambridge, Cambridge Univ. Pr., 2009, 474 p.

- CHRISTOFFERSEN, Jonas & MADSEN, Mikael Rask, *The European Court of Human Rights between Law and Politics*, Oxford, Oxford Univ. Press, 2013, 256 p.

- CONTE, Alex & BURCHILL, Richard, *Defining civil and political rights: the jurisprudence of the United Nations Human Rights Committee*, 2nd Ed., Burlington, Ashgate, 2010, 359 p.

- DECAUX, Emmanuel (Dir.), *Le Pacte international relatif aux droits civils et politiques: Commentaire article par article*, Paris, Economica, 2011, 996 p.

- DEMBOUR, Marie-Bénédicte, *Who Believes in Human Rights? Reflections on the European Convention*, Cambridge, Cambridge Univ. Pr., 2006, 340 p.

- DETRICK, Sharon, *A Commentary on the United Nations Convention on the Rights of the Child*, The Hague, M. Nijhoff, 1999, 790 p.

- DEWULF, Steven, *The Signature of Evil: (Re)defining Torture in International Law*, Antwerp, Intersentia, 2011, 617 p.

- DIJK, Pieter VAN, HOOF, Fried VAN, RIJN, Arjen VAN & ZWAAK, Leo (Eds.), *Theory and Practice of the European Convention on Human Rights*, 4th Ed., Antwerp, Intersentia, 2006, 1190 p.

- EGAN, Suzanne, *The UN Human Rights Treaty System: Law and Procedure*, Bloomsbury Professional, 2011, 550 p.

- EVANS, Malcolm & MURRAY, Rachel, *The African Charter on Human and Peoples' Rights. The System in Practice, 1986–2000*, Cambridge, Cambridge Univ. Pr., 2002, 419 p.

- FITZMAURICE, Malgosia & MERKOURIS, Panos, *The Interpretation and Application of the European Convention of Human Rights. Legal and Practical Implications*, Leiden, Brill, 2012, 303 p.

- FREEDMAN, Rosa, *The United Nations Human Rights Council: A Critique and Early Assessment*, Abingdon, Routledge, 2013, 332 p.

- FREEMAN, Marsha, CHINKIN, Christine & RUDOLF, Beate, *The UN Convention on the Elimination of All Forms of Discrimination Against Women: A Commentary*, Oxford, Oxford Univ. Pr., 2012, 292 p.

- FROUVILLE, Olivier DE, *Les procédures thématiques: une contribution efficace des Nations Unies à la protection des droits de l'homme*, Paris, Pedone, 1996, 139 p.
- GORBACHEV, Mikhail, *Perestroika: New Thinking for Our Country and the World*, November 1987, HarperCollins, 255 p.
- GUEST, Iain, *Behind the Disappearances. Argentina's Dirty War against Human Rights and the United Nations*, Philadelphia, University of Pennsylvania Press, 1990, 624 p.
- HAIDER, Dominik, *The Pilot-Judgment Procedure of the European Court of Human Rights*, Leiden, Brill, 2013, 347 p.
- HARRIS, David, O'BOYLE, Michael, BATES, Edward & BUCKLEY, Carla (Eds.), *Harris, O'Boyle and Warbrick, Law of the European Convention on Human Rights*, 3rd Ed., Oxford, Oxford Univ. Pr., 2014, 1080 p.
- HENNEBEL, Ludovic, *La jurisprudence du Comité des droits de l'homme des Nations Unies*, Brussels, Bruylant, 2007, 512 p.
- HENRARD, Kristin & DUNBAR, Robert, *Synergies in minority protection: European and international law perspectives*, Cambridge, Cambridge Univ. Pr., 2008, 462 p.
- HENRARD, Kristin & DUNBAR, Robert, *Synergies in Minority Protection European and International Law Perspectives*, Cambridge, Cambridge Univ. Pr., 2009, 476 p.
- JANIS, Mark, KAY, Richard & BRADLEY, Anthony, *European Human Rights Law: Text and Materials*, 3rd Ed., Oxford, Oxford Univ. Pr., 2008, 1016 p.
- JOSEPH, Sarah & CASTAN, Melissa, *The International Covenant on Civil and Political Rights: Cases, Materials, and Commentary*, 3rd Ed., Oxford, Oxford Univ. Pr., 2013, 1042 p.
- KELLER, Helen & ULFSTEIN, Geir (Eds.), *UN Human Rights Treaty Bodies: Law and Legitimacy*, Cambridge, Cambridge Univ. Pr., 2015, 490 p.
- KELSEN, Hans, *The Pure Theory of Law* (translated into English by Max Knight), Berkeley, University of California Press, 1962, 141 p.
- KEWENIG, Wilhelm, *Der Grundsatz der Nichtdiskriminierung im Völkerrecht der internationalen Handelsbeziehungen, vol. I (Der Begriff der Diskriminierung)*, Frankfurt am Main, Athenäum, 1972, p. 197.
- KOVACS, Peter, *International Law and Minority Protection. Rights of Minorities or Law of Minorities?*, Budapest, Akademiai Kiado, 2000, 174 p.;
- KOVACS, Peter (Ed.), *Minorités et droit international, Studia Iuris Gentium Miskolcinensia*, vol. III, Miskolc, 2008, 117 p.
- KRENC, Frédéric (Dir.), *Les mesures provisoires devant la Cour européenne des droits de l'homme. Un référé à Strasbourg*, Brussels, Larcier, 2011, 152 p.
- KRUCKENBERG, Lena, *The UNreal World of Human Rights: An Ethnography of the UN Committee on the Elimination of Racial Discrimination*, Baden-Baden, Nomos Publ., 2012, 186 p.
- LEMPINEN, Miko, *Challenges facing the system of special procedures of the United Nations Commission on Human Rights*, Turku, Abo Akademi, 2001, 307 p.
- LERNER, Natan, *The U.N. Convention on the Elimination of All Forms of Racial Discrimination*, 2nd Ed., Alphen a/d Rijn, Sijthof & Noordhoff, 1980, 259 p.
- LIEBER, Francis & HARTIGAN, Richard (Ed.), *Lieber's Code and the law of war*, Chicago, Precedent, 1983, 157 p.
- LILLICH, Richard & NEWMAN, Frank, *International Human Rights: Problems of Law and Policy*, Boston, 1979, 1030 p.

- LOUCAIDES, Loukis, *The European Convention on Human Rights. Collected Essays*, Leiden, Brill, 2007, 287 p.
- NMEHIELLE, Vincent O. Orlu, *The African Human Rights System: Its Laws, Practice, and Institutions*, Leiden, M. Nijhoff, 2001, 443 p.
- MAES, Gunter, *De afdwingbaarheid van sociale rechten*, Antwerp, Intersentia, 2003, 523 p.
- MARIE, Jean-Bernard, *La Commission des droits de l'homme de l'O.N.U.*, Paris, Pedone, 1975, 352 p.
- McKEAN, William, *Equality and Discrimination under International Law*, Oxford, Clarendon, 1983, 333 p.
- (Lord) McNAIR (Arnold), *The Law of Treaties*, Oxford, Clarendon, 1986, 800 p.
- McWHIRTHER, Darien, *The End of Affirmative Action: Where do we go from there?*, New York, Birch Lane Press Books, 1996, 188 p.
- MEDINA QUIROGA, Cecilia, *The American Convention on Human Rights: Crucial Rights and their Theory and Practice*, 2nd Ed., Antwerp, Intersentia, 2016, 374 p.
- MERRILS, John Graham, *Judge Sir Gerald Fizmaurice and the Discipline of International Law*, The Hague, Kluwer, 1998, 340 p.
- MEYER-BISCH, Patrice, *Le corps des droits de l'homme. L'indivisibilité comme principe d'interprétation et de mise en œuvre des droits de l'homme*, Freiburg, Editions universitaires, 1992, 401 p.
- MÖLLER, Jacob & ZAYAS, Alfred DE, *United Nations Human Rights Committee Case Law 1977–2008: A Handbook*, Kehl, Engel, 2009, 604 p.
- NEWMAN, Frank & WEISSBRODT, David, *International Human Rights: Law, Policy and Process*, Cincinnati, Anderson, 1990, 812 p.
- NOVAK, Manfred, *UN Covenant on Civil and Political Rights: CCPR commentary*, 2nd Ed., Kehl, Engel, 2005, 947 p.
- NOVAK, Manfred & McARTUR, Elizabeth, *The United Nations Convention against Torture: A Commentary*, Oxford, Oxford Univ. Pr., 2008, 600 p.
- ODELLO, Marco & SEATZU, Francesco, *The UN Committee on Economic, Social and Cultural Rights: The Law, Process and Practice*, Abingdon, Routledge, 2012, 328 p.
- O'FLAHERTY, Michael, *Human Rights and the UN: Practice Before the Treaty Bodies* (Nijhoff Law Specials), 1st Ed., The Hague, Springer, 2002, 256 p.
- OKAFOR, Obiora, *The African Human Rights System, Activist Forces and International Institutions*, Cambridge, Cambridge Univ. Pr., 2007, 352 p.
- PASQUALUCCI, Jo, *The Practice and Procedure of the Inter-American Court of Human Rights*, 2nd Ed., Cambridge, Cambridge Univ. Pr., 2012, 462 p.
- RAINEY, Bernadette, WHITE, Elizabeth & OVEY, Claire (Eds.), *Jacobs, White & Ovey, The European Convention on Human Rights*, 6th Ed., Oxford, Oxford Univ. Pr., 2014, 728 p.
- RAMCHARAN, Bertrand, *The Protection Roles of UN Human Rights Special Procedures*, Leiden, Brill, 2009, 224 p
- RIGAUX, Marie-Françoise & RENAULD, Bernadette, *La Cour constitutionnelle*, Brussels, Bruylant, 2008, 330 p.;
- SACHS, Albie, *The Strange Alchemy of Life and Law*, Oxford, Oxford Univ. Pr., 2009, 306 p.
- S.B.D.I, *L'effet direct en droit belge des traités internationaux en général et des instruments internationaux relatifs aux droits de l'homme en particulier*, Brussels, Bruylant, 1981, p.

- SCHABAS, William, *The Abolition of the Death Penalty in International Law*, 3rd Ed., Cambridge, Cambridge Univ. Pr., 2002, 506 p.
- SCHINDLER, Dietrich & TOMAN, Jiri, *The Laws of Armed Conflicts*, Leiden, M. Nijhoff, 2004, 1493 p.
- TULKENS, Francoise, KOVLER, Anatoly, SPIELMANN, Dean & CARIOLOU, Leto, *Judge Loukis Loucaides An Alternative View on the Jurisprudence of the European Court of Human Rights – A Collection of Separate Opinions (1998–2007)*, Leiden, Brill, 2008, 381 p.
- TYAGI, Yogesh, *The UN Human Rights Committee: Practice and Procedure*, Cambridge, Cambridge Univ. Pr., 2011, 909 p.
- VANDENHOLE, Wouter, *The Procedures Before the UN Human Rights Treaty Bodies: Divergence or Convergence?*, Antwerp, Intersentia, 2004, 331 p.
- VERDOODT, Albert, *Naissance et signification de la Déclaration universelle des droits de l'homme*, Louvain, Nauwelaerts, 1964, 356 p.
- VELAERS, Jan, *Van Arbitragehof tot Grondwettelijk Hof*, Antwerp, Maklu, 1990, 578 p.
- VELU, Jacques, *Les effets directs des instruments internationaux en matière de droits de l'homme*, Brussels, Swinnen (Prolegomena 2), 1981, 190 p.
- VERDUSSEN, Marc, *Les douze juges. La légitimité de la Cour constitutionnelle*, Brussels, Larcier, 2004, 95 p.
- VERDUSSEN, Marc, *Justice constitutionnelle*, Brussels, Larcier, 2012, 436 p.
- VIERDAG, Egbert, *The Concept of Discrimination in International Law*, The Hague, M. Nijhoff, 1973, 176 p.
- WELLER, Marc (Ed.), *Universal Minority Rights: A Commentary on the Jurisprudence of International Courts and Treaty Bodies*, Oxford, Oxford Univ. Pr., 2008, 576 p.
- WOUTERS, Jan (with the collaboration of Maarten VIDAL), *Cases van internationaal recht* (Cases of International Law), Antwerp, Intersentia, 2005, 607 p.
- XENOS, Dimitris, *The Positive Obligations of the State Under the European Convention of Human Rights*, Abingdon, Routledge, 2012, 272 p.
- YOUNG, Kirsten, *The Law and Process of the U.N. Human Rights Committee*, Ardsley, Transnational Publ., 2002, 355 p.

2.   *Articles*

- BILCHITZ, David, "Towards a Reasonable Approach to the Minimum Core: Laying the Foundations for Future Socio-Economic Rights Jurisprudence", *South African Journal on Human Rights*, 2003, pp. 1–26.
- BOLLYKY, Thomas, "R IF C > P + B: A Paradigm for Judicial Remedies of Socio-Economic Rights Violations", *South African Journal on Human Rights*, 2002, pp. 161–200.
- BUERGENTHAL, Thomas, "The Effect of the European Convention on Human Rights on the Internal Law of Member States", *International and Comparative Law Quarterly*, Suppl. 11, 1965, pp. 79–106.
- CHRISTIANSEN, Eric, "Adjudicating non-justiciable rights: socio-economic rights and the South African Constitution", *Columbia Human Rights Law Review*, 2007, pp. 321–353.

– CRAIG, Michael, "The International Covenant on Civil and Political Rights and United States Law: Department of State Proposals for Preserving the Status Quo", *Harvard International Law Journal*, 1978, pp. 845–886.

– DEARBORN, Charles, "The Domestic Legal Effect of Declarations that Treaty Provisions are not Self-Executing", *Texas Law Review*, 1979, pp. 233–251.

– DE BAERE, Geert, "The Court of Luxembourg acting as an asylum court", in André ALEN, Veronique JOOSTEN, Riet LEYSEN & Willem VERRIJDT, *Liberae Cogitationes (Liber amicorum Marc Bossuyt)*, Antwerp, Intersentia, 2013, pp. 107–124.

– DEMBOUR, Marie-Bénédicte, "*Gaygusuz* revisited: The Limits of the European Court of Human Rights' Equality Agenda", *Human Rights Law Review*, 2012, pp. 689–721.

– DE RUE, Maïté, "Les peines de perpétuité réelles sont contraires à la dignité humaine: la Cour européenne des droits de l'homme consacre un droit à l'espoir pour tous les condamnés (Cour eur. dr. h., Gde Ch., *Vinter e.a. c. Royaume-Uni*, 9 juillet 2013)", *Revue trimestrielle des droits de l'homme*, 2014, pp. 667–687.

– DUMONT, Hugues & HACHEZ, Isabelle, "Les obligations positives déduites du droit international des droits de l'homme: dans quelles limites?", in Yves CARTUYVELS ET AL., *Les droits de l'homme, bouclier ou épée du droit pénal?*, Brussels, Bruylant, 2007, pp. 45–73.

– EDELMANN, Bernard, "La Cour européenne des droits de l'homme: une juridiction tyrannique", *Recueil Dalloz*, 2008, pp. 1946–1953.

– FLAUSS, Jean-François, "Actualité de la Convention européenne des droits de l'homme", *Actualité Juridique Droit Administratif*, 2009, pp. 872–884.

– FITZMAURICE, Sir Gerald, "Some Reflections on the European Convention on Human Rights – and on Human Rights", in Rudolf BERNHARDT ET AL., *Völkerrecht als Rechtsordnung Internationale Gerichtsbarkeit Menschenrechte (Festschrift für Hermann Mosler)*, Berlin, Springer Verlag, 1983, pp. 203–219.

– GANNAGE, Léna, "A propos de l'absolutisme' des droits fondamentaux", in *Vers des nouveaux équilibres entre ordres juridiques (Liber amicorum Hélène Gaudemet-Tallon)*, Paris, 2008, pp. 265–284.

– GERARDS, Janneke, "The Prism of Fundamental Rights", *European Constitutional Law Review*, 2012, pp. 173–202.

– HAJIYEV, Khanlar, "The evolution of positive obligations under the European Convention on Human Rights by the European Court of Human Rights", in *The European Convention on Human Rights, a living instrument (Essays in Honour of Christos L. Rozakis)*, Brussels, Bruylant, 2011, pp. 207–218.

– (Baroness) HALE of Richmond (Edna), "Common Law and Convention Law: The Limits to Interpretation", *European Human Rights Law Review*, 2011, pp. 534–543.

– (Lord) HOFFMANN (Leonard), "The Universality of Human Rights" (Judicial Studies Board Annual Lecture, 19 March 2009), *Law Quarterly Review*, 2009, pp. 416–432.

– JOOSTEN, Veronique, "The Arab awakening: a wakeup call for the UN Human Rights Council", in André ALEN ET AL. (Eds.), *Liberae cogitations (Liber amicorum Marc Bossuyt)*, Antwerp, Intersentia, 2013, 974 p., pp. 317–330.

– LEHMANN, Karin, "In Defense of the Constitutional Court: Litigating Socio-Economic Rights and the Myth of the Minimum Core", *American University International Law Review*, 2006, pp. 163–197.

- LEQUETTE, Yves, "Des juges littéralement irresponsables", in Loïc CADIET, Pierre CALLE, Thierry LE BARS & Pierre MAYE (Eds.), *Mélanges dédiés à la mémoire du doyen Jacques Héron*, Paris, LGDJ, 2008, pp. 309–330.
- MAHONEY, Paul, "Reconciling Universality of Human Rights and Local Democracy – the European Experience", in *Grundrechte un Solidarität. Durchsetzung und Verfahren (Festschrift für Renate Jaeger)*, Kehl-am-Rhein, Engel, 2010, pp. 147–161.
- MARTENS, Paul, "L'irrésistible ascension du principe de proportionnalité" in *Présence du droit public et des droits de l'homme (Mélanges offerts à Jacques Velu)*, Brussels, Bruylant, 1992, vol. 1, pp. 49–68.
- MUREINIK, Etienne, "Beyond a Charter of Luxuries: Economic Rights in the Constitution", *South African Journal on Human Rights,* 1992, pp. 464–474.
- MYJER, Egbert, "One *Salduz* a year is enough. 20 Associative Thoughts on Judge Rozakis, Judicial Activism and the *Salduz* Judgment", in *The European Convention on Human Rights, a living instrument (Essays in Honour of Christos L. Rozakis)*, Louvain-La-Neuve, Bruylant, 2011, pp. 419–430.
- OPSAHL, Torkel, "Equality in Human Rights Law with particular reference to Article 26 of the International Covenant on Civil and Political Rights", in *Festschrift für F. Ermacora,* Kehl, 1988, pp. 51–64.
- PIETERSE, Marius, "Coming to Terms with Judicial Enforcement of Socio-Economic Rights", *South African Journal on Human Rights,* 2004, pp. 383–417.
- PIETERSE, Marius, "Resuscitating Socio-Economic Rights: Constitutional Entitlements to Health Care services", *South African Journal on Human Rights,* 2006, pp. 473–502.
- RAMCHARAN, Bertrand, "Equality and Non-Discrimination", in Louis HENKIN, *The International Bill of Human Rights: The Covenant on Civil and Political Rights*, New York, Columbia Univ. Pr., 1981, pp. 246–269.
- RIESENFELD, Stefan, "The Doctrine of Self-Executing Treaties and *U.S. v. Postal*: Win at Any Price?", *American Journal of International Law*, 1980, pp. 892–904.
- RIGAUX, François, "La loi condamnée. À propos de l'arrêt du 13 juin 1979 de la Cour européenne des droits de l'homme", *Journal des Tribunaux,* 1979, pp. 513–524.
- SAGAERT, Vincent, "De betekenis van Marc Bossuyt voor de Burundese rechtstaat: 'Munshingantahe' als eretitel" (and *post-scriptum* by Stanislas MAKOROKA), in André ALEN, Véronique JOOSTEN, Riet LEYSEN & Willem VERRIJDT (Eds.), *Liberae Cogitationes (Liber amicorum Marc Bossuyt)*, Antwerp, Intersentia, 2013, pp. 543–557.
- SCHABAS, William, "Article 6" and "Deuxième Protocole facultatif", in Emmanuel DECAUX (Dir.), *Le Pacte international relatif aux droits civils et politiques: Commentaire article par article*, Paris, Economica, 2011, pp. 179–199 and 869–882.
- SCOTT, Craig & ALSTON, Philip, "Adjudicating Constitutional Priorities in a Transnational Context: a Comment on *Soobramoney*'s Legacy and *Grootboom*'s Promise", *South African Journal on Human Rights*, 2000, pp. 206–268.
- SKELTON, James, "The United States Approach to Ratification of the International Covenants on Human Rights", *Houston Journal of International Law,* 1979, pp. 103–125.
- TOMUSCHAT, Christian, "Equality and Non-Discrimination under the International Covenant on Civil and Political Rights", in I. VON MUENCH (Ed.), *Festschrift für Hans-Jürgen Schlochauer,* Berlin, de Gruyter, 1981, p. 691–716.

- TULKENS, Françoise, "The European Convention on Human Rights between International Law and Constitutional Law", *Dialogue between Judges*, European Court of Human Rights, Council of Europe, 2007, Strasbourg, pp. 9–14.
- VAN HOOF, Fried, "The Legal Nature of Economic, Social and Cultural Rights: a Rebuttal of Some Traditional Views", in Philip ALSTON & Katarina TOMASEVSKI, *The Right to Food*, The Hague, M. Nijhoff, 1990, pp. 97–110.
- VÁZQUEZ, Carlos Manuel, "The Four Doctrines of Self-Executing Treaties", *American Journal of International Law*, 1995, pp. 695–723.
- VÁZQUEZ, Carlos Manuel, "Treaties as Law of the Land: The Supremacy Clause and the Judicial Enforcement of Treaties", *Harvard Law Review*, 2008, pp. 599–695.
- VERHOEVEN, Joe, "La notion d'"applicabilité directe' du droit international", *Belgian Review of International Law*, 1980/2, pp. 243–264.
- VIERDAG, Egbert, "The Legal Nature of the Rights granted by International Covenant on Economic, Social and Cultural Rights", *Netherlands Yearbook of International Law*, 1978, pp. 69–105.
- WATTHÉE, Sandrine, "L'affaire *Trabelsi*, ou comment la lutte contre le terrorisme prend le pas sur le respect par la Belgique de ses obligations conventionnelles", *Journal des Tribunaux*, 2013, pp. 727–729, & 2014, pp. 660–662.
- WEISSBRODT, David, "United States Ratification of the Human Rights Covenants", *Minnesota Law Review*, 1978, pp. 179–222.
- WESSON, Murray, "*Grootboom* and beyond: Reassessing the Socio-Economic Jurisprudence of the South African Constitutional Court", *South African Journal on Human Rights*, 2004, pp. 284–308.

II. GENERAL BIBLIOGRAPHY[524]

- ALFREDSSON, Gudmunder, GRIMHEDEN, Jonas & RAMCHARAN, Bertrand (Eds.), *International Human Rights Monitoring Mechanisms (Essays in Honour of Jakob Th. Möller)*, The Hague, M. Nijhoff, 2009, 725 p.
- ALSTON, Philip & GOODMAN, Ryan, *International Human Rights*, Oxford, Oxford Univ. Pr., 2012, 1632 p.
- ALSTON, Philip & MEGRET, Frederic (Eds.), *The United Nations and Human Rights: A Critical Appraisal*, 2nd Ed., Oxford, Oxford Univ. Pr., 2016, 800 p.
- BADERIN, Mashood & SSENYONJO, Manisuli, *International human rights law: six decades after the UDHR and beyond*, Burlington, Ashgate, 2010, 571 p.
- BAEHR, Peter, *Human Rights Universality in Practice*, Basingstoke, Palgrave Macmillan, 1999, 187 p.
- BANTEKAS, Ilias & OETTE, Lutz, *International Human Rights Law and Practice*, Cambridge, Cambridge Univ. Pr., 2013, 778 p.
- BASSIOUNI, Cherif & SCHABAS, William (Eds.), *New Challenges for the UN Human Rights Machinery: What Future for the UN Treaty Body System and the Human Rights Council Procedures?*, Antwerp, Intersentia, 2011, 480 p.
- BEITZ, Charles, *The Idea of Human Rights*, Oxford, Oxford Univ. Pr., 2011, 256 p.

---

524 Other books in English on international human rights protection.

- Bogusz, Barbara, Cholewinski, Ryszard & Cygan, Adam, *Irregular Migration and Human Rights. Theoretical, European and International Perspectives*, Leiden, Brill, 2004, 486 p.
- Bolla, Peter de, *The Architecture of Concepts. The Historical Formation of Human Rights*, Oxford, Fordham Univ. Pr., 2013, 309 p.
- Buergenthal, Thomas, Shelton, Dinah & Stewart, David, *International Human Rights in a Nutshell*, 4th Ed., St. Paul, Minn., West Publishing Co., 2009, 601 p.
- Chandler, David, *Rethinking human rights: critical approaches to international politics*, New York, Palgrave Macmillan, 2002, 246 p.
- Chowdhury, Azizur & Bhuiyan, Jahid, *An Introduction to International Human Rights Law*, Leiden, Brill, 2010, 316 p.
- Clapham, Andrew, *Human Rights: a very short introduction*, Oxford, Oxford Univ. Pr., 2007, 210 p.
- Condé, Victor, *A Handbook of International Human Rights Terminology*, 2nd Ed., Lincoln, University of Nebraska Press, 2004, 393 p.
- Coomans, Fons & Kamminga, Menno, *Extraterritorial Application of Human Rights Treaties*, Antwerp, Intersentia, 2004, 281 p.
- Costa, Karen da, *The Extraterritorial Application of Selected Human Rights Treaties*, Leiden, Brill, 2012, 334 p.
- Dershowitz, Alan, *Rights from Wrongs. A Secular Theory of the Origins of Rights*, New York, Basic Books, 2009, 273 p.
- Donnelly, Jack, *International Human Rights*, 4th Ed., Boulder, Westview, 2012, 296 p.
- Donnelly, Jack, *Universal Human Rights in Theory and Practice*, 3rd Ed., Ithaca, Cornell Univ. Pr., 2013, 336 p.
- Falcon y Tella, Fernando, *Challenges for Human Rights*, Leiden, Brill, 2007, 152 p.
- Falk, Richard, *Human Rights Horizons. The Pursuit of Justice in a Globalizing World*, Hoboken, Taylor and Francis, 2013, 269 p.
- Flood, Patrick, *The Effectiveness of UN Human Rights Institutions*, Westport, Greenwood Publ. Gr., 1998, 183 p.
- Forsythe, David, *Human Rights in International Relations*, 3rd Ed., Cambridge, Cambridge Univ. Pr., 2012, 370 p.
- Francioni, Francesco & Scheinin, Martin, *Cultural Human Rights*, Leiden, Brill, 2008, 380 p.
- Freeman, Michael, *Human Rights: An Interdisciplinary Approach*, 2nd Ed., Cambridge, Polity, 2011, 224 p.
- Gearty, Conor & Douzinas, Costas (Eds.), *The Cambridge Companion to Human Rights Law*, Cambridge, Cambridge Univ. Pr., 2012, 369 p.
- Goodale, Mark (Ed.), *Human Rights at the Crossroads*, Oxford, Oxford Univ. Pr., 2013, 256 p.
- Goodhart, Michael, *Human Rights: Politics and Practice*, 2nd Ed., Oxford, Oxford Univ. Pr., 2013, 512 p.
- Gould, Carol, *Globalizing democracy and human rights*, Cambridge, Cambridge Univ. Pr., 2004, 276 p.
- Griffin, James, *On Human Rights*, Oxford, Oxford Univ. Pr., 2008, 354 p.
- Hafner-Burton, Emilie, *Making Human Rights a Reality*, Princeton, Princeton Univ. Pr., 2013, 296 p.

- Halme-Tuomisaari, Miia, *Human Rights in Action: Learning Expert Knowledge*, Leiden, Brill Nijhoff, 2010, 280 p.
- Harvey, Colin, *Human Rights Law in Perspective. Humanity and Legality*, Oxford, Hart Publ., 2016, 220 p.
- Henkin, Louis, Neuman, Gerald, Orentlicher, Diane & Leebron, David (Eds.), *Human Rights. Documentary Supplement*, New York, Foundation Press, 2001, 1099 p.
- Henkin, Louis, Cleveland, Sarah, Helfer, Laurence, Neuman, Gerald & Orentlicher, Diane, *Human Rights*, 2nd Ed., New York, Foundation Press, 2009, 1682 p.
- Heyns, Christof & Viljoen, Frans, *The impact of the United Nations human rights treaties on the domestic level*, The Hague, KLI, 2002, 648 p.
- Hunt, Lynn, *Inventing Human Rights: A History*, Norton & Cy, 2008, 272 p.
- Jayawickrama, Nihal, *The judicial application of human rights law: national, regional and international jurisprudence*, Cambridge, Cambridge Univ. Pr., 2002, 965 p.
- Kälin, Walter & Künzli, Jörg, *The Law of International Human Rights Protection*, Oxford, Oxford Univ. Pr., 2009, 592 p.
- Kamminga, Menno & Scheinin, Martin (Eds.), *The Impact of Human Rights Law on General International Law*, Oxford, Oxford Univ. Pr., 2009, 288 p.
- Kao, Grace, *Grounding Human Rights in a Pluralist World*, Washington, Georgetown Univ. Pr., 2011, 248 p.
- Kende, Mark, *Constitutional Rights in Two Worlds South Africa and the United States*, Cambridge, Cambridge Univ. Pr., 2009, 337 p.
- Krause, Catarina & Scheinin, Martin (Eds.), *International Protection of Human Rights: A Textbook*, 2nd Ed., Turku, Åbo Akademy University, 2012, 677 p.
- Langford, Malcolm, Vandenhole, Wouter, Scheinin, Martin & Genugten, Willem van (Eds.), *Global Justice, State Duties: The Extraterritorial Scope of Economic, Social, and Cultural Rights in International Law*, Cambridge, Cambridge Univ. Pr., 2014, 498 p.
- Lutz-Bachmann, Matthias & Nascimento, Amos, *Human rights, human dignity, and cosmopolitan ideals: essays on critical theory and human rights*, Burlington, Ashgate, 2014, 175 p.
- Meister, Robert, *After Evil: A Politics of Human Rights*, New York, Columbia Univ. Pr., 2011, 545 p.
- Mertus, Julie, *The United Nations and Human Rights: A Guide for a New Era*, Abingdon, Routledge, 2010, 224 p.
- Moeckli, Daniel, Shah, Sageeta, Sivakumaran, Sandesh & Harris, David, *International Human Rights Law*, Oxford, Oxford Univ. Pr., 2nd Ed., 2013, 630 p.
- Normand, Roger & Zaidi, Sarah, *Human Rights at the UN: The Political History of Universal Justice*, Indiana Univ. Pr., 2008, 528 p.
- O'Flaherty, Michael (Ed.), *The Human Rights Field Operation: Law, Theory and Practice*, Burlington, Ashgate, 2007, 467 p.
- O'Flaherty, Michael & Ulrich, George (Ed.), *The Professional Identity of the Human Rights Field Officer*, Burlington, Ashgate, 2010, 486 p.
- O'Flaherty, Michael, Kedzia, Zdzislaw, Müller, Amrei & Ulrich, George, *Human Rights Diplomacy: Contemporary Perspectives*, Leiden, Brill Nijhoff, 2011, 320 p.
- Piccone, Ted, *Catalysts for Change: How the U.N.'s Independent Experts Promote Human Rights*, Brookings Institution Press, 2012, 225 p.

- RAMCHARAN, Bertrand, *The Security Council and the protection of human rights,* The Hague, Kluwer, 2002, 378 p.
- RAMCHARAN, Bertrand, *Judicial Protection of Economic, Social and Cultural Rights. Cases and Materials,* Leiden, Brill, 2005, 574 p.
- SCHUTTER, Olivier DE, *International Human Rights Law, Cases, Materials, Commentary,* 2nd Ed., Cambridge, Cambridge Univ. Pr., 2014, 1124 p.
- SHAWKI, Noha & COX, Michaelene, *Negotiating sovereignty and human rights: actors and issues in contemporary human rights politics,* Burlington, Ashgate, 2009, 238 p.
- SHELTON, Dinah, *Remedies in International Human Rights Law,* 2nd Ed., Oxford, Oxford Univ. Pr., 2005, 502 p.
- SHELTON, Dinah, *Advanced Introduction to Human Rights Law,* Cheltenham, Edward Elgar, 2014, 333 p.
- SHELTON, Dinah (Ed.), *The Oxford Handbook of International Human Rights Law,* Oxford, Oxford Univ. Pr., 2015, 1088 p.
- SIMMONS, Beth, *Mobilizing for Human Rights: International Law in Domestic Politics,* Cambridge, Cambridge Univ. Pr., 2009, 472 p.
- SMITH, Rhona, *Textbook on International Human Rights,* 5th Ed., Oxford, Oxford Univ. Pr., 2012, 440 p.
- STEINER, Henry, ALSTON, Philip & GOODMAN, Ryan (Eds.), *International Human Rights in Context: Law, Politics, Morals (Texts and Materials),* 3rd Ed., Oxford, Oxford Univ. Pr., 2007, 1492 p.
- TOFAN, Claudia, *International Human Rights Law, Documents,* Oisterwijk, Wolf Legal Publ., 2010, vol. 1, 934 p. & vol. 2, 844 p.
- TOMUSCHAT, Christian, *Human rights: between idealism and realism,* 3rd Ed., Oxford, Oxford Univ. Pr., 2014, 464p
- VINCENT, Andrew, *The Politics of Human Rights,* Oxford, Oxford Univ. Pr., 2010, 272 p.
- VINCENT, Raymond (Ed.), *Foreign Policy and Human Rights: Issues and Responses,* Cambridge, Cambridge, Cambridge Univ. Pr., 2009, 296 p.
- WEISSBRODT, David, Ní AOLÁIN, Fionnuala, FITZPATRICK, Joan & NEWMAN, Frank, *International Human Rights: Law, Policy, and Process,* 4th Ed., New York, LexisNexis, 2009, 1332 p.
- ZIEMELE, Ineta, *Expanding the Horizons of Human Rights Law. New Authors, New Themes,* Leiden, Brill, 2005, 301 p.

III. PUBLICATIONS OF MARC BOSSUYT

A. IN ENGLISH

- "Notes relating to the International Covenants on Human Rights", *Human Rights Journal,* 1977, pp. 297–309.
- "Case concerning Sovereignty over Certain Frontier Land" in Krystyna MAREK, *Digest of the Decisions of the International Court,* vol. II: International Court of Justice, The Hague, M. Nijhoff, vol. 1, 1977, pp. 606–621.
- "The United Nations and Civil and Political Rights in Chile", *International and Comparative Law Quarterly,* 1978, pp. 462–471; also reproduced in Richard

LILLICH & Frank NEWMAN, *International Human Rights: Problems of Law and Policy*, Boston, Little, Brown and Company, 1977, pp. 303–311.

- "The direct applicability of international instruments on human rights", *Belgian Review of International Law*, 1980/2, pp. 317–343; also published in S.B.D.I./B.G.I.R., *L'effet direct en droit belge des traités internationaux en général et des instruments internationaux relatifs aux droits de l'homme en particulier*, Brussels, Bruylant, 1981, pp. 79–105.

- "The Domestic Judge and the International Covenant on Civil and Political Rights", *Topical Law* (North London), October 1981, pp. 1–22; also published in *Summary of the Lectures of the twelfth study session of the International Institute of Human Rights*, Strasbourg, July 1981.

- "Human Rights in Suriname" (with John GRIFFITHS), *I.C.J. The Review*, July 1983, pp. 52–62.

- "Report of a United Nations Mission to Mauritania", E/CN.4/Sub.2/1984/23, Geneva, 1984, 18 p. & 7 annexes.

- "Judges and Judgements: 25 years of judicial activity of the Court of Strasbourg" (with Yolanda VANDEN BOSCH), *Belgian Review of International Law*, 1984–1985, pp. 695–712.

- "The Development of Special Procedures of the United Nations Commission on Human Rights", *Human Rights Law Journal*, 1985, pp. 179–210; also published in *Collection of Lectures, 16th study session*, International Institute of Human Rights, Strasbourg, 1–26 July 1985, 33 p.; excerpts reproduced in Frank NEWMAN & David WEISSBRODT, *International Human Rights: Law, Policy and Process*, Cincinnati, Anderson, 1990, pp. 123-129.

- "Human Rights and Non-Intervention in Domestic Matters", *I.C.J. The Review*, December 1985, pp. 45–52.

- "Coexistence in some plural European societies: Belgium, Part I", *The Minority Rights Group Report* No. 72, 1986, pp. 11–12.

- "The U.N. Human Rights Commission", in Karel WELLENS (Ed.), *Peace and Security: Justice and Development*, The Hague, Instituut Asser, 1986, pp. 77–80.

- "The Principle of Equality in Article 26 of the International Covenant on Civil and Political Rights", Armand DE MESTRAL ET AL. (Eds.), *The Limitation of Human Rights in Comparative Constitutional Law*, Québec, Y. Blais, 1986, pp. 269–288.

- *Guide to the 'travaux préparatoires' of the International Covenant on Civil and Political Rights*, Dordrecht, M. Nijhoff, 1987, 851 p.

- "Analysis concerning the proposition to elaborate a second optional protocol to the International Covenant on Civil and Political Rights aiming at the abolition of capital punishment", E/CN.4/Sub.2/1987/20, Geneva, 1987, 69 p.

- "Follow-up Report on the Mission to Mauritania", E/CN.4/Sub.2/1987/27, Geneva, 18 p.

- "International Protocols aiming at the Abolition of the Death Penalty", *Revue internationale de droit pénal* 1987, pp. 371–385.

- "The Death Penalty in the 'travaux préparatoires' of the International Covenant on Civil and Political Rights", in *Essays on the Concept of a "Right to Live"* (*in memory of Yougindra Khushalani*), Brussels, Bruylant, 1988, pp. 251–265.

- "Human Rights as an element of foreign policy", *Bulletin of Human Rights*, Geneva, United Nations, 1989, pp. 27–33.

- "For an Integrated Refugee Policy Better Adapted to Present Circumstances", in *Refugees in the World: The European Community's Response*, Utrecht, SIM (Special no. 10), 1989, pp. 37–44.
- "Two new regional conventions with respect to the prohibition of torture", in Franz MATSCHER (Ed.), *The Prohibition of Torture and Freedom of Religion and of Conscience: Comparative Aspects*, Strasbourg, Engel Verlag, 1990, pp. 81–92.
- "Belgium" (with Dick LEONARD), in *Minorities and Autonomy in Western Europe* (A Minority Rights Report), London, MRG, 1991, pp. 19–23.
- "International Human Rights Systems: Strengths and Weaknesses" in Kathleen MAHONEY & Paul MAHONEY, *Human Rights in the Twenty-first Century: A Global Challenge*, Dordrecht, M. Nijhoff, 1992, pp. 47–55.
- "Overview of Council of Europe standards on the status and rights of aliens, including refugees and asylum-seekers", in Council of Europe, *Seminar on the 'Legal Status of Aliens; European Standards and Unification Trends and their possible impact on Central and Eastern European Countries'* (Warsaw 7–9 November 1995) (DEMO-DROIT CR (96) 1), 17 p., & *Polish Yearbook of International Law*, 1995/1996, pp. 37–48.
- "The International Covenant on Civil and Political Rights and Children", in Eugeen VERHELLEN, *Collected Papers presented at the first International Interdisciplinary Course on Children's Rights*, Ghent, 1996, pp. 303–308.
- "United Nations Human Rights Procedures Regarding Burundi, Rwanda and Zaire (1994–1997)" in Karel WELLENS (Ed.), *International Law: Theory and Practice (Essays in Honour of Eric Suy)*, The Hague, M. Nijhoff, 1998, pp. 493–504.
- "Prohibition of Discrimination and the Concept of Affirmative Action" in *Bringing International Human Rights Law Home*, New York, United Nations, 2000, pp. 93–106.
- "Working Paper on the concept of affirmative action", E/CN.4/Sub.2/1998/5, Geneva, 1998, 10 p.
- "The concept and practice of affirmative action", preliminary report, E/CN.4/Sub.2/2000/11, Geneva, 2000, 22 p. & progress report, E/CN.4/Sub.2/2001/15, 2001, Geneva, 2001, 32 p. & final report, E/CN.4/Sub.2/2002/21, Geneva, 2002, 40 p.
- "The adverse consequences of economic sanctions on the enjoyment of human rights", E/CN.4/Sub.2/2000/33, Geneva, 2000, 43 p.
- "The Court of Arbitration", in Kas DEPREZ ET AL. (Eds.), *Multilingualism and Government: Belgium, Luxembourg, Switzerland, former Yugoslavia, South Africa*, Pretoria, Van Schaik, 2000, pp. 62–68.
- "Procedural Confusion at the Main Committee of the Durban Conference against Racism", *Human Rights Monitor*, 2001/56, pp. 12–15.
- "The Issue of Reparation for Slavery and Colonialism and the Durban World Conference against racism" (with Stef VANDEGINSTE), *Human Rights Law Journal*, 2001, pp. 341–350.
- "The concept and practice of affirmative action", in Ineke BOEREFIJN ET AL. (Eds.), *Temporary Special Measures. Accelerating de facto equality of women under article 4(1) UN Convention on the Elimination of all forms of Discrimination against Women*, Antwerp, Intersentia, 2003, pp. 65–74.
- *Out of the Ashes: Reparation for Victims of Gross and Systematic Human Rights Violation* (with Koen DE FEYTER, Stefan PARMENTIER & Paul LEMMENS (Eds.)), Antwerp, Intersentia, 2005, 522 p.

- "Hate Speech" & "Immunities" (with Stefan SOTTIAUX), in Dinah SHELTON (Ed.), *The Encyclopedia of genocide and crimes against humanity*, New York, Thomson Gale, 2005, vol. I, pp. 433–436 & vol. II, pp. 485–488.
- "Non-discrimination as enshrined in article 2, paragraph 2, of the International Covenant on Economic, Social and Cultural Rights", E/CN.4/Sub.2/2005/19, Geneva, 2005, 18 p.
- "The New Human Rights Council: A first appraisal", *Netherlands Human Rights Quarterly*, 2006, pp. 551–555.
- "Should the Strasbourg Court exercise more self-restraint? On the extension of the jurisdiction of the European Court of Human Rights to social security regulations, *Human Rights Law Journal*, 2007, pp. 321–332.
- "The South African Constitutional Court and socio-economic rights", in *Liège, Strasbourg, Bruxelles: parcours des droits de l'homme (Liber amicorum Michel Melchior)*, Limal, Anthemis, 2010, pp. 281–309.
- "Judges on thin ice: the European Court on Human Rights and the Treatment of Asylum Seekers", *Inter-American and European Human Rights Journal*, 2010, pp. 3–48.
- "Belgium condemned for inhuman or degrading treatment due to violations by Greece of EU Asylum Law, *M.S.S. v. Belgium and Greece*, Grand Chamber, European Court of Human Rights, January 21, 2011", *European Human Rights Law Review*, 2011, pp. 581–596.
- "The Full Effect of EU Law and of Constitutional Review in Belgium and France after the *Melki* Judgment" (with Willem VERRIJDT), *European Constitutional Law Review*, 2011, pp. 581–596.
- "The Court of Strasbourg acting as an Asylum Court", *European Constitutional Law Review*, 2012, pp. 203–245.
- "EU law and constitutionally and internationally protected rights", *Classical and Modern Trends in Constitutional Review*, Sofia, Feneya, 2012, pp. 53–61.
- "Is the European Court of Human Rights on a Slippery Slope?", in Spyridon FLOGAITIS, Tom ZWART, & Julie FRASER (Eds.), *The European Court of Human Rights and its Discontents: Turning Criticism into Strength*, 2013, Cheltenham, Edward Elgar, pp. 27–36.
- "The Independence of the Judiciary in Belgium", in Simon SHETREET (Ed.), *The Culture of Independence*, Leiden, 2014, pp. 139–145.
- "The Effectiveness of Human Rights Protection in a Multi-layered European System", in Mexican Supreme Court of Justice, *Dialogue between judges, Writings of the Summit of Presidents of Constitutional, Regional and Supreme Courts*, Mexico, 2014, pp. 23–32.
- "Social rights: a specific category of human rights?", in Mexican Supreme Court of Justice, *Dialogue between judges, Writings of the Summit of Presidents of Constitutional, Regional and Supreme Courts*, Mexico, 2014, pp. 359–373.
- "The European Court of Human Rights and irreducible life sentences", The *Trabelsi v. Belgium* judgment of 4 September 2014, *Human Rights Law Journal*, 2014, pp. 269–276.
- "Law and politics", in Jan DE BRUYNE, Isabelle VAN HIEL & Michaël DE POTTER DE TEN BROECK (Eds.), *Policy within and through law*, Antwerp, Maklu, 2015, pp. 35–44.

- "Judicial Activism in Strasbourg", in Karel WELLENS (Ed.), *International Law in Silver Perspective, Challenges Ahead*, Leiden, Brill/Nijhoff, 2015, pp. 31–56.
- "The European Union Confronted with an Asylum Crisis in the Mediterranean: Reflections on Refugees and Human Rights Issues", *European Journal of Human Rights*, 2015/5, pp. 581–605.
- "Categorical Rights and Vulnerable Groups: Moving Away from the Universal Human Being", *The George Washington International Law Review*, 2016, pp. 101–127.

B.   IN FRENCH

- "La distinction juridique entre les droits civils et politiques et les droits économiques, sociaux et culturels", *Revue des droits de l'homme*, 1975, pp. 783–820.
- *L'interdiction de la discrimination dans le droit international des droits de l'homme* (avec préface de Georges ABI-SAAB), Bruxelles, Bruylant, 1976, 262 p.
- "Le règlement intérieur du Comité des droits de l'homme", *Revue belge de droit international,* 1978–1979/1, pp. 104–156.
- "L'arrêt *Marckx* devant la Cour européenne des droits de l'homme", *Revue belge de droit international,* 1980/1, pp. 53–81.
- "La coopération internationale au développement", *Revue juridique du Rwanda,* 1981/3, pp. 307–314.
- "Droits linguistiques: une perspective européenne", *Manitoba Law Journal,* 1983, pp. 663–667.
- "Rapport d'une mission des Nations Unies en Mauritanie", E/CN.4/Sub.2/1984/23, Genève, 1984, 18 p. & Annexes 1–7.
- *Cours de droit international public et de droit des organisations internationales,* "Université Nationale du Rwanda" (Butare) et "Université du Burundi" (Bujumbura), 1984, 179 p.
- "La pratique en droit international public", in Travaux de l'Association Henri Capitant, *Le rôle de la pratique dans la formation du droit,* Paris, Economica, 1985, pp. 553–558.
- "Les affaires belges devant les organes de la Convention européenne des droits de l'homme", *Revue belge de droit international,* 1986/1, pp. 208–220.
- "Analyse de la proposition d'élaborer un deuxième protocole facultatif se rapportant au Pacte international relatif aux droits civils et politiques visant à l'abolition de la peine capitale", E/CN.4/Sub.2/1987/20, Genève, 1987, 73 p.
- "Rapport de suivi final sur la mission en Mauritanie", E/CN.4/Sub.2/1987/27, Genève, 1987, 18 p.
- "Les droits de l'homme en tant qu'élément de politique étrangère", *Bulletin des droits de l'homme,* Genève, Nations Unies, 1989, pp. 29–35.
- "La mise en œuvre de la nouvelle loi belge sur les réfugiés", *Revue belge de droit international,* 1989, pp. 171–187 & in *La Reconnaissance de la qualité de réfugié et l'octroi de l'asile,* Bruxelles, Bruylant (Collection de droit international, n° 25), 1990, pp. 171–187.
- "La Convention des Nations Unies sur les droits de l'enfant", *Revue universelle des droits de l'homme,* 1990, pp. 141–144.

- "Pour une politique intégrée en matière de réfugiés mieux adaptée aux circonstances actuelles", *Revue trimestrielle des droits de l'homme*, 1990, pp. 257–265.
- "Des malentendus au sujet de certains motifs d'irrecevabilité dans la procédure belge de reconnaissance du statut de réfugié", *Documentation-Réfugiés* 1993, Suppl. n° 208, Corresp. pp. 1–4.
- "La conformité à la Convention européenne des droits de l'homme des mesures d'éloignement du territoire de demandeurs d'asile déboutés" (avec Isabelle LAMMERANT), *Revue trimestrielle des droits de l'homme*, 1993, pp. 417–430.
- "Les demandeurs d'asile: Protéger les réfugiés tout en réduisant le nombre des étrangers illégaux", *Libéralisme*, 1993, pp. 33–45.
- "Les travaux du Comité des Nations Unies des droits de l'homme", *Revue trimestrielle des droits de l'homme*, 1994, pp. 31–40.
- "L'incompétence du juge civil des référés en matière d'asile", *Journal des procès*, 18 mars 1994, 18–24, et 1 avril 1994, pp. 12–14.
- "Article 14" in Louis-Edmond PETTITI, Emmanuel DECAUX & Pierre-Henri IMBERT (Eds.), *La Convention européenne des droits de l'homme, commentaire article par article*, Paris, Economica, 1995, pp. 475–488.
- "Nouvel ordre ou nouveau désordre international", *Libéralisme*, 1995, pp. 87–95.
- "La Belgique et la Commission des Droits de l'Homme de l'ONU (1986–1991)", in *La Belgique et 50 Ans de Nations Unies*, Bruxelles, Vif éd., 1995, pp. 47–56.
- "Le C.G.R.A. et les personnes déplacées de l'ex-Yougoslavie", *Revue du droit des étrangers*, 1995, pp. 467–477.
- "La Cour d'arbitrage: Contrôle d'égalité ou contrôle d'opportunité? A propos de la faculté de suspension par le Conseil d'Etat des décisions confirmatives du Commissaire général aux réfugiés et aux apatrides", *Revue trimestrielle des droits de l'homme*, 1996, pp. 551–571.
- Premier (118 p.), Deuxième (128 p.), Troisième (93 p.), Quatrième (93 p.), Cinquième (118 p.), Sixième (80 p.), Septième (133 p.), Huitième (p. 174) et Neuvième (p. 217) *Rapport(s) annuel(s) du Commissaire général aux réfugiés et aux apatrides* (années d'activité 1988, 1989, 1990, 1991, 1992, 1993, 1994, 1995, 1996).
- "La procédure d'asile en Belgique: Evolution récente", *Revue du droit des étrangers*, 1996, pp. 563–571 & in Société Française de Droit International, *Droit d'asile et des réfugiés* (Colloque de Caen), 1997, pp. 325–338.
- "La Commission des Nations Unies des droits de l'homme et la crise en Afrique centrale", *Revue de droit international comparé*, 1998, pp. 103–118.
- "La Belgique et le génocide rwandais: Responsabilités en droit international", *Journal des procès*, 20 février 1998, pp. 12–16.
- "Chronique de jurisprudence du Comité des droits de l'homme" (1993–1997), *Revue trimestrielle des droits de l'homme*, 1998, pp. 507–570.
- "Document de travail sur la notion d'action positive", E/CN.4/Sub.2/1998/5, Genève, 1998, 10 p.
- "L'interdiction de la discrimination et l'action positive", in Kalliopi KOUFA, *Might and Right in International Relations,* Thesaurus Acroasium, vol. XXVIII, Athènes-Thessaloniki, Sakkoulas Publ., 1999, pp. 325–344.
- "Les lois belges relatives à la répression du racisme", in Emmanuel DECAUX, *Le droit face au racisme*, Paris, Pedone (Publ. Fond. Marangopoulos, Série n° 4), 1999, pp. 118–125.

- "Préface" in Benjamin MULAMBA MBUYI, *Introduction à l'étude des sources modernes du droit international public*, Québec, Université Laval, 1999, pp. 13–17.
- "Conséquences néfastes des sanctions économiques sur la jouissance des droits de l'homme", E/CN.4/Sub.2/2000/33, Genève, 2000, 43 p.
- "La diversité culturelle au sein de la Commission des droits de l'homme des Nations Unies", in Claudio ZANGHI (Ed.), *I diritti dell'uomo alle soglie del terzo milennio: universalità et dialogo interculturale*, Messina, 2000, pp. 389–402.
- "La notion et la pratique de l'action positive", rapport préliminaire, E/CN.4/Sub.2/2000/11, Genève, 2000, 22 p., rapport de progrès, E/CN.4/Sub.2/2001/15, Genève, 2001, 32 p., & rapport final, E/CN.4/Sub.2/2002/ 21, Genève, 2002, 41 p.
- "La protection internationale des réfugiés à la lumière de la Convention de Genève relative au statut des réfugiés et de la Convention européenne des droits de l'homme", in Vincent CHETAIL (Ed.), *La Convention de Genève du 28 juillet 1951 relative au statut des réfugiés 50 ans après: Bilan et perspectives*, Bruxelles, Bruylant, 2001, pp. 239–256.
- "Protection internationale des minorités: le cas particulier de la Belgique", in *Droit constitutionnel & minorités*, Académie Internationale de Droit Constitutionnel, Recueil des cours, vol. XII, Tunis, 2003, pp. 15–39.
- "La définition du concept de 'minorités' en droit international", in Francis DELPEREE & Laslo TROCSANYI (Dir.), *L'unité et la diversité de l'Europe: les droits des minorités (Les exemples belge et hongrois)*, Bruxelles, Bruylant, 2003, pp. 21–35.
- "Les incidences de la Convention européenne des droits de l'homme sur l'application de la Convention relative au statut des réfugiés", in *Avancées et confins actuels des droits de l'homme aux niveaux international, européen et national (Mélanges offerts à Silvio Marcus Helmons)*, Bruxelles, Bruylant, 2003, pp. 11–28.
- "La prise en considération de la jurisprudence de Strasbourg par le Comité des droits de l'homme des Nations Unies" (avec Olivier LINS), in Gérard COHEN-JONATHAN & Jean-François FLAUSS (Dir.), *Le rayonnement international de la jurisprudence de la Cour européenne des droits de l'homme*, Bruxelles, Bruylant, 2005, pp. 83–99.
- "République démocratique du Congo: une Constitution pour une Troisième République équilibrée" (avec Nicolas BANNEUX, Evariste BOSHAB, Bob KABAMBA & Pierre VERJANS), in *Fédéralisme – Régionalisme 2004–2005 (La IIIe République Démocratique du Congo. Un nouveau régionalisme)*, pp. 81–101.
- "De la 'Commission' au 'Conseil' des droits de l'homme: Un nom pour un autre?" (avec Emmanuel DECAUX), www.droits-fondamentaux.org, janvier – décembre 2005, n° 5.
- "Étude sur le principe de non-discrimination énoncé au paragraphe 2 de l'article 2 du Pacte international relatif aux droits économiques, sociaux et culturels", rapport préliminaire, E/CN.4/Sub.2/2005/19, Genève, 2005, 18 p.
- "Commission des droits de l'homme: fallait-il réformer?", *Le Mensuel de l'Université*, juin 2006, 3 p.
- "Le mandat et le statut des experts indépendants", in Emmanuel DECAUX (Ed.), *Les Nations Unies et les Droits de l'Homme*, Paris, Pedone, 2006, pp. 209–216.
- "Le Conseil des droits de l'homme: une réforme douteuse?", in *Droit du pouvoir, pouvoir du droit (Mélanges offerts à Jean Salmon)*, Bruxelles, Bruylant, 2007, pp. 1183–1192.

- "Témoignage d'une présence belge au sein des organes des Nations Unies en matière de droits de l'homme", *Revue trimestrielle des droits de l'homme*, 2008, pp. 329–346.
- "La notion d'action positive", *La pauvreté: un défi pour les droits de l'homme*, Paris, Pedone, 2009, pp. 97–102.
- *Strasbourg et les demandeurs d'asile: des juges sur un terrain glissant*, Bruxelles, Bruylant, 2010, 189 p.
- "L'extension de la compétence de la Cour de Strasbourg aux prestations sociales: sur l'interprétation de l'article 14 de la Convention combiné avec l'article 1er du Protocole n° 1 dans les affaires *Gaygusuz, Koua Poirrez, Stec et autres, Burden* et *Andrejeva*", *Revue de droit monégasque*, 2009–2010, pp. 91–130.
- "Les travaux préparatoires", in Emmanuel DECAUX (Ed.), *Pacte international relatif aux droits civils et politiques: commentaire article par article*, Paris, Economica, 2011, pp. 1–9.
- "La modestie honore le juriste", *Revue belge de droit constitutionnel*, 2011, pp. 77–80.
- "Strasbourg et les demandeurs d'asile (*M.S.S. c. Belgique et Grèce, et Sufi et Elmi c. Royaume-Uni*)", *Annuaire international des droits de l'homme 2011*, Athènes, Ant. N. Sakkoulas, 2012, pp. 663–667.
- "Nationalité et minorités en droit international", in S.F.D.I., *Droit international et nationalité*: colloque de Poitiers, Paris, Pedone, 2012, pp. 145–163.
- "*You cannot try them, you cannot detain them and you cannot deport them* (Observations sous C.E.D.H., *M.S. c. Belgique*, 31 janvier 2012)", *Journal des tribunaux*, 2012, pp. 351–355.
- "Les rapports entre la Constitution belge et les traités", *Revue belge de droit international*, 2012, pp. 84–90.
- "Les droits sociaux: une catégorie spécifique de droits de l'homme?", in Leif BERG, Monserrat ENRICH MAS, Peter KEMPEES & Dean SPIELMANN (Ed.), *Cohérence et impact de la jurisprudence de la Cour européenne des droits de l'homme (Liber amicorum Vincent Berger)*, Oisterwijk, Wolf Legal Publ., 2013, pp. 43–58.
- "Des limites à la juridiction de la Cour de Strasbourg?", *L'homme et le droit (en hommage au Professeur Jean-François Flauss)*, Paris, Pedone, 2014, pp. 117–127.
- "Maintenir l'obligation du vote", *Revue belge de droit constitutionnel*, 2014, pp. 313–315.
- "*Tarakhel c. Suisse:* La Cour de Strasbourg rend encore plus difficile une Politique commune européenne en matière d'asile", *Revue suisse de droit international et européen*, 2015, pp. 3–6.
- "Perspectives extérieures sur le développement des libertés publiques et des droits de l'homme au Burundi", in Jean-Marie BARAMBONA, Stanislas MAKOROKA, Vincent SAGAERT & Raf VAN RANSBEECK (Dir.), *L'Etat du Burundi après 50 ans d'indépendance*, Bruxelles, Bruylant, 2015, pp. 327–333.

C. IN DUTCH

Recent publications additional to the full list reproduced in *Liberae Cogitationes (Liber amicorum Marc Bossuyt)*, Antwerp, Intersentia, 2013, pp. 971–974.

- "De rol van de asieljurisdicties in de Belgische asielprocedure" (met Lien De GEYTER), in Joëlle ROZIE, Filiep DERUYCK, Luc HUYBRECHTS & Filip VAN VOLSEM (Eds.), *Na rijp beraad (Liber amicorum Michel Rozie)*, Antwerp, Intersentia, 2014, pp. 39–52.

- "Rechterlijk activisme in Straatsburg", *Rechtskundig Weekblad*, 2014, pp. 723–733.
- "Straatsburg bemoeilijkt opnieuw het gemeenschappelijk Europees asielbeleid", *De Juristenkrant*, December 2014, p. 12.
- "Schuift het Hof van Cassatie een moeizaam bereikt compromis inzake samenloop van grondrechten terzijde? (noot onder Cass. 3e K., 15 december 2014), *Rechtskundig Weekblad*, 2014–2015, pp. 1624–1628.
- "Mensenrechten t.o.v. de doodstraf en t.o.v. niet-samendrukbare levenslange gevangenisstraffen", *Tijdschrift voor strafrecht*, 2015, pp. 59–65.
- "Hoe de EU de controle over de migratiebewegingen verloor", *De Juristenkrant*, October 2015, pp. 16–17.
- "De afschaffing van de doodstraf in Suriname", *Surinaams Juristenblad*, 2015, pp. 80–83.
- "Sergio Viera de Mello, De man die de wereld wilde redden", in Jan WOUTERS (Ed.), *Verenigde Naties: mensenwerk: 25 markante leiders*, Leuven, LannooCampus, 2015, pp. 76–82.
- "Noot onder *S.J.* t. Belgie (27 februari 2014; GK, 19 maart 2015) en de schorsingsprocedure in vreemdelingenzaken", *Tijdschrift voor Vreemdelingenrecht*, 2015, pp. 309–313.

IV. TABLE OF CONTENTS OF LIBERAE COGITATIONES (*LIBER AMICORUM MARC BOSSUYT*)

André ALEN, Veronique JOOSTEN, Riet LEYSEN & Willem VERRIJDT (Eds.)
ISBN 978–94–000–0353–8, Antwerp, Intersentia, 2013, 974 p.

ABOUT THE AUTHOR

Marc baron Bossuyt

Doctor juris (University of Ghent)
Docteur ès sciences politiques (University of Geneva)
Doctor honoris causa (University of Hasselt)
Diplôme d'honneur (University of Burundi)

Certificate of International Relations of the Bologna Centre
of the School of Advanced International Studies of the Johns Hopkins University
Diploma of International and Comparative Law
of the International Institute of Human Rights (Strasbourg)
Certificat d'études supérieures of the Graduate Institute of International Studies
(Geneva)

Former Chairperson of the UN Commission on Human Rights
Former Chairperson of the UN Sub-Commission on
the Promotion and the Protection of Human Rights
Former Chairperson/Rapporteur of the Working Group on the Declaration of
the World Conference against Racism, Racial Discrimination, Xenophobia and
Related Intolerance
Member of the UN Committee on the Elimination of Racial Discrimination

Former Visiting Professor
at the School of Law of the University of Santa Clara (California),
at the Faculties of Law of the *Université du Burundi* (Bujumbura) and
of the *Université Nationale du Rwanda* (Butare) and
at the College of Law of the National Taiwan University (Taipei)

Fellow at the Stellenbosch Institute for Advanced Study (STIAS)
Emeritus Professor of International Law of the University of Antwerp
Honorary Commissioner General for Refugees and Stateless Persons
Emeritus President of the Constitutional Court of Belgium